ENGLISH LANGUAGE SERIES

TITLE NO 11
Meaning and Form

ENGLISH LANGUAGE SERIES
General Editor: Randolph Quirk

Title no:

INVESTIGATING ENGLISH STYLE I
David Crystal and Derek Davy

THE MOVEMENT OF ENGLISH PROSE 2
Ian A. Gordon

A LINGUISTIC GUIDE TO ENGLISH POETRY 4
Geoffrey N. Leech

AN INTRODUCTION TO 7
MODERN ENGLISH WORD-FORMATION
Valerie Adams

COHESION IN ENGLISH 9
M. A. K. Halliday and Ruqaiya Hasan

AN INTRODUCTION TO ENGLISH 10
TRANSFORMATIONAL SYNTAX
Rodney Huddleston

MEANING AND FORM 11
Dwight Bolinger

Meaning and Form

DWIGHT BOLINGER

Harvard University

LONGMAN

LONDON AND NEW YORK

LONGMAN GROUP LIMITED *LONDON*

Associated companies, branches and representatives throughout the world
Published in the United States of America by Longman Inc, New York

© Longman Group Ltd 1977

First published 1977
Reprinted 1979

CASED ISBN O 582 55103 X
PAPER ISBN O 582 29104 6

Library of Congress Cataloging in Publication Data
Bolinger, Dwight Le Merton, 1907–
    Meaning and Form

    (English language series; no. 11)
    Bibliography: p.
    Includes index.
    1. English language—Semantics. 2. Surface struc-
ture (Linguistics) I. Title.
PE1585.B57   412   76-44857
ISBN O 582 55103 X

Printed and bound in Great Britain at
William Clowes & Sons Limited, Beccles and London

to LOUISE

Foreword

Few linguists have made so many original and insightful contributions to the study of contemporary English (prosody, grammar, lexicology) as Dwight Bolinger. His work is all the more impressive in proceeding from one who throughout his academic career was employed primarily not as a teacher of English, nor even of linguistics, but of Spanish. Not least within the uniqueness of Bolinger's scholarship has been his ability to keep up with the twists and turns and (at times) genuine revolutions in linguistic theory. And specifically, since he was until recently a doyen among Harvard professors, he was on the spot to absorb the ideas flowing up and down Massachusetts Avenue. But, as a man both deeply cultivated in literatures and languages and imbued with an outstanding intellect, he has been big enough – like Roman Jakobson, whose urbanities he also shares – to preserve a discriminating independence from rival schools to which lesser scholars have felt impelled to give wholeheartedly enthusiastic (if temporary) allegiance. And big enough too, of course, to give the fullest and most sympathetic credit on all sides.

William Labov has said that 'Speakers do not readily accept the fact that two different expressions actually "mean the same"' (*Studium Generale*, 23.77). Dwight Bolinger would presumably not merely associate himself with such speakers but would wish to go further and assert that linguists themselves should not 'readily accept' such a 'fact'. Certainly, the theme of this book is that there is no difference in form without some difference in meaning: and that certain forms have 'a meaning, from which certain aspects of syntax can be predicted, and not the reverse'.

Though content to describe himself as merely 'a diligent native speaker', he combines clinical skill and data-rich experience with the scientific intellect of the inquiring theorist. In consequence, working always in the spirit of 'Omnia probate – quod bonum est tenete', he challenges strongly and fashionably held views by confronting them with the incontrovertible data of usage, analysed with subtle perception.

The result is a disciplined body of studies which no grammarian of English can possibly afford to ignore and which constitutes a distinguished addition to this series. As English has increasingly come into world-wide use, there has arisen an acute need for more information on the language and the ways in which it is used. The English Language Series seeks to meet this need and to play a part in further stimulating the study and teaching of English by providing up-to-date and scholarly treatments of topics most relevant to present-day English – including its history and traditions, its sound patterns, its grammar, its lexicology, its rich variety in speech and writing, and its standards in Britain, the USA, and other principal areas where the language is used.

University College London   RANDOLPH QUIRK
February 1977

Preface

Despite a number of skirmishes over the past few years in which the troops arrayed on the side of meaninglessness have come off rather worse for the encounter, there has been no frontal attack on the theory that it is normal for a language to establish a lunacy ward in its grammar or lexicon where mindless morphs stare vacantly with no purpose other than to be where they are. The idea has been around for a good while. Traditional grammar recorded such things as *it* (*It is hard to decide*), *that* (*I know* [*that*] *it happened*), and *there* (*Across the street* [*there*] *is a candy store*) as having at most a grammatical function, with no meaning of their own. But contemporary linguistics has carried the fantasy to new heights, and expanded it with a new version of an old vision, that of synonymy: not only are there mindless morphs, but there are mindless differences between one construction and another. The transformation of that old vision is, literally, transformations: in its original form, one construction could be converted into another; in its newer form, an abstract structure could be converted into *x* number of surface structures – in either case without gain or loss of meaning. The resulting structures were the same; only the guise was different.

Though the full realization did not come till later, operations of this kind would not have been possible without heavy reliance on logic. The 'same meaning' (or zero meaning) that linguists were talking about was truth value. *I put on my coat* and *I put my coat on* report the same event. Nothing that is factually true or false about one can fail to be true or false about the other. But linguists are not logicians, and we surrender our birthright if we turn away from the very kinds of meaning that we are best equipped to deal with.

This book is a challenge to the fallacy of meaninglessness. It attempts to prove, by case studies, that any word which a language permits to survive must make its semantic contribution; and that the same holds for any construction that is physically distinct from any other construction. It re-affirms the old principle that the natural condition of a language is to preserve one form for one meaning, and one meaning for one form.

Palo Alto, California   DB
February 1977

Contents

Foreword   vii

Preface   ix

1 Introduction   1

2 *Any* and *some*   21

3 *Not any* and *no*   37

4 *It*   66

5 *There*   90

6 Apparent constituents in surface structure   124

7 Ergative *of* and infinitives of specification   135

8 Is the imperative an infinitive?   152

9 Imperatives are imperatives and *do* is *do*   183

References   201

Index   205

Chapter 1

Introduction

Every so often the scientific theorist finds it politic to climb down from the heights and appeal to common sense. Those of us who were parents in the 1930s well remember the theories of child-rearing that prevailed – asepsis was the ideal, the more untouched by human hands an infant was the better, and if some enterprising dealer in plastics could have found a way to wrap a fetus in cellophane it probably would have been done. Psychologists since then have well-nigh totally faced about, and a mother's love and kisses are again respectable as well as natural. Linguistics has seen more than one such retreat from artificiality. It was common sense that showed the mindlessness of twenty years ago, and that spurred the return to 'naturalness' a decade later.

This preamble is by way of saying that the thesis[1] I am going to sustain is not one that would surprise the man on the street. Tell him that if two ways of saying something differ in their words or their arrangement they will also differ in meaning, and he will show as much surprise as if you told him that walking in the rain is conducive to getting wet. Only a scientist can wrap himself up in enough sophistication to keep dry under these circumstances.

Here is how I mean to define my target. One of the principles – I could almost say fetiches – of current formal linguistics is the notion that underlying whatever communication one human being transmits to another is a deep structure in which every relationship relevant to meaning is set forth. The communication that gets transmitted is subject to all the accidents of transmission and is therefore a distortion of the bedrock structure. Among the possible distortions are actual bifurcations – two different ways of saying the same thing, two different surface structures, mapped onto a single underlying structure by means of different transformations. For instance, it has been claimed that the *to* of the infinitive and the *-ing* of the gerund were merely alternate complementizers and when you said *He likes to* *write* and *He enjoys writing* any difference there was existed only between the verbs *like* and *enjoy*, not between *to write* and *writing* – the two main verbs merely selected different complementizers. The difference between *to write* and *writing* became part of the automatism of language.

The other side of the picture – two things the same in form but different in meaning rather than the same in meaning but different in form – is better known because it appeals more to our sense of the unusual. It is the basis of most puns, the funeral home that advertises a lay-away plan, the athletic girl who loves the sun and air (son and heir), and any number of more professional curiosities that have been invented, such as Chomsky's *The shooting of the hunters was terrible.* Obviously if the accidents that strike the surface can produce two different things stemming from the same deep structure, they can also produce two same things stemming from different deep structures. The differences are of two kinds, constructional and homonymic, both of which result in ambiguity. The sentence *John said he was tired* can be taken to mean that John was referring to himself or to someone else. It is not that there are two words both spelled *he* that leads to the fork in the path, but that the grammar of *he* allows for reflexive or non-reflexive reference. This is constructional ambiguity, and linguistic literature abounds with examples, such as the Chomsky one just quoted. With homonyms, ambiguity arises because of a convergence of word forms (or, as with *metal* and *mettle*, sometimes because of a split). *He's an* [ˈænələst] can be taken as either *He's an analyst* or *He's an annalist. It's a fine grind* may refer to a desirable grind or to a pulverized one. Both kinds of ambiguity are commonplace: cases of more than one meaning attached to a single form far outnumber cases of more than one form attached to a single meaning (if indeed the latter exist at all) for the simple reason that the mind is freer than the tongue. Constructional ambiguity will concern us only incidentally, but homonymy will need our attention because in recent years it has frequently been assumed as a way of simplifying some complexity of syntax, without a proper semantic justification for saying that the form in question is 'really two (or more) different words'. *It's easy to play* is constructionally ambiguous like *John said he was tired;* but unlike *he, it* has been called two different words – very likely an unnecessary dissection.

It would be hard to quarrel with the doctrine of sameness and difference as an abstract scientific principle. The idea that things can be the same but different or different but the same is prerequisite to science – only by shutting our eyes to differences can we see that all legumes are a single family or that the gravitation of an apple hitting the earth is the same as that of a moon revolving about a planet. The problem is not in the principle but in the way linguists have sometimes interpreted it. I question whether any botanist would define his field so as to say that the variation among legumes has nothing to do with it; but linguists have tended to define linguistics so as to say that variation in surface structures that have the same deep structure is irrelevant to the one thing that matters most in language, namely meaning. They have insisted on absolute identity, with any difference defined out of the way.

This attitude has a peculiar fascination. It characterized much of the work in phonology until very recently. In dealing with the sound system of a language it is useful to think of an underlying system of contrastive units, phonemes or features, where a speaker, in two utterances of the same word, say, necessarily deviates within a certain range of tolerance without his hearer even being aware of it. Similarly one may find an identical system being used by another speaker, but with the physical traits of each signal differing slightly in ways that mark him as an individual or as the speaker of a different dialect, but with each unit still having the same communicative value as before. It is not too far-fetched to claim that cases like these are identical linguistically but different sociologically. The deviations can reasonably be defined out of the field.

What happens when these notions of systemic identity and irrelevant difference are carried up the ladder into morphology and syntax? With morphology it still makes sense to think of the plurality of *geese* and the plurality of *hens* as the same entity despite the difference in ways for forming the plural. Also, in describing the differences between speakers we would allow that if one says *eether* and another says *eyether* they are still using the same word; we know the origin of both and we can see the identity of usage. We may learn something of the speakers – their social group or their individual psychology – by observing the differences, but these can be ignored linguistically, in at least some contexts, since they do not affect the content of a communication. They may even be beyond the control of the speaker. He does not manipulate them to ring changes on his message.

Where the mischief begins is in syntax. Differences in the arrangement of words and in the presence or absence of certain elements are often assumed not to count. What is supposed to matter is the underlying deep structure, which is capable of producing, through transformations, divergent structures that mean exactly the same thing. The motive for assuming this is not only the search for simplicity, for ways of stating rules or laws just once instead of again and again, but also the yen that our modern linguist has for being a psychologist. If there is such a thing as a universal deep structure, it must reflect something about the human psyche, and many conjectures have been made about the human infant springing from the womb with his noun phrases and relative clauses all ready to light up as soon as they are plugged into a particular language.

Obviously the idea that even in syntax one could have identity within difference could not have gained currency without some empirical support. The classical case is that of the passive voice. If some differences of meaning are ignored, it is possible to say that *John ate the spinach* and *The spinach was eaten by John* are the same. They report the same event in the real world. The same entities are present and they are in the same relationship of actor and patient. But if truth value were the only criterion of identity in syntax we would have to say – as some have recently been trying to say – that *John sold the house to Mary* and *Mary bought the house from John* are just as much the same as the active-passive pair, and to seek some way of deriving them from a common base. Linguistic meaning covers a great deal more than reports of events in the real world. It expresses, sometimes in very obvious ways, other times in ways that are hard to ferret out, such things as what is the central part of the message as against the peripheral part, what our attitudes are toward the person we are speaking to, how we feel about the reliability of our message, how we situate ourselves in the events we report, and many other things that make our messages not merely a recital of facts but a complex of facts and comments about facts and situations. As William Haas remarks in his critique of attempts to spread the umbrella of logic over natural language,

> The undoubted meaningfulness of fictions and of deceptive or mistaken references is in fact meaningfulness of the *most general* kind. It extends over all sentences. It is, on the contrary, the sense of the standard type of propositions that represents a more specific kind of meaningfulness: they fulfil the *additional* condition of true-or-false reference (Haas 1975, 158–9).

The linguist cannot expect the logician, the anthropologist, or the psychologist to do his work for him, though he owes to them, and they to him, a recurring debt payable in mutual understanding.

If one wants to believe, as I do, that in syntax there is no such thing as two different surface structures with the same deep structure (that is, with the same meaning), how does one come to grips with the idea? Nobody has counted how many of these imagined cases of identity exist, so if you vanquish one there is always another one waiting for you. The only answer I know is to find the cases that have the greatest inherent plausibility, and on which the strongest claims of identity have been staked, and to take them on one by one. Each of the chapters that follow attacks a particular assumed equivalence or difference. The significance of the outcome will hardly be lost on generative grammarians, who of all recent theorists have made the most of exact paraphrase and its assumption of underlying identity. Yet others, including the author of this volume, have been equally guilty. After all, it was traditional grammar that first proclaimed the equivalence between active and passive and between attributive adjectives and reduced clauses. Always one's first impulse, on encountering two highly similar things, is to ignore their differences in order to get them into a system of relationships where they can be stored, retrieved, and otherwise made manageable. The sin consists in stopping there. And also in creating an apparatus that depends on the signs of absolute equality and absolute inequality, and uses the latter only when the unlikeness that it represents is so gross that it bowls you over.

Not all distinctions are quite so easy to prove as most of those covered in the separate chapters. One area is especially insensitive to SYSTEMATIC differences in meaning: that of the 'surface transformations', in particular deletion and pronominalization. I suspect that the reason is the fact that here the processes of transformation are a psychological reality. They intrude upon us whenever we echo anything in speech. Echoes may be distorted, but they tend to have one-to-one relationships to their sources. When a speaker replies to *Would you like to have some tea?* with *Yes I wóuld*, and is asked (by a third party, say) *Would what?*, we can observe him supplying the missing elements: *like to have some tea, of course*. One can almost say that *Yes I wóuld*, *Yes I wóuld like to*, *Yes I wóuld like to have some*, and *Yes I wóuld like to have some tea* are identical. No native speaker of English would be shocked at the use of 'same' to describe them (with a 'difference', of course, that 'does not count'). Yet there are functional differences. *Yes I wóuld like to have some*, unlike *Yes I wóuld*, is normal after a first refusal and then a change of mind, but not as a first response. The differences that one can detect in this kind of shortening and lengthening appear to be unpredictable from the inner structure of the sentence and to depend on some larger discourse relationship. The prosody may be involved, as in the successive truncations of the answer to *Who might have cut my hair better than John might have cut it?*

[1] Joe might have cut it better than John might have cut it.
[2] Joe might have cut it better than John might have.

[3] Joe might have cut it better than John might.
[4] Joe might have cut it better than John.
[5] Joe might have cut it better.
[6] Joe might have.
[7] Joe might.
[8] Joe.

All the answers use the same intonation curve, and when the answer is reduced to the monosyllable *Joe* it becomes a little awkward; the three-word answer *Joe might have* is about the lowest one can go in syllabic weight to accommodate the intonation comfortably. To continue with the matter of intonation for a moment, one can see a clear functional difference in two replies to the invitation *Why don't you go shopping with me?* One,

[9] I'd $l^{l\,i^{k^e}}{}_{t}{}^{o.}$

is polite and wistful. The other,

[10] I $don't$ ^{want} to go shopping with you.

is unmistakably rude. If the full answer is used on the first intonation,

[11] I'd $l^{l\,i^{k^e}}$ to go shopping with y^o $^{u.}$

one is more strongly impelled to finish with *but I can't*, and the whole reply sounds a bit brusque. I believe that the effect of repeating the full sentence in a case like this is one either of mocking the original speaker or pretending that he is so dense that it is necessary to repeat all words to make him understand. Combining the mockery with the low terminal pitch, which is normal intonationally because with no new information there are no pitch rises, gives a scornful finality just right for repudiation. Of course, if what is repeated does not echo another person's actual words, one has unadulterated finality. Compare the wistful intonation of

[12] I $^{wish\ mine}$ were as ^{nice} as $^{Ma}_{ry}$,s.

with the finality of

[13] I have to work it so that mine will be every bit as nice as Mary's is.

in which the addition of *is* is more appropriate. The effect of finality can be seen when complements are retained at the final low pitch: *He needs money and he means to have money; You'll accept what I tell you to do and you'll do what I tell you to do.*

There are other effects that can be got by repetition besides the extra bulk for intonational purposes and the mocking echo. One is the ancient device of plurality. If I say *She bought a red dress, a green one, and a blue one,* I give you a mere list of her purchases. But if I say *She bought a red dress, she bought a green dress, and she bought a blue dress,* you will infer that she bought excessively. One difference in form here comes from pronominalization, not deletion; but the two are the same in their main effects, namely in shortening and in not repeating the same words.[2] Another effect is that of separation. This is found when the element to be removed is not deleted but pronominalized. If I say *George came in the room and turned off the lights,* ordinarily I would be taken to mean that George performed the actions in sequence, as two parts of a complex plan. But if I say *George came in the room and he turned off the lights,* it is probably either two separate events that are conjoined or two linked events conceptually separated (for example, his coming into the room is reported, but his turning off the lights is complained about). As in so many other places, the *to* of the infinitive behaves in this same way, much like a pronoun. The phrase *the ability to read and write letters* is more likely to be interpreted as 'a letter-reading-and-writing ability' than as 'a reading ability plus a letter-writing ability'. But if the *to* is retained, *the ability to read and to write letters,* the probabilities are reversed – the *to* helps to divide *read* from *write-letters* and sets it up as an intransitive verb. Still another effect of repetition is admonitory, when used with someone's name, as in *Mary wants to eat my soup but Mary isn't going to get the chance.* I suspect that this is a side effect of the repetition of a personal name as a kind of reproof.

Except for the admonitory use, the effects of repetition mentioned thus far show a certain consistency. That is, we regularly have the option of repeating something in full to get extra intonational weight, to suggest plurality, or to indicate that a conjunction applies to a whole sentence rather than part of one. But admonitory repetition picks up a meaning through casual association – we repeat a person's name as a form of reproof in direct address, and manage to carry a suggestion of it over into indirect address. There are other such casual associations in our repeating or not repeating an element of a sentence. At the time that Dwight Eisenhower was suffering from heart attacks, a cynical cartoon of Richard Nixon was published which pictured the two men standing at the foot of a stairway and Nixon saying to Eisenhower, *Race you to the top of the stairs*. The omission of the subject *I* and the auxiliary is common in such invitations. I suspect that it comes by way of a blend with the imperative, which might also be used as an invitation in such a context, *Race me to the top of the stairs*. In any case, *Race you to the top of the stairs* is unambiguously an invitation; *I'll race you to the top of the stairs* is not. The regular deletion of the subject in the imperative gives, by reversal, an admonitory effect similar to the one just mentioned in connection with proper names, when the subject *you* is included: *You do as I say* is stronger than *Do as I say*, and *Come here, you* is stronger still than *Come here*. (Of course when the *you* is a vocative it merely contrasts with some other *you*, for example *You sit here, Jane, and you sit here, Mary*.) There are similar deletions in questions which have picked up special meanings. If I am sampling a food and say to you *Like a taste?* you are apt to interpret my invitation as less ceremonious and hence more sincere than if I said *Would you like a taste?*

It is obvious from these examples that deletions and pronominalizations may be specialized in function. An instance of particular specialization is the use of answers with deleted main verbs as strong affirmations or denials. In answer to *Do you claim that you were there on the night of August 22?* one may say, naturally, just *Yes*, or *Yes, I claim* etc, but the answer *I do* is the most positive. The KINDS of differences in meaning that one finds with structures that differ only by deletion or pronominalization may not be the same, or may not be as striking, as those involving change of order or change of lexical material. But these contrasts are obviously being exploited and it is not too far-fetched to suppose that even here there is some potential difference in function whenever there is a difference in form. And since deletion and pronominalization as processes of reduction imply a kind of identity with the original from which certain elements have been dropped, we can divorce ourselves from the transformationalists and join J. R. Firth (1964, 174) in questioning the validity of the concept. A reduction is a loss, yet *Mary says so but Mary is wrong* is marked by comparison with *Mary says so but she is wrong*; it is not the same, or less, but more. In the commonsense view, *Shut up* does not delete *you*; rather, *You shut up* adds it. The subjectless imperative has become a structure in its own right, and other 'deletions' may well have been firmed up in much the same way, or be somewhere along the road to it.

This says nothing of the sporadic occasions when a supposed deletion becomes a carrier for a totally different meaning – different in its truth value. Conditional tags using the verbs *want* and *wish* make little distinction between using or omitting the *to* of the infinitive – the differences, if any, are like the ones just discussed: *Do it if you want (to), Do it if you wish (to)*. But with the verb *like*, dropping *to* changes the meaning radically: *Do it if you like to; Do it if you like* – the first refers to a liking or fondness, the second to a choice. Adding *would* merges the two again: *Do it if you would like (to);* now both forms express choice. (These verbs are hobbled with strange restrictions: *I'll do it if I want*, but not *when I want*, though *I'll do it when I wish* is normal. On the other hand, *I'll do it if I like*, but not *I'll do it supposing I like*. All instances are normal when *to* is added.)

Where transformations have been set up at supposedly deeper levels the claim of identity-despite-difference is easier to disprove. And also the claim of difference-despite-identity (where the supposed difference overrides a genuine semantic relationship and true homonymy is not involved), which is the companion fallacy. The two go hand in hand, for an artificial identity in syntax may depend on an artificial difference in lexicon. These are two sides of a single universal, the Janus-faced one-form-one-meaning. It has exceptions, but as with all universals the exceptions are imbalances that a language tends to eliminate; we can no more live comfortably with precise synonymy than with the conflict of homonyms. So the chapters that follow will look equally at spurious identities and spurious differences.

As a foretaste of the fuller treatments I offer a few summaries of some other studies that have focused on the same problem.

1 The underlying identity of active and passive. Even the most ardent advocates of perfect paraphrase have retreated from their front-line position on this question, and now concede that there is some kind of difference in emphasis, a way of highlighting certain elements so that the two are not always interchangeable; or even admit – in a recent cross-linguistic study (Langacker and Munro 1975) – that elements such as *be* and *by* are not transformationally introduced particles but are meaningful in their own right. But as far as the English passive is concerned, the difference goes deeper. It involves the markedness of the passive voice with respect to the feature of transitivity (see Bolinger 1975). Why is it that one can say both *The dog walked under the bridge* and *Generations of lovers have walked under the bridge* but *The bridge has been walked under by generations of lovers* strikes us as at least tolerable while *The bridge was walked under by the dog* seems absurd? Or why is it that the passive of

Nobody is to camp beside this lake, This lake is not to be camped beside by any-body! seems acceptable, but the passive of *My sister camped beside the lake,* ★*The lake was camped beside by my sister,* is peculiar? After giving a set of examples like these to a class of seventy first-year college students, I found that when I had thrown out all the random responses there was a ten per cent consistent agreement on what the students felt was the reason for their willingness to accept a passive sentence with a preposi-tional verb – it had to represent something actually DONE TO something. The speaker has to be thinking of a patient that is somehow affected by the action. For generations of lovers to pass beneath a bridge makes it romantic. For a dog to walk under it is just that – you have a spatial relationship between dog and bridge, and nothing more. If a rancher warns that his lake is not to be camped beside by anybody he obviously has in mind the potential damage to the lake. But for someone's sister to camp there merely tells where she is. A little investigation shows that simple verbs are subject to the same restriction. We can say *George turned the pages* or *The pages were turned by George;* something happens to the pages in the process. But while we can say *George turned the corner* we cannot say ★*The corner was turned by George* – the corner is not affected, it is only where George was at the time. On the other hand, if one were speaking of some kind of marathon or race or a game in which a par-ticular corner is thought of as an objective to be taken, then one might say *That corner hasn't been turned yet.* I can say *The stranger approached me* or *I was approached by the stranger* because I am thinking of how his approach may affect me – perhaps he is a panhandler. But if a train approaches me I do not say ★*I was approached by the train,* because all I am talking about is the geometry of two positions. There are also power relationships involved. Though we can say both *Private Smith deserted the army* and *The generals deserted the army,* to say that *The army was deserted by Private Smith* is comical while *The army was deserted by all its generals* is normal. This shows, I think, that passivization cannot be defined on a particular set of verbs. It demands access to the speaker's intentions, to the meaning of whether or not an effect is produced.

2 The identity between *that* and zero and between *that* and *which* (or, the DIFFERENCE between demonstrative *that* and relative *that*). As far as I know, there has never been any doubt in any grammarian's mind about the absolute equivalence between sentences having and sentences omitting the relative word *that.* My way of wording this prejudices the case somewhat – to say that the word *that* has been omitted implies that it was there in the first place, and accordingly some semantic trace of it

may be left. The question is, does a sentence such as *I noticed you were there* mean the same as one such as *I noticed that you were there?* For traditionalist and transformationalist alike, they have been regarded as in free variation. I will not go into the various restrictions on this supposed variation, which are a long story, more than just to say that there do exist environments where a *that* is required and others where a *that* is excluded (see Bolinger 1972*a*). The most conspicuous instance of required *that* is one serving as subject in its own clause, in the case of adjective clauses: *★They arrested the man shot the policeman* requires an added *that*, but *They arrested the man the policeman shot*, where the *that* would be an object in its own clause, can do without it. That is the kind of restriction that can be stated nicely in transformational terms. The question is whether the process is merely one of introducing a *that* trans-formationally under set grammatical conditions, or one of meaning from which the grammatical restrictions flow as corollaries. One way of helping to decide the question – it is too complex for me to say that it will thereby truly be decided – is to look for minimally distinct pairs, one member of which contains a *that* while the other lacks it. The theory I am going on is that the word *that* is still – in very subtle ways – the same word that it was when it first began to be used to head subordinate clauses, namely a demonstrative. If we look at situations where speakers are volunteering information, where no question has been asked and no answer is implied, but what is being said comes out of the blue, it is unnatural for the word *that* to be used. If I step into a room and want to drop a casual remark about the weather I may say *The forecast says it's going to rain*. It would be odd for me to say *★The forecast says that it is going to rain*. But if you ask me *What's the weather for tomorrow?* I have a choice; *The forecast says that it is going to rain* is normal. If we think of *that* in its fundamental deictic or anaphoric use as a demonstrative, we see that it is appropriate when the clause in question does not represent a disconnected fact but something tied in with a previous matter to which *that* can point back, just as it does in *That man insulted me*, mean-ing the man referred to before. If I see you at the side of the road struggling with a tire and feel charitable I may go over and say to you, by way of an opener, *I thought you might need some help*. To say *I thought that you might need some help* suggests a question already brought up – if you were a huffy sort of fellow and looked up at me as if wondering what business it was of mine, then I might shrug my shoulders and say by way of answer to the implied question, *I just thought that you might need some help*. Look at it another way. Suppose the clause is used without its subordinating verb – the distinction between old and new crops up again. Take an exchange like

[14] I didn't know that. – Know what? – That Jack's held down six jobs at the same time.

Try leaving off the *that* in this case where a *that* anaphora has already been introduced. On the other hand, suppose no *that* anaphora is possible and the speaker is offering something new:

[15] You want to know something? – What? – Jack's held down six jobs at the same time.

The use of *that* here is just as odd as its omission in the other case. You will notice that the main verbs I used, *know* and *tell*, are both verbs that are perfectly free to take a clause introduced by *that*.

The other side of the problem of *that* and its omission is the supposedly suppletive relationship between *that* and the set comprising *who, whose,* and *which*. Just as *that* can be seen as basically demonstrative, so the other relatives can be seen as basically interrogative, and as lexemes in their own right, whose interrogative origin of course is a historical fact. The contrast between *that* and *which* shows up in a minimal pair such as the following:

[16] This letter that came yesterday, that you remember had no stamps on it, was postmarked four weeks ago.
[17] *This letter that came yesterday, that incidentally had no stamps on it, was . . .

The normal use of *incidentally* is to call a hearer's attention to a side topic which is new to the discourse. It is incompatible with anaphoric *that*, but quite compatible with a word that raises a new 'question'. We could if we wished use *which* in the first example, to refresh the hearer's memory, bringing the topic up anew; but there is hardly any choice in the second. The same contrast may be seen between *that* and *who*, for example in relation to intonation. In the example *I want to get word to him as soon as possible about someone else that (who) I knew was available*, the most compatible intonations are the following:

[18] . . . someone ^else^ that I knew was available.

[19] . . . someone ^else^ who I knew was a^vail^able.

In the first, availability is not at issue; it has been brought up before. In the second, the hearer is informed of it.

The independent meaning of a *that* or a *which* is a tough point to get across because of its very subtlety and the infrequency with which using one or the other or neither is a matter of life and death. Unfortunately we have tended too often to see the importance of a question of language in terms of the importance of the message. The two are not related.

3 Identity of the infinitive and the gerund. I have already mentioned this point. For a long time transformationalists held that the infinitive and gerund were automatic variants whose only claim to a difference was that they were selected by different governing verbs. That notion has now been given up, perhaps in part because of the evidence cited in Bolinger 1968*a*, including examples such as the following:

[20] To wait would have been a mistake.
[21] *To wait has been a mistake.
[22] Waiting would have been a mistake.
[23] Waiting has been a mistake.

There is evidently some such feature as 'hypothetical' attaching to the infinitive. Kempson–Quirk (1971, 551–6) confirm this in a series of test sentences. But like other old articles of faith the notion of a suppletive relationship between the two verb forms dies hard, and one indirect manifestation of it was still lurking around as recently as 1971 (Dingwall 1971; see Bolinger 1977). I refer to the idea that there need not be any feature present in the verbs that take infinitive complements that causes them to do so, and similarly with the verbs that take gerunds. Whatever features may distinguish the infinitive from the gerund are not matched by compatible features in the respective governing verbs. Proof of this is supposed to be found in the fact that there are pairs of synonyms one member of which takes infinitive complements and the other gerund complements. An example of such a pair is *refuse* and *spurn*. Since there seems to be no relevant difference in meaning between them, the choice of different complements must be arbitrary, so the reasoning goes:

[24] He refused to accept the job.
[25] *He spurned to accept the job.
[26] He spurned my helping him.
[27] ?He refused my helping him.

The problem here is to show that the minimal pair *He refused to accept the job* and **He spurned to accept the job* once more embodies a difference in meaning, only now the difference produces an anomaly in one of the sentences. More precisely, there is something about the meaning of the verb *spurn* that is incompatible with the meaning of the infinitive. Suppose we try to get a fix on *spurn* and *refuse* by looking at some of the other complements that go with them. We can say *He refused the offer, He refused the invitation . . . bid, advice*. We cannot say **He refused the idea*, **He refused the solution*, **He refused the truth* – but with *spurn* these are all right. We can say *After having it on trial he refused it*, but we cannot say **After owning it for years he refused it*. Again, *spurn* is all right. There is obviously something about the meaning of *refuse* that faces somehow in a different direction from that of *spurn*. I hypothesize that it is a feature (if you like to call such things features) that might be called 'future orientation'. One can refuse an offer, and accordingly refuse a gift, a car, a dog, or even an idea if it is thought of as something offered. But one may not refuse something that one already possesses. The feature of future orientation fits the hypothetical meaning of the infinitive. There are other pairs like *refuse* and *spurn* that show this same contrast of orientation. Take *remember* and *recall*. They are synonyms in sentences like *I remembered my adventure* and *I recalled my adventure;* but whereas *Remember to phone me* is normal, **Recall to phone me* is not. *Remember*, like *refuse*, embodies that future orientation. It brings things AHEAD OF one's mind, not back of it. If I say *At that moment I remembered my wife*, *remember* may well suggest something to be done. But in *At that moment I recalled my wife* all we have is a backward look. The companion pair of *remember–recall* is *forget–overlook: He forgot his sister when he went* tells us that an action he was supposed to carry out in the future was left undone. *He overlooked his sister when he went* merely tells us that she failed to get his attention. The picture of language as an automaton in which you punch the button reading *refuse* and an infinitive pops into the slot is false to the facts. The infinitive has a meaning and *refuse* has a compatible meaning. There is nothing more mysterious about the harmony between *refuse* and the infinitive than there is between *to drink* and *coffee*.

4 The identity of *-one* and *-body*. Rather than suppletion this is a case of assumed free variation: the authors of the handbooks, including Jespersen, could see no difference, for example, between *someone* and *somebody*. The willingness to probe no further probably reflects the supposed status of these indefinites as function words. Since the same disregard, as we have seen, was bestowed on *that* (and also, as we shall

see in Chapter 4, on *it*), we can profit by one more demonstration that grammaticization may make meaning more abstract, but does not obliterate it.

To test the use of *-one* and *-body* I gave a series of tests (Bolinger 1976) of which the simplest was the following, using thirteen graduate students who were presented with two different situations and asked to choose the more suitable indefinite.

First situation:

[28] 'Who's the present for?' I asked.

He gave me an intimate look. 'Somebody' / 'Someone' } very special, very dear to me,' he said. Of course it had to be me, but I concealed my blushes.

Second situation:

[29] 'Who's the present for?' I asked.

'Oh, { somebody,' / someone,' } he said, as if meaning it was none of my business. 'You don't know him. Her. Them.'

The vote was unanimous, with *someone* for the first and *somebody* for the second. Knowing what we know about pronouns it should not surprise us that meanings having to do with distance, intimacy, and the relationships between the speaker and others should be built into them, and that appears to be what has happened with the indefinites. My hypothesis about *-one* is that it is marked for nearness, in both a spatial and a psychological sense. After a more elaborate test another group was asked to comment on their own reactions. Several did so, and the gist of the answers conformed to the hypothesis. As one worded it, '[*-one*] intimacy, definiteness, individuality; [*-body*] distance, indefinite reference, collectivity'. It should go without saying that the *-one* of the indefinite compounds has unmistakable semantic ties to the word *one* as an independent indefinite pronoun, as in *What can one say?*

5 The difference between *remind* and *remind*. Most of the older morphemic splits – *that₁* and *that₂*, *it₁* and *it₂*, etc – were perpetrated on relatively defenseless grammatical morphemes, in order to accommodate some hypothesis about syntax (such as that relative clauses were the same whether a *that₂* was present or absent, a claim that no one dared make about *that₁*). But with the advent of generative semantics, other parts of

the lexicon have been exposed to attack. Now it is paraphrase relationships between the underlying structures of individual words that must
be accounted for. If *Mary reminds me of Joe* is viewed as essentially the
same as *Mary strikes me as being like Joe*, then we have a basis for deriving
both *remind* and *strike like* from the same 'remote structure'. What then
happens to the other senses of *remind*? Well, they have to be dismissed as
irrelevant: 'there are really several verbs in English whose phonological
shape is *remind*' (Postal 1970, 38).

The potential for mischief is now multiplied, for the range of possible
remote structures for a word is as wide as the linguist's ingenuity in
contriving them and making a plausible case, given semantic facts that
are very difficult to define. With the standard paraphrases in SYNTAX,
there was at first always a relationship to an existing kernel sentence,
and later to a deep structure that at least bore SOME resemblance to an
existing sentence. When a given string is made up of elements (words
mostly) it is rather difficult to analyse it without coming out with the
same elements, more or less, that you start with; but when the analyst
supplies the elements, objective safeguards tend to break down. So it is
with *remind*. We can approach the question in two ways. (i) The form
of the word is a more or less empty shell, with a potentially indefinite
number of meanings – therefore the word is really as many words as
there are meanings: if this can be done with *draw* 'sketch' and *draw*
'pull', why not with *remind* and *remind*? (As in *He reminded me of my
brother; He reminded me of my appointment*.) (ii) The form of the word is
an indication that all the senses may be related, and this possibility
should yield only to the strongest proofs to the contrary. If we assign
remind the meaning 'A causes z to think of B, where B has some connection to A' (Bolinger 1971a, 524) the various senses are pulled together and
differences are relegated to another level, that of INFERENCE. Given a
context in which nothing obstructs our taking 'connection' in as strong
a sense as we please, the connection between A and B extends to
'resemblance'. It is no accident that English is not the only language
embodying the same variety of subsenses in its word for 'remind'.

6 The identity of active and pseudo-passive. It has been claimed (Mihailović 1967) that there is no difference in meaning between the types
He accidentally drowned in the river and *He was accidentally drowned in the
river*. But there is a difference, even without an agent expressed or implied. If we say *He stupidly drowned* we view him as an actor in the
causal chain, even though he may not have been a willing or even a
conscious one – we can add *He stupidly drowned; why couldn't he have*

been more careful? But to say *He was stupidly drowned; why couldn't he have been more careful?* is odd – we are more apt to say *why couldn't they have fenced off the safe area so he could have told how far to venture out?* The pseudo-passive, like the real passive, puts the responsibility on other shoulders than those of the victim.

7 The identity of verb + particle + NP and verb + NP + particle. This brings us to the 'movement transformations' and the supposed lack of any difference in meaning after the movement has occurred. Specifically, *She threw away the key* and *She threw the key away* are taken to reflect the same deep structure and to have the same meaning. Two theoretical preconceptions here combine to yield a false conclusion. The first is the fondness for switchyard solutions: for the linguist who likes mechanical ways of dealing with data, movement transformations are irresistible. The second is the aversion to categorizing a word in more than one way at the same time. An adverb is an adverb and has adverbial functions, an adjective is an adjective and has adjectival functions. But functions and categories are not always so happily wedded to each other. In *She threw away the key*, *away* is purely adverbial; but in *She threw the key away* it becomes somewhat adjectival, modifying *key* as to location. There is a partial change in the constituents of the sentence (Bolinger 1971*b*, especially Chapter 7). This can be seen in a pair of sentences that John Beatty tried on a number of sailors: *They hauled in the lines but didn't get them in* and *★They hauled the lines in but didn't get them in*. The informants agreed that the first was possible, the second not. Obviously, assuming that *lines in* means that they were in, to say they were not got in is contradictory. What is true of adverbs, adjectivalizing them so to speak, is equally true of adjectives, which can be adverbialized: *They cut open the melon* ('opened the melon by cutting'), *They cut the melon open* ('cut it so that it was open'). True, these are subtle differences, but who says that semantic distinctions have to be gross?

8 The identity of adjective + noun and noun + *be* + adjective. There is a natural logic in the concluding line of an exchange such as the following:

[30] I'm not going to clean your *dirty floors.* – Who says my *floors are dirty?*

Given the discourse equivalence of the predicative and attributive uses of the adjective, one can understand why a grammarian should be tempted to find a grammatical equivalence as well. This is another movement transformation, with the predicative construction regarded as more basic than the attributive. But it has been clear for some time that the relationship between these two structures is not as obvious as it once appeared (see especially Bolinger 1967). In fact, the supposed deep structure actually gives us less information than the surface structure; one can see this by the behavior of a great many adjectives. Take one such as *loose*. I may say *The dog is loose*, meaning that he is not tied up. I can say *Where is the dog that's loose?* but I am not apt to say **Where is the loose dog?* On the other hand I can say *A loose dog is apt to be a danger to the neighborhood*. Or take an adjective such as *handy*. *The tools are handy* is ambiguous – it may mean tools that are made in such a way that they are very useful, or it may mean just that the tools happen to be easy to reach. But if we say *the handy tools* we select just one of these meanings, the one that refers to how the tools are made, the way they really are. An adjective that is placed before the noun is not just any adjective that can occur after the verb *be*, but is one that can be used to do more than describe a temporary state – it has to be able to characterize the noun. **Where is the loose dog?* is an unlikely sentence because it refers to a temporary state. *A loose dog is apt to be a danger to the neighborhood* is normal because we are making a generalization in which it is necessary to characterize certain dogs AS IF they formed a class. We can say *the people asleep* but not **the asleep people* because we are not characterizing them, only telling how they are at the moment. But when the adjective *aware* began to be used as a synonym of *alert*, it was able to move before the noun: *He's a very aware person*. An adjective that can only refer to a temporary state has to follow the noun: *money galore*. Even if we play with the deep structure so as to set up more than one source for the obvious differences, it still does not follow that *an empty house* means the same as *a house that's empty*. Sometimes they are interchangeable, but other times they are not, for the simple reason that the explicit predication in one makes a difference in the way the information is presented to the hearer.

If the cases I have cited are truly the examples of fallacy that I believe they are, what is at the root of them? I would say that the cause is a confusion of competence and performance, exactly the reverse of the kind that has been claimed by many transformationalists. Instead of there being an underlying sameness in active and passive, with the differences being relegated to style, focus, or whatnot, there is an underlying difference with the samenesses being due to performance variables. If you are asked *What happened to the train?* and you answer *It was wrecked by the engineer*, you could just as well have answered *The engineer wrecked it*. There is nothing in the performance situation that cannot be satisfied by one answer as well as by the other. But in the series

[31] The train was wrecked. – Did they arrest the conductor?
. . . .

you are going to prefer *It was wrecked by the engineer* to *The engineer wrecked it*. The fact that a contrast that we carry in our competence is relevant does not mean that it is relevant all the time. It only means that it is there when we need it. If a language permits a contrast in form to survive, it ought to be for a purpose. When we look at what has happened historically to the accidental contrasts that have popped up, at the avidity with which speakers seize upon them to squeeze in a difference of meaning, come what may, we should form a proper appreciation of linguistic economy. It is not normal for a language to waste its resources.

False difference stems from the same confusion of competence and performance as false identity. Now we find a single overarching meaning which performance variables imbue with local tinges that pass for distinct senses. The deception is like what happens when we meet an acquaintance in an unexpected setting: we may not recognize him. Take the perfect tense. It is a single form using a single auxiliary *have*. Does it have a single meaning? Context may fool us into thinking it does not, that it must be assigned separate senses including 'hot news' and 'there are occasions on which *x* happened' (McCawley 1969, 9). Thus *Max has been fired, and so has Fred* would not be used to report Max's recent firing and Fred's repeated experience of being fired, or vice versa, but only one of the two kinds of firing for both persons. But the fact is that the senses CAN be mixed:

[32] *Edith:* Max has been fired!
     Ethel: So have I. Many times.
[33] *Arthur:* I've been arrested!
     Adam: Who hasn't? The cops don't like beards.
[34] I've never been arrested but Ray just has.[3]

This tells us that the perfect has a meaning that covers both apparent sub-senses and that performance variables cue us to the speaker's intention. *Max has been fired* is as neutral to the distinction in question as the nominalized *the firing of Max*.

This book is about the principle of one meaning, one form, which Raimo Anttila has been re-emphasizing as the 'seeing' half of linguistic change. The blind half, including manifestations of phonetic adaptation and inertia, may continuously cause us to stumble into allowing two meanings for a single form or two forms for a single meaning, but we do not live happily with either accident and only tolerate the one while moving immediately to repair the other. We shall understand this more clearly as we come to appreciate the work on lexical invariance and related matters in the tradition of Roman Jakobson, William Diver, Anna Hatcher, and Erica García, and carried on by Robert Kirsner, Sandra Thompson, Joan Hooper, Talmy Givón, Linda Waugh, and others of their generation.

Notes

1 Adapted from 'Meaning and Form', in Transactions of the New York Academy of Sciences, Series II, Volume 36, No 2, February 1974.

2 In other respects as well. Certain quantifier pronouns are the same as quantifier adjectives, and appear to be the result of deletion, *eg, He has some money* reduced to *He has some*. The syntax of the *to* of the infinitive, when the lexical infinitive itself is dropped, is quite similar to that of the personal pronouns, *eg, I hated IT but I had TO.*

3 One thing that does need explaining is why the perfect has to be truncated differently depending on whether the more inclusive 'continuous' subsense precedes the 'point action' one:

I've never been arrested but Ray just has.
Ray's just been arrested but I've never been.
*Ray's just been arrested but I never have.

Chapter 2

Any and *some*

1 Introduction

In this chapter I take a fresh look at 'Linguistic Science and Linguistic Engineering', *Word* 16 (1960) 374–91, which was a rejoinder to Lees 1960*a*. The grammar of *any* and *some* was the prime example in Lees's criticism. As the skirmishing paragraphs in the original are no longer of any interest, I omit them. I have made a few other changes to smooth out the text, but without modernizing it to the extent of substituting terms that have recently come into favor; part of the value of the original, I think, is that it identified a few things that are considered important now but were not much in the wind back then when sentence grammar was the linguist's cynosure: presuppositions (called 'suppositions'), factivity (the 'factual *know*'), higher sentences (*Isn't it true that* versus *Is it true that not*), and lexical invariance.

The evidence I gave (not much of it was new – it would have sufficed to cite Jespersen and Poutsma) dealt effectively enough with Lees's particular objections, but syntax, though beaten, has refused to die. I argued that Lees's syntactic *some-any* rule would not work. Two recent studies agree with that conclusion but offer syntactic explanations of a more subtle kind. The first is Lakoff 1969, which applies the syntactic notion of higher sentences. It correctly points out that sentences of the type *If you eat some* (*any) *spinach I'll give you $10* and *If you eat any* (*some) *candy I'll whip you* prove that the choice between *any* and *some* hinges on a kind of positive or negative expectation. But the expectation is given a material form: underlyingly the two sentences have abstract performative verbs, and are related to *I warn you that if you eat any candy I'll whip you* and *I promise you that if you eat some spinach I'll give you $10*. This is an interesting proposal, and the speaker who has a warning or a promise in mind is certainly apt to make the choices indicated. But to say that 'the choice of which sentence is grammatical is dictated by the meaning of the main verb' is again to throw the decision in the lap of syntax. Nothing is dictated except the meaning of *any* and *some*, as can be seen in the following:

> I warn you that if you do something like that I'll whip you.
> I promise you that if you do anything bad I'll come to your rescue.
> I promise you that if you get any good grades at all I'll give you $10.

In the first, the hearer has given some positive indication, by word or deed, of performing the forbidden action; the action is more particularized than if *anything* were used, which would make the prohibition more inclusive. In the second, it is the relative unlikelihood, in the speaker's mind, of his interlocutor's being guilty of a bad action, that makes him choose *anything* – his feeling could be shown as a kind of scale between *some* and *any*: 'It isn't likely that my friend will do something bad – in fact, it isn't likely that he will do anything bad at all', where *anything* sweeps the horizons for all possibilities and finds them doubtful. In the third example the speaker uses *any* because just one or two good grades are enough and it makes no difference what part of the range they are from. In all three examples the speaker picks WORDS to suit the MEANINGS he has in mind. He does not first ideate a performative which then automatically triggers a *some* or an *any*.

Labov 1972 does in a thorough way what my original article only adumbrated. It discriminates the features of *any* by a reasoned logical analysis and shows how they react with contextual conditions to produce acceptable and unacceptable utterances. The features are features OF *any*: the lexical integrity of the word is respected. The correspondence of *any* and *some* finds its proper perspective: it is 'a product of discourse considerations, rather than an automatic suppletive fact' (799). The problem that Labov set out to handle was the unacceptability of sentences like *Anyone wouldn't go to his party despite the acceptability of the affirmative *Anyone would go to his party* and of negations in which *any* is commanded by a non-factual, for example *If anyone didn't go to his party . . .*, *For anyone not to go to his party . . .*, and so on. He states this as a rule: 'Whenever an unstressed indeterminate *any*, without a negative feature of its own, is not commanded by a negative or non-factive feature, it may not be followed by a negative' (782). The logical proofs as far as I can see are unassailable. The only doubtful thing is the categoricalness of the rule itself. It is a sort of last gasp of syntax. Given the tenor of the article, which is anything but categorical, it is as if Labov found himself forced to concede that this one relic of syntactic categoricalness had resisted his onslaught. So it may be a comfort to him to discover that even here there are exceptions, which do not conflict with his general logical position. Consider the following:

[1] Anybody shouldn't wánt to, I would think.
[2] Anybody mightn't want to but still do it anyway.
[3] Anybody could hardly be blamed for doing thát!
[4] Anybody wouldn't think you had a care in the world.
[5] Anybody hadn't better try that with mé!
[6] Hell's bells, anybody would never be thát foolish!
[7] Any géntleman wouldn't use such language.

All these have modals, which Labov found conducive to *any* in affirmative sentences. In addition each one has something else that pushes it toward greater acceptability. In [1] it is the tentativeness of the tagged higher sentence; the result is less assertive, more non-factual. In [2] the modal itself, being epistemic, attaches to a higher sentence, which gives, under-lyingly, the 'command' that Labov specifies; on top of that there is a parallel affirmative which would be destroyed if *nobody* were used: *No-body might want to but still do it anyway*. In [3] there is again an epistemic (*hardly* negates it: *It is hardly fair for anybody to be blamed for doing thát*), on top of which *hardly* lacks any straightforward affirmative counterpart, so that with *nobody* we would come out with the rather unsatisfying *Nobody could very fairly (easily, rightly) be blamed for doing thát*; besides which *nobody* is too categorical – what we want to say is *It is true of anybody that* . . . . In Scots we would not have to make do with the explicitly distributive *any* but could use the merely indefinite *a body*: *A body could hardly be blamed for doing thát!* And this can stand in more gracefully for a particular individual: *A body – meaning John – could* etc. Indefinite *a man* is like *a body*. There are other kinds of following negatives that are equally awkward to change, for example when a change from *any* to *no* would compel a later change from *no* to *any*: *Anybody (a body, a person, a man) is no more to be trusted with a billion dollars than with an atomic bomb* is better if anything than *Nobody is any more to be trusted* etc. In [4] there is negative raising: *Anybody would think you hadn't a care in the world.* In [5] and [6], as in [3], we have proof that an *any* plus a negative is not quite the same in meaning as a *no, none*. *Nobody had better try that with mé!* is a remark ABOUT the situation rather than one addressed TO it. We can imagine [5] being said with a threatening look at all the anybodies within hearing. Similarly with [6]: *Nobody would ever be thát foolish!* forecloses the possibilities whereas [6], with *anybody*, keeps them open: it makes a better exclamation, and its tentativeness can be seen in the greater ease with which a *would they?* can be tagged. As for [7], the accent on the noun shows that we have the equivalent of a limiting clause – *Anybody who is a gentleman wouldn't use such language* – which is explicitly provided for in Labov's rule (the *any* is determined).

The gradient becomes very steep at the point of Labov's rule for negative attraction, but it is not a vertical cliff. Discourse considerations are still in operation, and the syntactic rule is still variable. The constant is the meaning of *any*, which Anthony (forthcoming) defines as 'counter-specification'.

2 *Any* and *some* as independent words

The problem of *any* and *some* lies precisely athwart the line that separates syntax from lexicon. In one view (adopted by Lees 1960*a*) it belongs to syntax and should be dealt with transformationally. In the other it belongs to lexicon and its relationship to such matters of syntax as negation and interrogation is incidental. What follows is meant to show that lexicon has the first claim, and *any* is not a form that is automatically triggered by a negative or an interrogative.

Some can occur in environments that supposedly should allow only *any*. This can be dealt with by an old dodge – 'free variation'; the difference, if any, is stylistic. But a brief look at conducive negation is enough to show that more than 'style' is involved. (Conduciveness is the process of cuing an expected answer, as in *Isn't it a lovely day?* or *It's a lovely day, isn't it?*) The difference in the following is unmistakable:

Didn't you publish some poetry back in 1916? = Isn't it true that you published some poetry back in in 1916?
Didn't you publish any poetry back in 1916? = Is it true that you didn't publish any poetry back in 1916?

The first is conducive; the speaker already holds the belief, and an affirmative answer is expected. The second is non-conducive; it expects yes or no equally. (Nowadays we would recognize that something is presupposed here – the speaker has inferred non-publishing as an explanation for some fact that has come up: *That year was when I was hardly recognized as a poet any longer. – Why? Was it that you hadn't published any poetry that year?*, equivalent to *Why? Didn't you publish any poetry that year?* But presupposition is not belief. The speaker holds no brief for either yes or no.) A ludicrous example, touching on the 'private verbs' and 'public verbs' noted by Joos, is *Why don't you love me any more?* and *Why don't you love me some more?* The use of *some* and *any* is an incidental clue to conducive versus non-conducive negation.[1]

3 The relevance of accent and mass-count

Lees states, 'except for *any* under contrastive primary stress with the meaning "whatsoever, no matter which, etc"', *some* in assertions alternates with *any* in questions and negatives.' The matter of accent ('stress') has at least as much to do with *some* as with *any*, and invokes the question of mass-count because the usual adjunct form of *some* with mass (and plural) nouns is [sm̩], while the usual adjunct form with singular countables is [sʌm]. This whole matter is of doubtful relevance, but Lees is obliged to exorcise it to escape from the type *Any man would do that*, which otherwise would disprove his thesis.

In the first place, even having obviously the meaning that Lees assigns, *any* does not have to be under 'contrastive primary stress', *eg: Maybe yóu wouldn't do that, but any mán would* has the contrastive accent on *man*.

In other contexts as well, however, the *some-any* distinction is maintained, regardless of accent or type of noun. We can say that *any* is accented as any other word is accented – to focus on its meaning; and where *any* is accented, *some* is accented. The accent is overlaid along with the rest of the speech melody, and does not affect the underlying difference.[2] In the following I posit that [sm̩] is the plural and mass equivalent of the indefinite article, and that [sʌm] with a singular countable is the emphatic equivalent of the indefinite article. Note how *a-any* and *some-any* ignore these lines:

a, any, one
Do you see a man over there? No, I don't see any. Yes, I see one. Do you see any MP around anywhere? No, I don't see any. Yes, I see one. Here, with singular countables, *a-any* reproduces the *some-any* contrast in questions: *Do you see a man over there?* suggests that the speaker thinks he may see one. *Do you see any MP around?* evinces concern over the presence of whatever such individual.

[sm̩], *any*, [sʌm]
Did you hire some clerks (some help)? No, I didn't hire any. Yes, I hired some. Do you see any MPs (any supervision)? No, I don't see any. Yes, I see some.

Another example of the kinship of this type with the preceding one: *I got the idea that there might be a call for me, but as it turned out there wasn't any; I got the idea that there might be some* [sm̩] *calls for me, but as it turned out there weren't any.*

[sʌm], *any,* emphatic but not contrastively accented, singular countable
Was there any (some [sʌm]*) attempt at escape? There wasn't any attempt at escape. There was some* [sʌm] *attempt at escape. What was the argument about – some dame? No, it wasn't about any dame; one of them called the other a liar. Was any (some* [sʌm]*) exception made? No, they wouldn't make any. Has any (some* [sʌm]*) rule been violated? No, there hasn't been any rule violated. Is there any (some* [sʌm]*) cure for it? No, there isn't any cure for it.*

[sʌm], *any,* emphatic but not contrastively accented, plural
Were there any (some [sʌm]*) attempts at escape? There weren't any attempts at escape. There were some* [sʌm] *attempts at escape. He did it, but not without some* [sʌm] *misgivings. He did it without any misgivings.* The meaning of *some* is 'a certain few'.

[sʌm], *any,* emphatic but not contrastively accented, mass

Lo   had   to be some ox   e   fish would have. di
  ok. There   ygen the r or the   ed.

Some emphatic here means 'some-little-old', 'some-or-other'. Unemphatic [sm̩] could of course be used in the same context. *No, there wasn't any oxygen there.*

Contrastive accent can of course be added to [sʌm], as well as to *any.*

4 *Some-any* versus inherent negatives

I maintain that *some* and *any* do not have affirmation and negation built into their meaning, but what correlation there is between the two systems is a matter of semantic compatibility. This does not mean that negation, for example, is never built in. A kind of polarizing force attaches itself more or less permanently to certain expressions, pairing them off with others in a negative-affirmative contrast (or, more properly, in a negative-unmarked contrast, as we now prefer to view such 'polarity items'). Usually, though not always, one can read 'negation' as including 'questions' and 'conditions'. Some examples of built-in negation follow, divided into verbs and non-verbs.

Verbs

(1) *Mind* versus *object: Do you mind (object)? No, I don't mind (object).* **I mind his raising all that fuss* (but the rejoinder *Yes, I do mind* is normal). *I object. If you mind (object), I won't do it.* (2) *Budge* versus *move:* **Will they budge? Will they move? They won't budge (move).* **He budged. He moved. If he so much as budges (moves) one inch, hold him.* (3) *Care* versus *like: Would you care (like) to go? I wouldn't care (like) to.* **I'd care to. I'd like to. If you'd care (like) to wait a minute, I'll show you in.* (4) *Let on* versus *confess, reveal, indicate,* etc: *Did he let on (reveal) what the real reason was? He didn't let on (reveal) what it was.* **He let on what it was. He revealed what it was. If you dare let on what the real reason is, I'll fix you.*[3]

Non-verbs

(5) *Long* versus *a long time: Will they be long (a long time) in getting there? They weren't long (a long time) in getting there.* **They were long in getting there* (but emphatic formulas are normal: *He was there long before I was; They were too long in getting there*). *They were a long time getting there. If it's going to be long (a long time), let's sit down.* (6) *Far* versus *a long way: Is it far (a long way) from here? It isn't far (a long way) from here.* **It's far from here* (but again with emphasis: *It's far, far away from here; It's terribly [too] far from here*). *It's a long way from here. If you have far (a long way) to go, start early.* (7) *Very* versus *pretty, awfully, rather,* etc. This polarization is not complete. (Also it is more heterogeneous: *awfully* is unmarked – for example, *He is awfully bright, He isn't awfully bright;* but *pretty* and *rather* are marked for affirmative – for example, *It's pretty good,* **It isn't pretty good; She's rather tall,* **She isn't rather tall.*) In my speech it has gone only far enough to make me feel a bit uncomfortable with a sentence like *It's very new* unless *very* is quite emphatic. But *Is it very new?, It isn't very new, If you pull very hard it's liable to break,* etc, strike me as normal. (8) *Quite* versus *completely:* This polarization has been blurred by the reintroduction of *quite* from prestige dialects. I can recall the sensation of prissiness that a sentence like *It's quite good* once gave me, the most natural thing being *not quite: It isn't quite over yet, He isn't quite as heavy as he was.* Even questions here are not part of the core of my dialect, unless expecting a roundly negative answer: *Did you really think he was quite as good as he used to be?* (9) *Much* and *many* versus *a lot, a good (great) many, a great deal: Do you have much (many, a lot) to finish? I don't have much (many, a lot) to finish.* **I have much (many) to finish* (but again with emphasis: *I can think of many reasons why Chessman should not be executed; I have too much to finish*). *I have a lot (a good many, a great deal) to finish. If you have much (many, a lot) to finish,*

leave it for tomorrow. I find *Much of that material is unacceptable* to be more normal than *Much of that material is acceptable,* unless the latter comes as a denial of another's remark to the contrary.[4]

The independence of *any* from built-in negation can be seen in sentences where *any* and one of the polarized expressions occur together. Conditions, for example, are a normal place for *any* (see *pp* 159–63), but must carry a negative implication if *many* is to be accommodated easily: *If many of them are OK, I'll eat my hat; ?If many of them are OK, I'll be glad; If any of them are OK, I'll eat my hat (I'll be glad).* Similarly with the more indefinite *whenever* and the more definite *every time: Whenever there are many complaints, they appeal to me; *Every time there are many complaints, they appeal to me; Whenever (every time) there are any complaints, they appeal to me.* Or, with *mind: Whenever they mind, I refrain; *Every time they mind, I refrain; Whenever (every time) they raise any objection, I refrain.*

Although the *some-any* pair is not to be classed with *mind, budge, much,* and the like, it does have affinities with certain other pairs, notably the following:

Either-both: Do you want either (both)? I don't want either (both). I want either (both). If you want either (both) you can have them. Either-both differs from *any-some* in that it is definite; that is, *any*=one or another, *either*=the one or the other, *some*=a portion, a selection, *both*=the two.

Either-too: Do you want that one either (too)? (For me, *either* expects a negative answer here.) *I don't want that one either. *I don't want that one too.* (Normal as 'I don't want that one in addition to the other', or with *don't want*=reject, especially if reordered as *That one too I don't want.*) *I want that one either. I want that one too. If you want that one either (too), you're wasting your time* (again with *either* implying negation). This is perhaps the most definitely polarized pair of all: witness the childish *He is too!, He isn't either!,* where *too* is merely an emphatic affirmative and *either* an emphatic negative.

*Ever-sometimes: Do they ever (sometimes) ask for more? Don't ever say that again. *Don't sometimes say that again* (but *He doesn't go there sometimes* 'He stays away sometimes'). *I agree with them ever.* (*Ever since* is a relic of *ever* 'always': *I've agreed with them ever since.*) *I agree with them sometimes. If they ever (sometimes) ask for more, don't say no.*

To these can be added the compounds *anybody-somebody, anyone-someone, anything-something, anywhere-somewhere.* Given the compound *sometimes,* we see *ever* as a morphological reshaping of *at any time.* And there is a similar reshaping with the adverbial use of *any* and *some*. *Any* takes on the emphatic *at all*, as in *Is it any better? Is it at all better?* But here the *some-any* family overlaps the set of polarized forms, since *at all* has a built-in negative. As for *some*, its adverbial uses are dialectally restricted; *somewhat* occurs in the literary standard and *a little, a bit, a trifle* are colloquial. The best pairing is with *any* and *a little: Is it any (a little) better? It isn't any better.* *It isn't a little better* (normal to negate a prior affirmation). *It's any better. It's a little better. If it's any (a little) better, I'll take it.*

The *some-any* set can be diagrammed as follows:[5]

UNITARY			DISTRIBUTIVE	NEGATIVE	
Unemphatic adjunct	Emphatic adjunct	Non-adjunct		Adjunct	Non-adjunct
a, an	sʌm	one	any	no	none
sm̩	sʌm	sʌm	any	no	none
a little (somewhat, a trifle, a bit)			any (at all)	no (nowise, not one bit)	
sometimes			ever	never	
both			either	neither	
too			either	neither	
and			or	nor	

Though the family resemblances here are unmistakable, we have something less than a paradigm. Even disregarding the morphological dispersion in several of the forms, there are differences in degree of polarization. A feeble implied negative is enough to induce an *any* versus a *some*, but *either* almost requires that the negative be explicit: *I would dislike saying anything like that,* but *I would dislike saying that, either; ??I would avoid saying that, either; ?I would be reluctant to say that, either.*

5 *Any* in affirmations, *some* in negations

I have already given some examples of *any* (without 'contrastive primary stress') in affirmations. To give an idea of the contexts favoring it, I add a few more:

Sentences in which a modifying clause restricts the 'whateverness' of *any: Go anywhere you like. Turn any evidence you have over to the police. The insulation is to keep out any air that might get in. It kills any insects that may be around. A seismograph detects any tremors that may occur. What are those isotopes good for? – They trace any foreign matter in the system. I'll shoot anybody that tries it (anything that moves). I'll buy any stocks you designate.*

Initial *-ing* clauses with an over-all suggestion of tentativeness or doubt: *Having to hurt anyone is contrary to his nature* (versus *Having to hurt someone actually pleases him). Buying anything now is likely to prove a bad investment. Landing anywhere around here is going to call for pretty skilful flying.*

Subordinate clauses with tentative adverbs: *Whenever I say anything, she shuts me up. Where it makes any difference, he knows how to be tactful. Wherever you find any indication of radioactivity, mark the map.* The obvious case is *if* and its synonyms: *If (in case, supposing) it makes any difference, we can try some other way.* (This is related to questions: compare *Had he seen anyone?* and *Had he seen anyone, he would have told us.*)

Simple affirmations in which a whateverness, a non-particularity, is implied: *Any other man would have accepted. Any rust would ruin the motor – that's why we have to keep it so clean. It corrects any list to starboard. It compensates for any errors. It equalizes any injustices. You're wrong – neither Russians nor Americans are as rigid as you say; both sides would welcome any real indications of friendliness. Parents are always proud of any accomplishments of their children. Be frank; remember, they'll see through any deception on your part. They'll be here any minute now.* We are tempted to overlook instances of this kind because we tend to conceive of an action as particularized, as referring to one occurrence or set of occurrences rather than to a possibility of occurrence. Thus *★The man consumed any sandwiches* is unusual because we think of sandwich-eating as referring to a given occasion; but *The acid consumed any rust* is normal because it covers an indefinite number of occasions, and the 'whatever' meaning of *any* applies.[6]

Lees stars *★We didn't eat something.* This is a possible sentence, as is any other where the negation does not penetrate to the thing but affects the action as a whole: *Why is your mother mad at you? – Because we didn't eat something [that she told us to eat]* – meaning, of course, 'We neglected to eat something'. In *I was embarrassed because I didn't know some important people who were there,* either there was an affirmative desire to know some or the reference is to a particular group that was there – the negation goes to the action as a whole, not to the noun.

6 *Some* in questions

A question that serves to prompt – typically an invitation to positive action – calls for *some*. In the following, *any* is unacceptable: *Good morning, will you have some breakfast? Will you please give me some sugar for my cereal? May I have a couple of tickets for some friends? What do you say we go buy her some flowers? Why don't you stay awhile and have some tea? Shall we go in and have some hamburgers? May I leave something for somebody who is coming by at four o'clock to pick it up?*

Suppositions likewise call for *some*. A prior fact is assumed: *What are you looking so happy about? – did your dad bring you something? What did they give you to drink – some ginger ale?* A man encountering his crushed hat on the seat of a chair says *What happened here? – did somebody sit on it? What's the matter – don't you like me or something?* ('Is the explanation that you don't like me or something of the kind?') In the paired sentences *Did you hear that something (anything) happened last night?* and *Did you know that something happened last night?* I find *anything* more difficult with the factual *know* than with the conjectural *hear*, but when *did you know* is replaced with *do you know*, commonly used in the sense 'so far as you know' and hence again conjectural, *anything* is normal: *Do you know that anything happened last night?* Suppositions reveal a bit of real rather than transformational history. In *Did you know that something happened last night?* we have *Something happened last night – did you know it?*

Conducive questions and expectations are subtypes of suppositions. *Didn't you pick up some kind of bug in Mexico?* can be paraphrased to make the supposition explicit: *You picked up some kind of bug in Mexico, didn't you?* An expectation can be made explicit by tagging *I hope*: *Did you bring some milk, I hope?* (**Did you bring any milk, I hope?*)

7 *Any* without explicit negation

The barest suggestion of a negative, without the presence of an explicitly negative word such as *no, not, nobody, never,* etc, makes a favorable climate for *any*. In *It's been a week since I bought any*, the implication is that I haven't bought any for a week. In *This doctrine was first put out in any detail in 1935,*[7] we understand that it was not put out in any detail earlier. In *He has more than anybody else*, nobody has more than he. In *Stop him before he does anything foolish* the meaning is that he should be kept from doing anything foolish. And note this verb *kept from*, and *prevent*, and many others which imply negation: *We avoid any such complications; He has waived any privilege under the contract; You'll have to relinquish any and all claims.* This occurs most easily in complex sentences in which the main clause implies a negative, even just a negative emotion: *I'm sorry I said anything, He's sore that anybody would turn him down, I wonder that anybody even looked at her, They're afraid to go anywhere, She hates to apologize to anybody, I defy you to prove anything, I doubt that he wants anything, The idea of his doing anything for me!, How strange that anyone would believe that!* (even *How nice that anyone would believe that!* if there had been some doubt of its likelihood).

Minimal contrasts show how subtle the negative and affirmative shadings may be in order to induce a *some* or an *any.* In *Don't do anything I wouldn't do, anything* is a bit more likely than *something;* but in *Don't go and do something I wouldn't do,* the *go and* is just positive enough to tip the balance slightly in favor of *something.* In the series *not more than, barely, scarcely,* and *hardly,* we find a gradient in which *some* is favored at one end and *any* at the other:

> I had not more than eaten some of the fruit when . . .
> I had barely eaten some (any) of the fruit when . . .
> I had scarcely eaten any (some) of the fruit when . . .
> I had hardly eaten any of the fruit when . . .

To define 'negation' under these circumstances becomes exceedingly difficult. Our only formal, and none too reliable, clue is the selection of the word *any* itself, but then to say that *any* is required in negative contexts becomes a circular rule.[8] The effect of this is to enable us to use the same rule to derive *some* that Lees used to derive *any.* We have an 'affirmative' context, *ie,* one in which there is no formal negative; but negation is implied. We then add a formal negative, and get *some.* In the following four sets the choices are not uniformly obligatory but they are certainly plausible:

He accepts some.	He refuses any.
He doesn't accept any.	He doesn't refuse some.
He has some.	He lacks any.
He doesn't have any.	He doesn't lack some.
I'm for something like that.	I'm against anything like that.
I'm not for anything like that.	I'm not against something like that.
I'll demand some profit.	I'll forgo any profit.
I won't demand any profit.	I won't forgo some profit.

For both ends of the inverted rule in a single sentence, take *I don't mind some wine, but I do mind any hard liquor.*

Embedded clauses are no exception, in spite of Lees's assertion that 'even when the indefinite word appears in another sentence embedded within the main sentence, it is still restricted to *some* in assertions, *any* in Q's and negatives'. This is true (with exceptions already noted) of *I'm willing to accept some* and *I'm not willing to accept any.* But the rule is reversed in *I'm loth to accept any* and *I'm not loth to accept some, I'm averse to accepting anything* and *I'm not averse to accepting something, I'm ashamed to accept anybody's help* and *I'm not ashamed to accept somebody's help,* etc.

8 A logical model of *some-any*

Some and *any* contrast too often in identical environments for the difference between them to be attributed to 'style'. If we are looking for an alternate to *any* that is truly stylistic – assuming that style includes contrasts of emphasis, speech level, and the like, but excludes the truth values – our choice would fall on the word *no* (*none*) replacing *not any, eg, There's no time to waste = There isn't any time to waste, He'll get no recommendation from me = He won't get any recommendation from me,* etc. (In subject position it is normally *no* and not *not any* that occurs in simple predications: *No man can believe that = *Not any man can believe that = There isn't any man who can believe that.*) ' "Boston is not far from any city" . . . is as good a reading as "Boston is far from no city" . . .' (Quine 1941, 100).

The logical difficulty of *some* in negations is its unsuitability for categorical negation: 'When a statement involves "some" (or in particular "something"), attachment of "not" to its main verb does not in general produce a denial of the statement . . . "Something does not bore George" is by no means the denial of "Something bores George". Whereas the latter goes into symbols as:

[1] $\exists x$ x bores George,

the former does not express the denial:

[2] $\sim\exists x$ x bores George;

it expresses rather another quantification:

[3] $\exists x$ $\sim x$ bores George

to the effect that there are at least some things in the world that do not bore George' (Quine 1941, 99).

The idiomatic rendering of [2] is *Nothing bores George,* or, to put the sentences in a form that more closely resembles our previous examples, *There is something that bores George, There isn't anything (there is nothing) that bores George, There is something that doesn't bore George.*

Applying this to Lees's *We didn't eat anything, We didn't eat something,* we get, for the first, 'There was no x such that we ate x', or $\sim \exists x$ We ate x, and for the second, 'There was an x such that we did not eat x', or $\exists x \sim$ We ate x. The latter is no good for categorical denial because it fails to tell us whether the other somethings were eaten or not.

This comes about through the distributive nature of negation, and explains why the distributive lexemes *any, either, ever* are suitable where the collective lexemes *some, both, too* are unsuitable except on the less frequent occasions when the speaker limits the scope of the negation. 'Whereas conjunction combines statements two or more at a time, denial applies to statements one at a time. Statements can be denied jointly, however, by denying them severally and conjoining the denials' (Quine 1941, 13). This is what *any (either, ever)* enables the speaker to do: *any* means (and this has nothing to do with contrastive accent) just what Lees says it means, 'whatsoever, no matter which'. Its use with negation enables us to 'deny statements severally and conjoin the denials' – *I don't have any friends* means 'I don't have friend A + I don't have friend B + I don't have friend C + ... ∞ – I don't have whatever friend may be indicated'.

Any, therefore, is extremely USEFUL to negation and hence highly frequent IN negation but is not in a one-to-one mechanical relationship with negation as singular -*s* in a verb is to singular -∅ in a subject noun. The relationship is one of semantic compatibility, of ontological, not grammatical, sense.

The relationship to questions is similar. A *some* indicates a particularity, an assumed something (more often than not an existent something, a bit of real, not transformational, history). The sequence *You know something? – Joe got married* is nonsense with *anything.* An *any* opens the entire field to inquiry. *Are you going anywhere?* infers nothing, particularizes nothing. *Are you going somewhere?* does infer something, so that *What's the big hurry – are you going somewhere?* is a logical sequence, but *What's the big hurry – are you going anywhere?* is a non-sequitur.

The best statement that can be made about *any* is in lexical terms. It is hard to improve on the one given by Jespersen (1933, 17.9.1): '*Any* indicates one or more, no matter which; therefore *any* is very frequent in sentences implying negation or doubt (question, condition).'

9 Conclusion

There is no denying that the association of *any* with negation is intimate enough so that, through reinterpretation by speakers of limited experience, it may in some idiolects be on its way to becoming as proper to syntactic transformations as to lexicon. We have already seen how far the *either-too* pair has gone. What one hears from younger speakers is of course pertinent in this regard. I noted from a fifteen-year-old the question *Why didn't you give ús any?*, surprising to me because the context was one expecting the item to be given and I would have said *Why didn't you give ús some?* But this encroachment does not conflict with the idiomatic interpretation, and I doubt that it has progressed far enough yet to call for a new accounting.

Notes

1 From the perspective of later transformational-generative grammar the contrast at this point could still be handled syntactically in terms of the absence or presence of negation in the embedded sentence, roughly, *You published some poetry* versus *You didn't publish any poetry* in the first pair, and *You don't love me any more – why?* versus *Love me some more, why don't you?* in the second.

2 The one place where prosody makes a striking difference is in the type *I don't want to go anywhere*, with rise–fall–rise on the last word, meaning 'I don't want to go just anywhere'. But even this is not totally unambiguous, and the rise–fall–rise is not required; *cf* the announcement by President Truman on 20 February 1952: 'I have made no commitments to England to send American troops anywhere in the world', with two almost contradictory meanings and no necessary difference in the intonation.

3 See F. W. Bradley, 'A Word List from South Carolina', *Publications of the American Dialect Society* No 14 (1950), *p* 44.

4 An incidental point of some interest is what constitutes a polarity item. We might, for example, be tempted to include the pair *yet-already*; but actually it does not belong. Rather, these two words conjugate with affirmation and negation in terms of their meaning, which in itself is neither affirmative nor negative. *Yet* expects a state of affairs to have been reversed prior to the time of reference. *They aren't here yet* implies that the state of their not being here was expected to be reversed by now; *He's here yét* implies that the state of his being here was expected to be reversed by now. (The accent on *yet*, optional in the negative sentence but required in the affirmative, is itself based on the nature of the expectations and does not affect the meaning of the word except to focus on it.) The expectation with *already* is that a state of affairs that is true at the time of reference actually should have become true later. *He's here already* (*already here*) expected this affirmation to come true later, but it has come true now. Since it is true at the time of reference, *already* is forced to be affirmative. If there is a negative, as in *He's not eating already* (*already not eating*), the

negation is affirmed as a unit: *not eating=fasting*. As with *some*, the affirmativeness of *already* compels conducive negation in questions: *Aren't they here already?=They're here already, aren't they?* But *yet* is ambiguous, at least when it is accented: *Aren't they here yét?= They're still here, aren't they?* (conducive) or *Is it still true that they are not here?*

5 I disregard in the table the restricted distribution of forms where there is no contrast. For example, in the *a little* row, *no* occupies the whole negative slot although it is adjunct only – there is no non-adjunct to contrast with it as in the case of *no-none*. Also, though *at all* is emphatic, *ever* is not necessarily unemphatic (*Don't you go there éver? Don't you go there at áll?*), therefore the 'distributive' column has no separation for emphasis. I add *and-or-nor* to complete the picture, though *or* and *nor* alternate in exceptional ways.

6 The kinship between this last set of examples and the first with its modifying clauses might now suggest a syntactic treatment, which is to assume a non-recoverable underlying clause. Thus *Any rust would ruin the motor=Any rust that there might be would ruin the motor.* But this does not explain the unacceptability of ⋆*I'm sure that when he came in John noticed any woman*, since when the clause is given, the sentence is acceptable: *I'm sure that when he came in John noticed any woman that was there.* Without the clause, we have no clue to non-particularity (unlike such a case as *I'm sure that John would have noticed any woman*), and the perfective verb is too strong an indication of the opposite, that is, of particularity. The clause makes a nice explicative paraphrase, but what *any* responds to is non-particularity.

7 *Language* 37 (1961) 195.

8 The choice of *any* to determine the negativeness of something else is indeed sometimes practical, as in the case of *if not* and *unless: If you don't say anything (something) I'll scream* versus *Unless you say something I'll scream.* Or *few* and *a few: Few need any* versus *A few need some.*

Chapter 3

Not any and no

A good deal has been written about negative hopping, negative transportation, negative raising, or negative absorption, as it has been variously called (and to which I add negative leftshifting for reasons that will become obvious), in which a negative that apparently belongs to a 'lower' verb comes to be attached to a 'higher' one. In

> [1] I want not to suffer.
> [2] I don't want to suffer.

the speaker must have a positive desire not to suffer, so that the negative would seem to belong to the lower verb; yet in [2] he expresses himself as if he wouldn't mind suffering – he just doesn't go out of his way to want it.

Negative leftshifting is not a unique phenomenon. We find also the leftshifting of affirmation or emphasis:

> [3] I believe he really did make that mistake.
> [4] I really do believe he made that mistake.

Also interrogative leftshifting:

> [5] Do you suppose he's coming? – *Yes, I do.
> [6] Do you suppose he's coming? – Yes, he is,

(The respondent ignores the question-form of *suppose* and answers 'Is he coming?')[1] Something similar happens with *shall*, as Jespersen 1909–49 points out (4.7.2.5), and also with *can:*

> [7] I hope I shall see you.
> [8] I shall hope to see you.
> [9] It seems I am unable to work.
> [10] I seem to be unable to work.
> [11] I can't seem to work.

And what about *a hot cup of tea* for *a cup of hot tea?*

In the flush of their discovery of this phenomenon, transformational grammarians were wont to assume that sentences thus related were perfect paraphrases and could be linked transformationally. Of late there have been second thoughts – Horn 1974 and Epstein 1975 make the best case for a difference in meaning, to which I add a contrasting pair by way of corroboration:

[12] I don't think he likes it, maybe he does, but I don't think so.
[13] *I think he doesn't like it, maybe he does, but I think not.

the *maybe* attached to *likes* produces no contradiction when the negative is not attached to *likes* as well but to the higher verb. Yet despite the potential difference, speakers' behavior proves that negation is not very firmly anchored:

[14] Some rotten old count that never keeps appearing 'keeps never appearing'. (Heroine in Peter Sellers' film 'The Bobo', 1967)
[15] (Fifteen-year-old speaker hears mother remark that some customers refuse trading stamps:)Why shouldn't anybody want them? 'Why should anybody not want them?'

I shall have little more to say about leftshifting, which I have brought up at this point only to distinguish it from the really neglected phenomenon that I intend to treat here: negative rightshifting.

Rightshifting was broached by Labov 1972 in a pregnant two-page aside to his monograph on negative attraction and negative concord. His treatment is a springboard for mine. In its simplest form, rightshifting relates two such sentences as the following:

[16] People are starving because *there aren't any jobs.*
[17] People are starving because *there are no jobs.*

The alternation is between Neg . . . *any* and *no(ne)*. For convenience I shall abbreviate this to *not any* versus *no*. It is understood that *not* and *any* are generally separated.

To make sure that there is no confusion with leftshifting, I offer a sentence in which either phenomenon might occur, *I want you not to see anyone,* yielding

[18] I don't want you to see anyone (leftshifting) =
[19] I want you to see no one (rightshifting).

Want is a 'Neg-raising' verb (Horn 1974). With a main verb that is not a

Neg-raiser, only rightshifting can occur, for example *tell* as in *I told you not to see anyone:*

[20] I told you to see no one (rightshifting) ≠
[21] I didn't tell you to see anyone.

Labov considered rightshifting of a nature to be described transforma-tionally, and he set up two restrictions on its operation, both designed to prevent the Neg from shifting into subordinate clauses. The first was aimed at adjective clauses. In sentences like

[22] I hate an office that doesn't have any windows.
[23] Here's a document not bearing any signature.
[24] He'd rather have a suit without any vest.

the negative in [22] is already in the clause, and can rightshift as easily as in [23] and [24]:

[25] I hate an office that has no windows.
[26] Here's a document bearing no signature.
[27] He'd rather have a suit with no vest.

But in a sentence like this one of Labov's,

[28] I'm not going to sign a petition that any half-baked Stalinist wrote.

the negative is to the left of the noun *petition*, and is blocked; therefore

[29] I'm going to sign a petition that no half-baked Stalinist wrote.

while grammatical, means something different. (The version *I'm going to sign no petition that any . . .* is a normal instance of rightshifting that does not attempt to penetrate a subordinate clause.)

The second restriction was aimed at noun clauses. It did not interfere with infinitives, so that pairs like

[30] I didn't force John to do anything!
[31] I forced John to do nothing!

or even like

[32] He didn't order George to tell Arthur to ask Sam to do anything like this!
[33] He ordered George to tell Arthur to ask Sam to do nothing like this!

may have the same reading, but two such sentences as

[34] I didn't say that John painted any of these!
[35] I said that John painted none of these!

are hard to interpret as synonymous.

While these restrictions are typical of some of the real difficulties of rightshifting, they are far from being any sort of filter through which good sentences may pass and bad ones are strained out. The first restriction is violated by this pair:

[36] In this medicine you have a remedy that is good for all sorts of ailments. – In this medicine you don't have a remedy that's good for anything, my friend.
[37] In this medicine you have a remedy that is good for nothing, my friend.

The second restriction is violated by this one:

[38] You told John you would help him. – I didn't tell John I would do any such thing.
[39] I told John I would do no such thing.

Furthermore, given a context, many sentences that violate neither restriction may be unacceptable with rightshifting:

[40] What are you doing there? Eating oranges? – I'm not eating any oranges, no indeed; I can't stand them ≠
[41] *I'm eating no oranges, no indeed; I can't stand them.

But there is no problem with

[42] How are you getting your vitamins these days? –Well, I'm not eating any more oranges, I can tell you that. From now on it's tomato juice =
[43] Well, I'm eating no more oranges, I can tell you that. From now on it's tomato juice.

(As will be seen later, in [43] the speaker is assuming that his interlocutor may have in mind that he is still eating oranges.) Nor is there any problem with

[44] What are you doing here? Eating oranges? – I'm not doing anything and not eating anything. So why don't you mind your own business?

[45] I'm doing nothing and eating nothing. So why don't you mind your own business?

I believe it is futile to assume a transformational relationship, and more so to try to write restrictions on it, without some theory of what the constructions mean. There is a lexical contrast, *not any* versus *no;* and there is a syntactic contrast, negating the verb versus negating the alternatives. It should hardly be surprising if this turned out to have semantic consequences, with or without a logical, truth-value difference.

1 Cases in which logical equivalence is lacking

A necessary first step is to set aside the kinds of sentences in which the syntactically non-negated verb is semantically non-negated as well: that is, in which the action of the verb actually takes place – the negation in the complement does not involve it.

Canceled negation
In the kind of leftshifting whose alter ego is 'negative raising', the higher verb that receives the negation is negated along with the lower verb. That is, in a sentence such as *I don't suppose they did it* the negation can be interpreted with the higher verb – the supposition that they did it is negated on the basis of their actually not having done it. With canceled negation, we know, either from our knowledge of the world or from indications in the context, that the action takes place; the negative therefore logically belongs to the subordinate verb, and can be regarded as leftshifted:

[46] How did they happen to starve? – They didn't live where any food could be garnered =
[47] They lived where no food could be garnered.

If they lived where no food could be garnered, obviously they did not live where any food could be garnered; the other possible meaning of [46], that they did not live anywhere, is ruled out as nonsense. If the leftshifting analysis of [46] is accepted, then basic to both [46] and [47] is presumably [48]:

[48] ?They lived where not any food could be garnered.

The problem of [48]'s acceptability will be looked at later. For the moment, the only question is whether a PROCESS of leftshifting occurs here.

It probably makes more sense simply to accept [46] at face value: the scope of the negation is the entire sentence, and the hearer does not psychologically dissect a *did live*, which he knows to be the case, but instead draws an inference, much as he would do in an exchange like *Was John robbing a bank? – Well, he wasn't picking daisies.*

Canceled negation occurs in sentences that are basically definitional. To paraphrase the preceding example:

[49] The place where they lived wasn't a place where any food could be garnered =

[50] The place where they lived was a place where no food could be garnered.

Similarly:

[51] You say that Joe is no good as a liar. It seems to me that he is pretty good at it. – Trouble is, he doesn't tell lies that anybody believes, only lies that are too fantastic to be credible =

[52] Trouble is, he tells lies that nobody believes.

Here the context rules out the possibility of his telling no lies at all. The definitional paraphrase is

[53] Joe's lies aren't lies that anybody believes.

[54] Joe's lies are lies that nobody believes.

Two more examples, one disambiguated by knowledge of the world and the other by immediate context:

[55] How do you feel about murder? – Murder isn't something that any decent society condones =

[56] Murder is something that no decent society condones.

[57] I can understand your hating to have Jones as a fellow-worker – somebody who never shows up at the office. – Oh, he shows up all right. He just doesn't show up when any jobs are waiting for him =

[58] He just shows up when no jobs are waiting for him.

If these were cases of rightshifting, they would violate Labov's first restriction.

Idioms

The negation is attached to some part of the complement. Examples:

[59] He got there in nothing flat ≠ He didn't get there in anything flat.

[60] Don't worry, I'll have this finished in nó time ≠ I won't have this finished in any time.

[61] It was no go ≠ It wasn't any go.

I do not include among idioms those collocations whose lack of a *not any* counterpart is due to chance – semantically they could just as well have one. Thus *I'll have none of it* is stereotyped in the sense 'I'll not permit it' (not idiomatic because *I'll not have* is used freely with a nominal complement, *eg*, *I'll not have any of your lip*, *I'll not have that kind of behavior around here*); it does not match, or does not match very well, with *I'll not have any of it*, otherwise a perfectly good potential carrier of the special meaning. While idioms and stereotypes with *no* are probably in the majority, the opposite case can be found:

[62] I'm not getting any younger.

[63] Don't take any wooden nickels.

Privatives

A *with* plus negation easily becomes a privative:

[64] I took a bath with no soap = I took a bath without any soap ≠ I didn't take a bath with any soap.

[65] The judge let them off with no penalty (scot-free).

[66] The mole can see with no light.

Underlying sentential complements

A complement that refers to an event may be caused to refer to a non-event by being independently negated. So for event nouns:

[67] I will accept no reprisals 'I will accept there being no reprisals' or 'I will not accept any reprisals'.

[68] The weatherman predicts no rain 'He predicts that there will be no rain' (unusual as 'He doesn't predict any rain').

[69] I promise you no punishment 'I promise that you will not be punished' (pragmatically odd as 'I don't promise you any punishment').

And for adverbial modifiers of events:

[70] John can make a success under no pressure 'He can make a success when he is under no pressure' (less likely, 'He can't make a success when he is under any pressure').

[71] John is really happiest in no job at all 'He is happiest when he is not working' (less likely, 'He isn't happiest at any job').

2 External negation

In external negation the speaker denies something that has supposedly been affirmed. One sign of this is the use of *some* rather than *any;* another is a special intonation, or punctuation, to show that the thing denied is quoted:

[72] You ate some mushrooms. – I did not 'eat some mushrooms'.

With external negation, the bars to using at least SOME forms of *no* rather than *not any* are virtually down. Examples [33], [35] and [37] show this. Supplying a context for [33], we have

[73] He ordered George to tell Arthur to ask Sam to weld these pieces. – He ordered George to tell Arthur to ask Sam to do nothing like this!

Other examples:

[74] You ate ten oranges. – I didn't eat any ten oranges!=
[75] I ate no ten oranges!
[76] You approved of John's painting all of these. – I didn't approve of John's painting any of these!=
[77] I approved of John's painting none of these!
[78] You're convinced he helped both sides? – I'm not convinced he helped anybody!=
[79] I'm convinced he helped nobody!

There is an intonational difference, for example between [76] and [77] and between [78] and [79]. To take the [76–77] pair,

[80] I did n't approve of John's painting any of these!

[81] I ap proved of John's painting none of these!

Without the latter intonation, an example such as [77] or [79] would tend
to be seen as having the negation confined to the subordinate clause. (One
such as [75] may use a fall-rise because of the numeral; it could well be
followed by *I didn't even eat six!* with a straight fall.) The basis for the
intonation will be discussed later.

External negation is basically speaker's negation. There is less motive
for a speaker to take up someone else's denial of a third party's affirmation,
and accordingly [83] is less likely than [82]:

[82] You claimed that Gregg had written the will. – I claimed that
Gregg had written nothing!

[83] He claimed that Gregg had written the will. – ?He claimed that
Gregg had written nothing!

If the speaker identifies himself with another's point of view, however, a
third-person verb is normal:

[84] He approved of John's painting none of these! (Speaker doesn't
want John to paint them either.)

The non-first-person affects the passive:

[85] ?It was conceded that he had said nothing!
[86] ?It was insisted that he accuse nobody!
[87] ?You were told that I was fond of nothing!

(These are all normal if the negative is viewed as unshifted.) But again, if
the speaker's viewpoint is strongly involved, there is no problem:

[88] It has been proved that he saw the crime committed. – It has been
proved that he saw nothing!

Factive verbs tend to be unsatisfactory for a different reason – a contradiction seems to result:

[89] You're glad that John ate all the dessert. – *I'm glad that John ate
nothing!

Here there is no intention on the second speaker's part to negate, in any
sense, the action of the subordinate clause, which both speakers assume to
have happened; in this respect it differs from [77] and [84]. And it differs
from [79] and [82] in the non-factivity of the latter – both non-helping
and non-writing would suit the second speaker perfectly well, even though
he does not assert that particular negation.

In all these examples except [74–75] we are dealing with a peculiar kind of negation, one that skips an intermediate verb. Thus whereas *It has been proved that he saw nothing!* can be interpreted as logically equivalent to *It hasn't been proved that he saw anything!*, the form

[90] It has been proved that he didn't see anything.

can only be equivalent to the OTHER reading of the first sentence. Why is it that a more remote negation – one at the end of the sentence – can have an effect that a closer one cannot?

I believe that the answer lies in the accentual prominence of the negation at or near the end. This is coupled with a formulaic use of the indefinites *nothing, nowhere, nobody, no one,* along with certain other expressions that lead a double life: *nothing of the sort (kind), no such (thing), nonsense, not at all, fiddlesticks, poppycock,* etc. Most of them have the possibility of either being integrated with the sentence proper or forming part of the overarching higher sentence implied in external negation, *It is not the case that* (which of course can be expressed in various ways). *Nothing of the sort* has this freedom:

[91] John is a liar. – Nothing of the sort! =
[92] Nothing of the sort is true! =
[93] John is nothing of the sort!

Nonsense belongs only with the higher sentence (**John is nonsense!*) The *klang* effect of the nuclear accent plus the echo of these higher-sentence formulas enables the sentence-bound indefinites *nothing, nowhere, nobody, no one* (and sometimes *none*) to behave as if they were exclamatory sentence-free negatives such as *nonsense.* We note that nominals negated with *no* are extremely difficult here:

[94] He found proofs that clinched the argument. – ??He found proofs that clinched no argument!

this is almost impossible as a categorical denial using a straight downglide (the most propitious intonation), such as can easily be managed with any of the following:

[95] He found proofs that clinched nothing!
[96] He found proofs that did nothing of the sort!
[97] He found proofs that clinched fiddlesticks!
[98] Poppycock!
[99] Nonsense!

No plus noun is too specific to use as a blanket denial, besides lacking the advantage of the nuclear accent on the negative. Even *no place*, for all that it competes successfully with *nowhere* on other fronts, poses no competition here:

[100] You said you were going to live abroad. – I said I was going to live nowhere! (=I didn't say I was going to live anywhere!)

[101] *I said I was going to live no place!

On the other hand, *no such place*, given the formulaic nature of *no such* (compare *He's crazy. – No such thing!*), might be used. The stereotyping of the negative indefinites with no attached nouns explains the difficulty of such an example as [35].

Given these possibilities, we are not surprised to find them extending to factives:

[102] You should be ashamed! You're glád that Eileen bumped off her boyfriend! – I'm glad that Eileen did nothing of the sort! (=I'm not glad that Eileen did anything of the sort!)

[103] I'm glad (that) nothing!

[104] I'm glad (that) fiddlesticks!

[105] I'm glad that Eileen bumped off fiddlesticks!

[106] Like héll I am!

[107] He knew you had the mumps. – He knew I had nothing! He had no way of knowing!

[108] *He knew I had no mumps! (OK as 'He knew I didn't have the mumps'.)

Formulaic external negation is no respecter of clause types. We have seen noun clauses and adjective clauses, and adverb clauses are just as amenable:

[109] You'll tell me when you get the reply. – I'll tell you when I get nothing!

Formulaic indefinite negatives are also found in disjunctions where, for emphasis, all alternatives except one are ruled out:

[110] I'll play chess or nothing.

[111] I'll live in Chicago or nowhere.

As before, *no* plus noun is unusual:

[112] *I'll play chess or no game.

[113] *I'll live in Chicago or no place.

But *no* plus noun is possible if *at all* is given the nuclear accent:

[114] I'll play chess or no game at all.
[115] I'll live in Chicago or no place at all.

3 Proximity to the verb

The formulaic denials are clearly examples of external negation – one may even think of the negation at the end coming where it does in part by virtue of its externality. But examples such as [116–119] are also external negations and are not restricted to certain formulas:

[116] He lost fifty dollars. – He lost no fifty dollars!
[117] They climbed a mountain. – They climbed no mountain! They weren't there long enough!
[118] At least they found some of them. – They found none of them!
[119] This is a lot better. – This is no better!

The formulaic negatives can occur within a subordinate clause, but *none*, *no* plus noun, and *no* plus comparative are sensitive to any syntactic break. In [116–119] the negation occurs in the essential complement of the verb, but as embeddings go deeper it becomes more and more difficult to construe any negative other than a formulaic one with the main verb. This is true even of infinitive complements:

[120] You ordered John to write some letters. – I ordered John to write no letters!
[121] You asked me to order John to write some letters. – ??I asked you to order John to write no letters!

(But [121] with a formulaic negative is normal:

[122] I asked you to order John to do no such thing!)

Similarly with prepositional phrases:

[123] This letter comes from the husband of a friend of yours. – This letter comes from no husband of a friend of mine!
[124] *This letter comes from the husband of no friend of mine!

And prepositional phrases under infinitives or *-ings*:

[125] You asked me to write a letter to a friend of yours. – I asked you to write no letter to a friend of mine!

[126] ??I asked you to write a letter to no friend of mine!
[127] You saw him dropping a tablet in a glass of water. – I saw him dropping no tablet in a glass of water!
[128] ??I saw him dropping a tablet in no glass of water!

(Here the dialects with multiple negation have all the advantage: *I never seen him drop no tablet in no glass of water!*) As for the barrier of a clause, it seems to be impenetrable except by formulaic negatives, as can be seen in the following contrasts:

[129] You know that we'll have to rent a house. – *I know that we'll have to rent no house! (OK I know that we'll have to rent nothing!)
[130] He has a dog that bit a policeman. – *He has a dog that bit no policeman! (Starred in the relevant sense. OK He has a dog that bit your old man!)
[131] They'll bide their time until they get a break. – *They'll bide their time until they get no break! (OK They'll bide their time until nothing!)

Whether the reason is syntactic (involving, perhaps, short-term memory) or semantic (involving some closer degree of entailment), it appears that for a negative to negate a whole proposition it cannot be rightshifted too far. This is only an impression, and more needs to be done to set the boundaries, but it is enough to show that except for the formulaic negatives, rightshifting has more restrictions than the two proposed by Labov.

4 A cline of externality?

I have leaned rather heavily up to this point on unmistakable cases of external negation in order to give the negative the greatest freedom to migrate. When everything in the sentence is 'old stuff' except the negative itself, negation becomes the overarching new information. External negation represents the extreme of givenness. Is it perhaps true that all cases of rightshifting depend on there being some degree of this quality?

The obvious first step away from literal external negation would be toward something the speaker views as not actually claimed but as in the mind of his interlocutor. In example [43], *How are you getting your vitamins these days? – Well, I'm eating no more oranges, I can tell you that*, the second speaker seems to be rebutting what he assumes that the other speaker might be thinking. By way of contrast, imagine a guest who has been served fruit by a hostess who knows nothing of his habits, and who offers him oranges for a second time; he replies with [132], not with [133]:

> [132] I'm not having any more oranges, thank you – my eye is on one of those apples over there.
>
> [133] *I'm having no more oranges, thank you – my eye etc.

[133] would sound rude, as if to imply that the hostess ought to know better.

A narrative context is a likely spot for complete lack of any presupposition – all the information is new:

> [134] I went for a drive but I didn't bump into any fellow from my own outfit so I gave up and came back to barracks.
>
> [135] *I went for a drive but I bumped into no fellow from my own outfit so I gave up and came back to barracks.

The same is true of most commands – we don't expect our hearer to assume what we are telling him to do:

> [136] Go take your walk, but don't stumble over any rock.
>
> [137] *Go take your walk, but stumble over no rock.
>
> [138] You feel how unsteady the earth is? – don't build any house here!
>
> [139] *You feel how unsteady the earth is? – build no house here!

Nevertheless there is a significant type of command – 'gnomic imperatives', they might be called – in which *no* is normal:

> [140] Speak no evil.
>
> [141] Post no bills.
>
> [142] Accept no substitutes.
>
> [143] No smoking.
>
> [144] No trespassing.

Such commands are in the realm of what one 'should know better than to do' – there is a presupposition about public behavior. But the same goes for private behavior where the demands are obvious, given the situation:

> [145] Don't make any noise; she's asleep.
>
> [146] ?Make no noise; she's asleep.
>
> [147] You've been warned: make no sound, or you may be caught.
>
> [148] That's an interesting summary, but don't say any more – I'd rather see the movie and get the story for myself.

[149] *That's an interesting summary, but say no more. . . .
[150] He lied, he cheated, he abused his children, he wrote bad checks, he . . . – Say no more! You've convinced me!

We seem to have here a kind of externality that might be paraphrased 'It is to be supposed that you will not' (or, leftshifted, 'You are not supposed to'). Some of the examples seem curt, and that is apt to happen with commands that carry a presupposition, but it is not inherently the case:

[151] Have no fear.
[152] ?Don't have any fear.
[153] Dream no unpleasant dreams.
[154] Don't dream any unpleasant dreams.

Here [151] and [153] are reassuring; there is actually a negative suggestion, psychologically speaking, in [154].

A command being given is more apt to be wholly new than one reported, hence a contrast like

[155] While I'm gone, don't see any of your friends.
[156] ?While I'm gone, see none of your friends.
[157] I told you to see none of your friends!

But with presupposition built in, we get

[158] While I'm gone you're seeing none of your friends. That's understood, right?

Questions behave similarly. A negative question may call either for new information or for confirmation of something presupposed:

[159] We couldn't take a vote, there wasn't a quorum. – I don't believe you. Weren't there any new members present, to make up the necessary number?
[160] ?Were there no new members present?
[161] We couldn't take a vote, there wasn't a quorum. – I can well believe you. Were there no new members present? Is that why?

Given the context of [159] – where the speaker asserts his disbelief and accepts no assumptions – [160] is inappropriate. But as a confirmation of his suspicions, the same form is appropriate in [161]. In the following pair, the first question asks something for confirmation while the second brings up a new topic – if rightshifting were used it would suggest that the hearer ought to have had the sense to think of it:

[162] It was spooky there with nobody around. I was desperate for

company. – Had you seen no one? No one at all? (= Was it because you had seen no one?)

[163] It was spooky there with nobody around. I was desperate for company. – Couldn't you find anything to read? That might have cheered you up a bit.

Examples such as [163] suggest a gradient in which the rightshifted negative is the most categorical, and *any* is between that and a question with *some: Couldn't you find something to read?* would be equally appropriate.

In [164] and [165] the speaker has drawn an inference and is asking for confirmation:

[164] Have you no manners, child?
[165] Is there no end to his impertinence?

The person asked [164] is given little opportunity to protest; but if asked *Haven't you any manners, child?* the response *Of course I have!* would be appropriate.

As for answers, when they are directed to what the speaker takes to be a presupposition on the hearer's part (as in [43]) they may use *no*. In the following there is no presupposition:

[166] In warm weather I just can't stand to be in the kitchen, but my family expects two hot meals a day. How do yóu manage? – I just don't cook anything (?I just cook nothing). They get cold meals and like it.

And similarly with [167]; but in [169], the answer could appropriately be preceded with *Agh – we might have known!*

[167] I tested out Solution B against all the ones we rejected, and guess what I found: it doesn't work any better than the others do.
[168] ? . . . and guess what I found: it works no better than the others do.
[169] How did Solution B turn out? – It's no better than the others.

There need be no explicit question, of course; the same contrast occurs:

[170] When he woke the next morning I heard him scream, 'I can't see anything! I'm blind!'
[171] *When he woke the next morning I heard him scream, 'I can see nothing! I'm blind!'
[172] As I told you, the poor man can see nothing; he's been blind for years.

In [167–172] it is the context that tells us what is new and what is not, but that information can just as easily come from our knowledge of the world:

[173] I'm eating, and getting no nourishment.
[174] ?I'm eating, and getting no toothache!
[175] I'm eating, and not getting any toothache!
[176] They're at the carnival, but having no fun.
[177] ?They're at the carnival, looking for nothing, just fooling around.
[178] They're at the carnival, not looking for anything, just fooling around.
[179] They're at the movies, but seeing no film – it's a TV presentation this time.
[180] ?They're at the movies, but seeing no vaudeville this time.
[181] They're at the movies, but not seeing any vaudeville this time.

It is expected that food will nourish, that carnivals will amuse, and that movies will show film. To justify [174] would call for a fairly elaborate contextualization, whereby eating would naturally lead to a toothache; [175] is normal, and INFORMS us that there is some connection between eating and toothache – the connection is not presupposed. If movies nowadays routinely showed vaudeville, [180] would be normal.

A rightshifted negative finds a rhetorical use with speakers who set up straw men in the form of assumed presuppositions and proceed to knock them down:

[182] This is no honest man standing up for his rights. This is no folk hero, no champion of the underdog, no knight in shining armor, but the meanest of the mean, the lowest of the low, of self-serving politicians.

The presence of an expletive adjective expressing a value judgment signals a presupposition and is easily accompanied by rightshifting. Thus a person who dislikes all pianos may generalize the class as *tinpanny* – he assumes that his interlocutor ought to share his prejudice when he uses such an adjective in pre-position:

[183] ?OK, I'll entertain you, but I'll play no piano – it'll have to be an accordion or an organ.
[184] OK, I'll entertain you, but I'll play no tinpanny piano – it'll have to be an accordion or an organ.
[185] ?He said he would rent no apartment – he hates the noise.

[186] He said he would rent no stupid apartment – he hates the noise.
[187] ?I'll go, but I'll wear no necktie.
[188] I'll go, but I'll wear no damned necktie.

These examples of pejorative generalization bring out another fact, which is that potentially generalizing nouns, that is, mass nouns (especially abstract ones) and plurals are more frequent in *no* rightshifting than singular – especially concrete singular – nouns are. This can't be because *no* and *any* are barred from singular:

[189] There wasn't any bulb in the lamp.
[190] There was no bulb in the lamp.

(A lamp is supposed to have a bulb.) Instead, I believe it is because the broader the reach of a noun, the more we are apt to harbor preconceptions about its referent. For example, picking oranges (but hardly picking a single orange) is a normal occupation for someone in an orange grove:

[191] She's in the orange grove, but picking no oranges.
[192] ?She's in the orange grove, but picking no orange.
[193] She was at her desk, but writing no letters.
[194] ?She was at her desk, but writing no letter.

(A normal contextualization for the last sentence would be someone's prior statement that she WAS writing a letter – the reply has an outright external negation; *I can assure you* would be an appropriate addition.) Some instances of abstract nouns (including abstract count nouns) are so common as almost to achieve the status of collocations: *no sign* (of something), *no trace, no notion, at no time,* etc:

[195] I find no value in this.
[196] Your invention serves no purpose.
[197] He has no idea of how to earn a living.

The less tied to the here and now, the better. Thus *having money* is long-term, *having dimes* is not:

[198] ?She can't use the vending machine – she has no dimes.
[199] She can't use the vending machine – she doesn't have any dimes.
[200] She can't buy the house – she has no money.

This is relative. The first sentence is practically normal, but a little unexpected by comparison with the others. The same goes for the '?' signs in the following:

[201] Why don't they admire her? – ?She has no nice clothes.

[202] Why don't they admire her? – She has no dignity.

[203] Why is the new economic policy not being adopted? – ?It will produce no goods.

[204] Why is the new economic policy not being adopted? – It will produce no benefits.

[205] How come you didn't eat? – ?They brought no food.

[206] How come you didn't profit? – Our investment brought no return.

[207] ?It's too hard to read – there's no lamp anywhere around here.

[208] It's too hard to read – there are no lamps anywhere around here.

[209] It's too hard to read – there's no light.

Other examples of abstractions:

[210] I have no intention of waiting.

[211] I had no thought of injuring them.

[212] He has no reason to dislike you.

[213] I have no time for foolishness.

[214] There was no suspicion that anything was wrong.

[215] He promised to do no wrong.

[216] They volunteered no information.

[217] It's no use.

[218] There was no way out.

[219] There are no means to do it.

[220] I have no compunction in denouncing them.

[221] There is no time like the present.

While all these have acceptable *any* counterparts, they ring a bit truer as they stand. Several count as collocations, and examples are to be found with full idiomatic status:

[222] It's no matter.

[223] *It isn't any matter.

5 A yes and a no versus a not and a take-your-pick

In an outright external negation the negative is the only new element and accordingly the whole proposition is negated:

[224] You told him our secret. – I told him nothing!

[225] You told him our secret. – Like fun I told him!

But there is another side to the relationship of rightshifted negation to presupposition in all its phases, namely the contrast between *no* and *not any* simply as words in their own right. We have now been told repeatedly[2] that *any* is not a suppletive variant of *some* but is an independent distributive in all its uses, including the apparently suppletive *I want some* and *I don't want any*. The use of *any* with negation is not, basically, a matter of negative concord but of the logical necessity of negating a collectivity item by item in order to achieve an unambiguous total negation (*He doesn't have all of them* is compatible with *He has some of them; He doesn't have any of them* is not).

So *any* looks to all the possibilities, and is not inherently negative. We noted of example [163] that it can be used to convey a kind of affirmative 'might be'; a *some* instead of the *any* would make little difference:

> [226] I'm bored with this place. – Aren't there any books you can read? I can think of lots of things to do!

The negation on the verb can negate the verb without detracting from the essential affirmativeness of *any*, as can be seen in the following, where the speaker is about to leave on a trip and is talking to himself:

> [227] I hope I haven't forgotten anything – let's see, there's the key, and the food for the cat, and the card for the mailman . . .
> [228] *I hope I have forgotten nothing – let's see, there's the . . .

With *anything* the speaker ranges over all the affirmative possibilities, which he hopes to deny. With *nothing* the possibilities are immediately foreclosed.[3] To motivate a sentence like [228] calls for presupposing a situation in which the question has already come up and the negative can now settle the matter – a neighbor, sure of his facts, might say to our traveler, a mite impatiently, *You have forgotten nothing*. For another instance of the 'openness' of *any*, imagine a wife complaining of her husband's inertia on a Sunday afternoon and saying

> [229] He just doesn't do ánything. Sits there all afternoon watching football.
> [230] He just does nóthing. Sits there all afternoon watching football.

Where [229] protests, looks toward what might be even though it isn't, [230] is resigned, implying 'that's how it is'.

'Openness' and 'foreclosure' are revealed intonationally. *Any* favors an inconclusive (that is, terminal rising) intonation, *no* a falling one:

[231] I hope I have n't for got ten anything.

[232] No o, you have n't for gotten anything.

[233] You've for gotten noth ing.

It is the openness of *any* that makes it appropriate for new information and neutral where presupposition is concerned. Neg . . . *any* denies an affirmation. Aff . . . *no* affirms a negation. The positive verb conveys a positive attitude; Aff . . . *no* is confident, downright, certain – most appropriate for use with negations that are 'just naturally that way'. In [234] the speaker's attitude does not change on passing from the first verb to the second; in [235] it does:

[234] I will sit down and say nothing.
[235] I will sit down and not say anything.

The fact that the action may be logically negated does not abrogate the positive attitude – which is to say that a truth-value logic is insufficient to explain rightshifted negation.

But it can also happen that the action itself is not negated, even logically. That is, the construction always has the option of signifying something 'going on'. In [236], the action proper is not inhibited, even though it fails to be fulfilled (*see* is not a 'success' verb here); but in [237] it is inhibited:

[236] I strained my eyes but saw nothing.
[237] Why do you keep holding your hands in front of my eyes so I can't see anything?
[238] *Why do you keep holding your hands in front of my eyes so I can see nothing?

It is inhibited also in [239]:

[239] Rheumatism, failing eyesight – he's not getting any younger.
[240] ?Rheumatism, failing eyesight – he's getting no younger.

Nowhere has developed an erewhonian sense:

[241] Where did John come from? – He didn't come from anywhere; he's been here all the time.

[242] ?He came from nowhere; he's been here all the time.

He came from nowhere would normally be taken in the sense that he did
come, but it was from out of the void – he made a mysterious appearance.
Similarly:

[243] It was a Barmecide feast; they were (busy) eating nothing.

There was eating but no food. And similarly

[244] I got there late and found them (industriously) doing nothing.

[245] I sat there looking at nothing (staring into vacant space).

The positive verb makes it possible to create a something out of a nothing.
We recognize this in semi-facetious speech:

[246] What did you get out of his talk? – I got a great big nothing (a
whole lot of nothing, a bellyful of nothing).

Likewise in a form of cleft sentence, preserving the positive verb:

[247] They offered me nothing ⟹ What they offered me was nothing.

[248] They didn't offer me anything ⇏ *What they didn't offer me
was anything.

The presence of a modifier of real action, as in [243] and [244] and in

[249] They were carefully and judiciously inspecting nothing.

of course gives the show away. Yet the logical equivalence may still be
there, and instead of reporting a real happening (but a zero outcome) the
speaker may be conveying roughly the same meaning as with a sentence
containing no negative. For example, *I don't want for anything* and *I want
for nothing* both signify 'I have all I need', and *She didn't get anywhere* and
She got nowhere signify 'She failed'. The tags show us how the speaker
regards the choices (the tag is to be read with a rise-fall intonation):

[250] *I want for nothing, do I?

[251] *I want for nothing, don't I?

[252] *She got nowhere, did she?

[253] *She got nowhere, didn't she?

[254] She got exactly nowhere, didn't she?

The negative form is sufficient to spoil the negative tag in [251] and [253] (that is, we expect a reversal of polarity in a conducive tag), and the positive attitude is sufficient to spoil the affirmative tag in [250] and [252]. It is not until an adverb clinches the positive, in [254], that the negative tag becomes normal. Contrast these examples with others in which the speaker views the action as negated, and the only contribution of the positive verb is the assurance it conveys:

[255] It makes no difference, does it?
[256] They had no money, did they?
[257] They lost no time, did they?

The relative isolation of the verb as a positive item is reflected in a tendency for the rightshifted negative to form part of a collocation, to 'idiomatize' to a certain degree. The whole sentence then takes on a positive cast in spite of its negative form. (Not all collocations are affected – *to make no difference*, as the tag in [255] shows, is still felt as negative over-all; similarly *to pay no attention, have no use for, hold no brief for*, etc.) The following can be glossed affirmatively and all are awkward with a conducive tag of either polarity:

[258] That man is nobody's fool (?is he?, *isn't he?) 'He is pretty clever'.
[259] He stops at nothing (*does he?, *doesn't he?) 'He will venture anything'.
[260] They left no stone unturned (*did they?, *didn't they?) 'They did everything possible'.

The positive cast may become securely positive, as in *nothing but*= '100 per cent':

[261] She'll give him nothing but trouble, won't she?

The ties within a collocation may be very faint, but still detectible. *Do nothing* and *say nothing* outrank *eat nothing, buy nothing*, etc:

[262] What shall I do? – Do nothing. Let things ride.
[263] What shall I say? – Say nothing. Least said, soonest mended.
[264] Where shall I go? – ?Go nowhere.
[265] What shall I take? – ?Take nothing.

The doubtful examples could be normalized with a context, but *do* and *say* require no help. *Do nothing* is viewed as a positive act – 'let things ride', exactly as in [262]. *Say nothing* is 'keep quiet'.

Besides the idioms and collocations that bind the negative to the complement and leave the verb free to signify a positive action, there are of course the syntactic obstacles that were noted earlier. In the following,

[266] They did it with no trouble.
[267] We woke after sleeping no more than two hours.
[268] It was a fish that had no fins.

the negative is separated from the main verb phrase, and the most obvious interpretation is that the constituent of which it forms an immediate part is the one negated. To use it to negate the main verb, that is, to mean 'they didn't do it', 'we didn't wake', and 'it wasn't a fish', would entail great difficulty in processing. What we found earlier was that with the negative not part of the essential complement of the verb, only the most favorable conditions (a clear-cut external negation, where everything but the negative has already been processed, plus – generally – a formulaic negative) would allow the negation of the verb. Even something as close as a single infinitive complement is difficult unless the speaker is denying something already stated:

[269] ?I wanted to accommodate them, but as they had asked to go nowhere I didn't feel obliged to offer. (OK had asked nothing)
[270] They had asked to go to the circus. – They had asked to go nowhere!

If the most obvious interpretation is that of a negated complement – a reflection of type and depth of embedding plus other factors – even a completely explicit external negation and a usually effective indefinite negative (such as *nothing*) may not get by. But the speaker may then resort to the formulaic negatives that imply ridicule:

[271] It's a mammal that has fins. – *It's a mammal that has nothing! Don't you know a fish when you see one?
[272] It's a mammal that has fins. – It's a mammal that has your grandmother! Don't you know a fish when you see one?

6 *Not any* as a constituent

Up to this point, examples of the two forms of negation have been associated with complements, where there is relative freedom of choice between them. When the negative accompanies the subject of the main verb, there is no such freedom. The *no* forms reign almost supreme:

[273] None dare say that I have failed.
[274] ?Not any dare say that I have failed.
[275] Nobody really cares.
[276] ?Not anybody really cares.
[277] No books were on display.
[278] ?Not any books were on display.

But the restriction is not confined to main-clause subjects, as can be seen in cases like

[279] They bought no provisions.
[280] *They bought not any provisions.
[281] The facts were revealed to no one.
[282] *The facts were revealed to not anyone (not to anyone).

The restriction on *not* and *any* occurring side by side is strong enough even to render doubtful certain sentences in which the *not* of *not any* ought to be interpretable as a constituent of the verb phrase. This is the case with *is* (*was*) *not* and *have not* (*have* for possession), which may still, in Modern English, postpose a *not* that belongs with the verb. As long as the morphological and phonological signals are made to point clearly enough to *not* as a constituent of the verb phrase, there is no problem. Two obvious ways of doing this are (1) to decrease the distance between *not* and the verb through contraction, and (2) to increase the distance between *not* and *any* by inserting a disjuncture, which is normal in emphatic denials:

[283] There wasn't any trouble.
[284] There was too much trouble. – There was nót . . . any trouble!
(*Compare* There was nót, I repeat, nót, any trouble!)

A third, weaker, alternative is to add a modifier between *any* and the noun, which seems to have the effect of obscuring *any* by attracting the accent to the modifier. Compare the following, with and without such a modifier:

[285] There was not any further attempt.
[286] ?There was not any attempt.
[287] He is not any great hero.
[288] ?He is not any hero.

With *have*, the conditions are clearer. Only contraction is strong enough to preserve constituency with the verb phrase:

> [289] They had too much money. – *They had not any money! (OK
>   They hadn't any money!)

(Auxiliary *have* of course is not affected: *He had not so much as spoken.*)

The prohibition on *not any* does not extend to *hardly any*, further evidence that the restriction is morphosyntactic. *Hardly* may appear as readily after as before the verb:

> [290] They hardly bought any provisions.
> [291] They bought hardly any provisions.
> [292] Hardly any books were on display.

It would appear that the syntax of *not any* is such that the *not* must attach itself to a verb if one is available. (The same is true of *not* plus a noun complement except in Neg-Aff contrasts:

> [293] *I want not money.
> [294] I want not money but [yes] recognition.
> [295] I want not money so much as [yes] recognition.)

But a speaker can omit the verb and *not any* then gets by:

> [296] Who's been around? – Not anybody, and it's damned lonesome.
> [297] *Not anybody's been around, and it's damned lonesome.
> [298] What do you want? – Not anything, for the moment.
> [299] *I want not anything, for the moment.

It is a fair guess that the mischief-maker is the prohibition in Modern English against adjoining *not* after any verb except an auxiliary, which has been overgeneralized to exclude the same arrangement when the *not* belongs to the complement; that is, **want-not* drives out *want not-*.

As in example [284], *not any* in its graceless position becomes normal with emphasis:

> [300] Not ány books were on display!
> [301] The facts were revealed nót to ányone!
> [302] They demanded feats that nót ány óne person could accomplish.

This, plus the lack of any restriction on *hardly any*, gives us the opportunity to test *any* for its contrast in meaning with *no*, which turns out to be the same 'openness' as before:

> [303] Hardly anybody came, but we still had a good time.

[304] ?Almost nobody came, but we still had a good time.
[305] What do you expect to find on the bargain shelf? – Not any books – pamphlets, maybe.
[306] What do you expect to find on the bargain shelf? – ?No books – pamphlets maybe.

Hardly anybody looks up, *almost nobody* looks down; and the affirmative possibilities are more in mind in [305] than in [306], though with a longer pause in [306] after *books*, to signify a shift in viewpoint and a new thought, the result is normal. If the sentence forecloses the alternatives, *any* becomes odd:

[307] What can I do for you? – Nothing, thank you.
[308] What can I do for you? – ?Not anything, thank you.

The affirmativeness of *any* is revealed syntactically in coreference with *as* and *that:*

[309] What they found was, unfortunately, not any cache of precious metal as they had hoped, but only some rusted iron scrap.
[310] ?What they found was, unfortunately, no cache of precious metal as they had hoped, but only some rusted iron scrap.
[311] How many do you need? – Ten or eleven. But not any less, if that [=any less] is what you had in mind.
[312] ?. . . But no less, if that is what you had in mind.

7 Conclusion

Negation – along with several other adverbial satellites such as interrogation, emphasis, and restriction (*only, just*) – is a shifter. Since denying any one of two or more conjoined elements may, under certain logical conditions, amount to denying the conjoined series as a whole, it often makes little practical difference where the negative element is attached. This has given rise to one well-studied phenomenon, leftshifting. But in terms of the number of verbs and types of sentences affected, the opposite phenomenon, rightshifting, is much more widespread. It involves the alternation of *not any* and *no*, along the following lines:

1 *Not any* (that is, Neg . . . *any*) is the negation of a set of open possibilities; *no* (that is, Aff . . . *no[ne]*) is the affirmation of a foreclosed negation. Correlated with this is the fact that:
2 *No* is used in logically affirmative sentences (the action takes place) some

detail of which is negated. The detail may range from the entire complement, as in *They were (busy) eating nothing* (a Barmecide feast), to some fragment, such as the instrumental in *He took a bath with no soap*.

3 Alternatively, *no* is used in logically negative sentences where the affirmativeness of the verb is interpreted not factually but as a positive attitude: the speaker is more assured, more categorical. This leads to:

4 A tendency for *no* sentences to be directed to things that are generally presupposed or are regarded by the speaker as already held in mind (including what is totally presupposed, that is, the external negation of something previously said or claimed). This results in:

5 A higher frequency of inclusive concepts (abstractions, mass nouns, plurals) and a lower frequency of singular, particular, concrete concepts. On the side of external negation it also results in:

6 Formulaic negation, using the indefinites *nothing, nowhere, nobody, nothing of the sort, no such thing*, and expressions of ridicule (*fiddlesticks, your old man*, etc) more or less integrated into the syntax of the sentence and occupying the position of the nuclear accent.

7 Syntactic complexity interferes with using *no* to negate, logically, the main verb, but formulaic negation overrides much of the interference, suggesting that a negative at the end lends itself to being taken as 'exterior'.

8 The *not* of *not any* is attracted to the verb if one is present, and rules of position and contraction relative to the verb then apply.

The behavior of the negative is suspiciously like what happens in factoring and multiplication. If we set the first quantity as the main verb and the second as the complement, we get, for Neg . . . *any*,

$(-v) (c_1 c_2 \ldots c_n)$ [Negation of a set of open possibilities]

and for Aff . . . *no* the following steps:

$(+v) (-c_1 -c_2 \ldots -c_n) =$ [Affirmation of a distributed negative]
$(+v) -(c_1 c_2 \ldots c_n) =$ [Negative factored out – 'foreclosure', = denial of fact of open possibilities]
$-(+v!) (c_1 c_2 \ldots c_n)$ [Negative shifted, affirmativeness of verb reinterpreted attitudinally]

The semantic developments reported here agree with – and could almost have been predicted from – Vachek's assessment (1976, 93–5) of the history of Neg . . . *any* and Aff . . . *no* in English. It was chiefly the appearance of *any* that made it possible to eliminate multiple negation as a sign of negative concord and reserve it for reversal of polarity (*He didn't eat nothing* is no longer ambiguous as between he did have food and he did not have food), at the same time opening the way for a new set of meanings for the negative indefinites (*no, none,* etc). *Any,* as Vachek points out, 'combines the features of universality within certain limits and of potential realizability of the asserted relation in all implied individuals'; in the *no* type, on the other hand, the verb is neutral as regards polarity. I have modified this only to the extent of claiming that while the verb may be neutral in that sense, it at least conveys a positive attitude. In other words, what we have is a sweeping metaphor in the language, very like what happened with intonation, where the deep fall in pitch that fundamentally signifies 'finality' in the sense 'through speaking' has come to signify 'finality' in attitude: 'nothing more to be said, issue closed'. The two are fitting companions in that *no* generally uses precisely this intonation.

What *no* means for style is a balancing act in which now the positive and now the negative end of the seesaw can be tilted up.

Notes

This chapter has benefited singularly from the criticisms of Talmy Givón, and also from comments by Michael Anthony. They are absolved from responsibility for any misuse I have made of their help.

1 Furthermore, with questions just as with negations the main verb may be adverbialized, and the interrogation, like the negation, is carried along with it when it is tagged:

> I don't suppose he's coming ⟶ He isn't coming I don't suppose.
> Do you suppose he's coming ? ⟶ Is he coming do you suppose ?

2 Anthony forthcoming, Labov 1972, Lakoff 1969, Vachek 1947. See also Chapter 2 in this volume.

3 Vachek 1947 describes the *any-no* contrast in essentially the same terms: 'the *no*-type represents what may be called a simple universal negation, whereas the *any*-type expresses the so-called "consistent universal negation", which tries to stress more thoroughly the idea that each and every case covered by a given universal negative proposition participates in it'. From review by Paul Garvin, *Language* 27 (1951) 194–5.

What I have called 'foreclosure' in the *no* type of negation is described by Poldauf (1964, 372–3) as 'deliberate'.

Chapter 4

It

The theme of this chapter is the value of *it* as a referential pronoun.[1] Two main uses are considered: the 'pronominal copy' in constructions such as *It is hard to say*, and 'weather' expressions such as *It is hot down here*. My claim is that in both of them *it* remains a pronoun whose meaning contrasts with its absence.

Charles-James Bailey (1969) notes that certain sentences with *it that* which are doubtful in the affirmative become acceptable in the negative:

[1] ?I believed it that the election hurt them.
[2] Not for a moment did I believe it that the election hurt them.

It can be shown that the degree of acceptability here relates to *it* as an anaphoric pronoun. This is a point of some importance for the type of generative-transformational analysis that assumes a common deep structure for sentences containing *it* . . . *that* and sentences from which 'the *it* has been deleted'. What I intend to show is that sentences with *it* differ in meaning from sentences without *it*, and that the difference can be assigned to *it* as a member of the set that includes *he, she,* and *they*. If [1] is unacceptable, it is because an anaphoric reference has been made when none is appropriate.

The case will be more convincing if other mutations beside negation turn out to have the same effect on acceptability. So, for certain auxiliaries:

[3] *I understand it that the election hurt them.
[4] I can understand it that the election hurt them.
[5] *Do you believe it that the election hurt them?
[6] Would you believe it that the election hurt them?

Likewise for sentence modifiers that restrict the possibilities:

[7] ?It's that he's a Republican that I find so objectionable.
[8] It isn't that he's a Republican that I find so objectionable.
[9] It's just (only, merely, simply) that he's a Republican that I find so objectionable.

Also emphasis, which proves that affirmativeness is not the cause of unacceptability:

[10] I positively do believe it that the election hurt them.

Likewise a mere interchange of subjects, which suggests that no rule of syntax is involved:

[11] He won't believe it that I am better than he is.
[12] ?I won't believe it that he is better than I am.

(Both sentences are normal without *it*.) Finally, just a change of context may make a difference:

[13] He had to go and blab it that I was seen out with a blonde last night.
[14] I can't hear what that fellow's blabbing. – Wendell, I wouldn't have believed it of you! He's blabbing (*it) that you were seen out with a blonde last night.

To be anaphoric, *it* must refer to some fact already broached. Looking at these examples we see that this is precisely the reason why [2], [4], [6], [8], [9], and [13] are normal: the sentences are about a topic that has already been introduced. In [4], for example, *can understand* is obviously a comment on a prior topic. As for negation, it is likely to be concerned with something already affirmed – though not necessarily: one would not enter a room bearing news of an election and announce to those present **I do not believe it that the election hurt them*. But the same sentence would be normal in contradicting someone.

What of [11] and [12]? In [11], as a proper egotist, I maintain that I am better than he is: *it* = *the fact;* it remains a fact regardless of his views. In [12], I am unlikely both to accept and reject my own proposition in the same breath. If *the fact* replaces *it*, the acceptability ratings remain the same.

Many more proofs can be found that 'expletive' *it* retains at least some value beyond that of plugging a grammatical hole. Following are a few.

1 Factive verbs

If it is true that *it* has a referent, we should expect it to be favored with factive verbs. Typical factives are those concrete verbs that are extended metaphorically to notional complements:

[15] *He can't swallow that you dislike him.
[16] He can't swallow it that you dislike him.
[17] *She hid that she was involved.
[18] She hid it that she was involved.
[19] *He let out of the bag that I was the one they were looking for.
[20] He let it out of the bag . . .
[21] *He spilled that you were the thief.
[22] He spilled it that you were the thief.

Other factives generally conform:

[23] *They pooh-poohed that we were responsible.
[24] They pooh-poohed it that we were responsible.

If the factive verbs in [15], [17], [19], [21], and [23] are replaced by non-factives such as *understand* or *doubt*, the result is normal; but *it* may be used with these same verbs when the topic has already been introduced, for example

[25] He can't understand that you dislike him.
[26] He can't understand it that you dislike him.

Emotional factives such as *love, hate, admire,* and *welcome,* which (with *that* clauses) are limited to what is already present to the mind, require *it:*

[27] *I just love that you are moving in with us.
[28] I just love it that . . .
[29] *We welcome that we are to have the benefit of your criticism.
[30] We welcome it that . . .[2]

Factivity is not related directly to the problem of *it*, but only as a matter of probabilities. A factive verb implies the factuality of its complement in the mind of the speaker, not the shared knowledge of it between speaker and hearer. Thus the verb *know* is generally not used unless the speaker accepts the complement as true (in *John knows they're guilty* it is the speaker and John, not the speaker and the hearer, who share the prior knowledge), but it can still be used for something that the hearer may be learning for the first time. *Know* accordingly does not normally use *it* (except in the passive voice, which will be looked at later):

[31] He knows (*it) that I can best him.

Similarly with other verbs that report facts, that is, make something present to the mind that was not present before:

[32] They divulged that they were moving in with us.

With the verbs of reporting in the following, the contrast is between something previously unknown and something already settled:

[33] You might at least have announced that you were moving in on us.
[34] You might at least have announced it that you were moving in on us.
[35] Did you find (*it) out that the check was bad?
[36] When did you find (it) out that the check was bad?

Emotional factives that broach something new do not use *it:*

[37] Joe, I'm glad you're here.
[38] *Joe, I'm glad of it that you're here.

But if the complement refers to something already introduced, *it* is used:

[39] If he asks you to help him, just say you regret (*it) that you can't.
[40] You shouldn't regret it that you were helpful.

The use and non-use of *it* enables us to make a distinction in factive verbs between attitudes and feelings. An attitudinal verb such as *be sorry* is not as strongly factive as a verb that expresses just one's emotional reaction, such as *resent:*

[41] I'm sorry she did that, if she did.
[42] *I resent it that she did that, if she did.
[43] *I resent that she did that.
[44] I resent it that she did that.

Resent requires *it*, and is also the verb that will not admit a questioning of the fact.[3]

2 Suppositions, suasions, and past versus future

Where factives more often than not require *it*, and reports have a choice, suppositions – normally having to do with bringing forward something new – generally exclude *it:*

[45] Who would have thought (it) that things would turn out this way?
[46] Who would have supposed (*it) that things would turn out this way?
[47] He pretended (*it) that he was the one.
[48] I presume (*it) that you are Dr Livingstone.
[49] I was the one who guessed (it) that you would win.
[50] I guess (*it) that you will win.

Suppose and *pretend* seem to be affected absolutely, the other verbs (including *imagine, theorize, hypothesize, conjecture,* as well as *presume* and *guess*) relatively.

As can be inferred from [49] and [50], the tense of the verb is an important factor. What has already happened is more apt to be on the boards, conversationally:

[51] *I don't expect it that he will be there.
[52] I never expected (it) that he would be there.

Verbs of suasion look to the future and are strongly affected by the tense:

[53] I suggest (*it) that they wait.
[54] I suggested (it) that they should wait.
[55] We don't intend (*it) that you shall be inconvenienced.
[56] We didn't intend (it) that you should be inconvenienced.
[57] Are you going to order (*it) that he be fired tomorrow?
[58] I was the one who ordered (it) that he should be fired tomorrow.

This is not to say that a future tense excludes *it;* but where *it* is used, the matter has already been broached or predetermined:

[59] Since we are agreed on the action, I shall take the responsibility of ordering it that he be fired.
[60] Clerk, this set looks to be about what we want. Do you guarantee (*it) that it won't cause any trouble?
[61] Clerk, the last set we bought developed a short circuit after we'd only used it a couple of weeks, and I hate to bring stuff in for repair all the time. – We guarantee (it) that you will not have any trouble.

Nor does a past tense necessarily require *it.* If the matter is not already shared as definite, *it* is unacceptable:

[62] They didn't carry out your wishes because I didn't recommend (*it) that they should make the attempt.

3 *How come?* versus *why?*

Presumably *how come* is a reduction of *how comes it that*, which can still be used synonymously (*cf* the Merriam *Third* definition 'How does it happen that?' and Bartlett, 1848, 'How came it?'). The *it*, now lost, is nevertheless retained semantically in the contrast with *why*. *How come?* asks about something previously established, but *why?* is neutral in this respect (and also includes purpose). It is difficult to arrange a context that is queried about and at the same time is impossible to view as a fact, so that most of the time the two are interchangeable: but responses to commands, which are not factual, demonstrate the difference:

   [63] You should help me. – Why? (How come?)
   [64] Help me! – Why? (*How come?)

4 Extraposition

The extraposition of cleft sentences provides some of the best evidence for the meaningfulness of *it*. The evidence from other types of extraposition – subject *that* clauses and infinitives, mostly – is mixed.

   Cleaving a sentence that is totally lacking in a prior basis for the information referred to is difficult to do. The interchange

   [65] When will we know? – It's tomorrow that we'll know.

is normal because we are able to understand that the time of knowing has been previously established. But in

   [66] When will you tell me? – *It's tomorrow that I'll tell you.

the speaker is asking for information that has no prior basis. Similarly we can imagine a sympathetic bystander in Uncle Tom's Cabin asking – concerning Eliza as she leaves her home – *Where will she go?* but the answer

   [67] *It is to Canada that she will go.

is unacceptable because there is no prior *it*. (Compare *It was to Canada that she went*.) The neatest proof of prior information is the contrast in the answers to original and reclamatory questions, the latter by definition laying a basis since they repeat what has already been said. There is a difference between *who?*, which may as readily have a prior basis as not, and *who else?*, which virtually has to come out of the blue unless it is reclamatory:

Speaker A	*Speaker* B
[68] Who came?	It was John.
[69] Who else came?	*It was Mary.

The first interchange is possible because it can easily happen that A and B have the mutual understanding that a person of 'it' identity came. In the second, 'who else' is a new and unexpected reference. On the other hand,

A	B
[70] Who else came?	Mary.
[71] Who else (did you say) came?	It was Mary.

with the normal continuous rise of the reclamatory question, has an acceptable *it* referring to something already known. Similarly in

[72] Someone else came. – Yes, it was John.

As for the extraposition of infinitives, while a pair such as

[73] To give in now would be fatal.
[74] It would be fatal to give in now.

are interchangeable in many contexts and look as if they might be in free variation, actually the *it* again relates to some kind of prior basis. Consider the following answers to the question *What do you think of running him as a candidate?*:

[75] *To do that would be a good idea.
[76] To run him as a candidate would be a good idea.
[77] It would be a good idea to do that.

In [75], the use of *that* forces the anaphora – the speaker has to be picking up the idea from his interlocutor and is therefore obliged to use *it* and the construction in [77]. But [76] is possible where the speaker is turning the question over in his mind and treating it as his own idea. While the lines are not as sharply drawn, we note a similar contrast in the following pairs, where the first member is normal but the second is felt as a mild non-sequitur (and is marked with the query, though it is not unacceptable):

[78] Try to realize this simple fact: to give in now would be fatal.
[79] ?Try to realize this simple fact: it would be fatal to give in now.
[80] I agree with you all the way: it would be fatal to give in now.
[81] ?I agree with you all the way: to give in now would be fatal.

The question of factivity has a more drastic effect on the infinitive than on the clauses examined previously, and is seen in connection with perfective verbs (the 'tense' factor also noted earlier).[4] If the event has already happened, a prior basis has to be assumed and *it* is required:

[82] I would have no trouble at all; to convince him would be easy.
[83] *I had no trouble at all; to convince him was easy.
[84] I had no trouble at all; it was easy to convince him.
[85] To assist you would be a pleasure.
[86] *To assist you was a pleasure.
[87] It was a pleasure to assist you.
[88] To show up now might present certain dangers.
[89] *To show up then presented certain dangers.
[90] It presented certain dangers to show up then.

Extraposition with *that* clauses (aside from cleft sentences) is more complex. Whereas with the infinitive the extraposed element is usually the topic, as is shown by the relative height of the accents in the most frequent intonation,

[91] It's ^{nice} to play ^{bad} minton.

(*badminton* would almost certainly be contrastive if *bad-* were higher in pitch than *nice*),[5] with a *that* clause the extraposed element can just as readily be the comment:

[92] It's ^{nice} that you ^{let} them.

Accordingly from the standpoint of functional sentence perspective the motivation for an *it* is weaker: if it stands in for the comment it is by definition less known. The low referential value of *it* is suggested by the greater ease with which it can be suppressed before a clause, by comparison with an infinitive:

[93] ?'Sfunny to hear you say that.
[94] 'Sfunny you didn't know.
[95] ??Funny to hear you say that.
[96] Funny you didn't know.

At the same time, the test of future reference again shows a contrast when the *that* clause represents something more known or less known:

[97] ?It would be inexcusable that they should run away.
[98] It would be inexcusable that they should do such a thing.
[99] ?It would be regrettable that they should resign on the spur of the moment.
[100] It would be regrettable that they should resign on the spur of the moment like that.

The addition here of anaphoric *such* and *like that* creates a stronger tie with what has already been talked about.[6]
    Where extraposed *that* clauses are most frequent is with the passive of verbs of information:

[101] Somebody will announce (it) that the president has been indicted.
[102] *That the president has been indicted will be announced.
[103] It will be announced that the president has been indicted.

If the information value of the verb is increased, extraposition is not necessary:

[104] That the president has been indicted will not be announced.
[105] That the president has been indicted will be denied.
[106] That the president has been indicted will be loudly proclaimed.

So it appears that semantic weight, and not the 'knownness' of the content of the clause, is what forces extraposition and with it the addition of *it*. Here we have the strongest case for *it* as a grammatically introduced particle.

5 *It* matched with other substantives

It is the pronominal neuter counterpart of the definite article. The kinship between them can be seen in the responses to the following questions, in both of which the speaker has assumed that his hearer shares knowledge of an identity:

[107] Did you hear it? – Did I hear what?
[108] Did you hear the noise? – Did I hear what noise?

A number of abstract nouns, with *the* added, can double for *it* in the same constructions:

[109] Not for a minute did I believe the story (believe it) that she had disappeared.

[110] What abóut the fact (what abóut it) that I wasn't there? You annoyed you didn't see me or something?

[111] The fact will be announced (it will be announced) that the president has been indicted.

This includes a number of idioms:

[112] He spilled the beans (spilled it) that you were involved in that operation.

[113] They finally got the idea (got it) that I meant them no harm.

Also idioms that are relatively specific to *it* but in which another nominal can be substituted. These are common as verbal expressions in which if there were no nominal the verb proper would be separated from its complement:

[114] I have it (I have the word) on good authority that you are to be selected.

[115] She gave it away (gave the game away, gave the fact away) that we had played the joke.

[116] They let it be known (let the fact be known) that their next move would be an economic one.

[117] I intend to make it public (make the news public) that I am a candidate.

[118] They bruited it about (bruited the rumor about) that arson was involved.

[119] Our interview brought it (brought the fact) into consciousness that we had a deep rapport.

(The idiomaticity of *bring* is flexible: it allows any directional adverb that can be applied to a conversation – *up, out, into the open,* etc.) And there are idioms where no other nominal can replace *it*:[7]

[120] I take it that you wanted something else.

The significance of this interchange of nominals is that it broadens the question of supposedly meaningless particles. Though *it*, being smaller and more defenseless, is easier to dismiss as a mere space-filler, actually there is almost as much reason to dismiss *the fact*. The only GRAMMATICAL requirement is that there be something in an otherwise empty slot; as a rule, some other nominal will serve as well as *it*. This is just as true in the most obvious cases of pronominal substitution:

[121] About John's leaving, I don't believe that (that business, that crap, it).
[122] I don't believe it (that, etc) about John's leaving.

What of course strikes us as rather special, grammatically, about *it* is that in subject position it has to be separated from *that*, though not elsewhere; the other nominals have an option:

[123] I resent it that you take that attitude.
[124] I resent the fact that you take that attitude.
[125] The fact that you take that attitude is to be resented.
[126] The fact is to be resented that you take that attitude.
[127] *It that you take that attitude is to be resented.
[128] It is to be resented that you take that attitude.

Yet this is probably a trivial difference, perhaps attributable just to the prosody of English. *It* is normally stressless, but in initial position followed by an obligatorily stressless *that* it would have to be stressed. A parallel development is the archaizing of *he who* – if someone says this, we are immediately conscious of the sound of it.

The point is that although in some cases *it* (or some other nominal) is required by the grammar, the sense of 'neuter definite' never CONFLICTS with the meaning of the construction in which it occurs, and as often as not it contributes. Among the nominals that can be used, *it* is simply the ultimate in abstractness. We have been so accustomed to think of all pronouns as mere stand-ins that it is hard for us to see them – *it* especially – as only the end of a gradient, along which are ranged many 'nouns', some of them fairly close to the end: *the fact* near *it*, *the fellow* near *he*, etc.

And there is always the potential for some referential value. Even an idiom that is destroyed by dropping *it* can exhibit it, for example the idiom in [120]. *Take it that* is mostly used as a performative to introduce tentative assertions, that is, statements that are put forward for confirmation and are based on an inference that the speaker draws from knowledge presumably shared by his interlocutor.[8] The idiomatic use of *bring* cited earlier has the choice of using or omitting *it*, with the expected effects:

[129] He brought out that he was the one responsible.
[130] *Why don't you bring out that you were the one responsible?
[131] Why don't you bring it out that you were the one responsible?

In [129] the fact is newly introduced. In [130] and [131] the context implies that the facts have already been established, which creates a conflict in [130].

6 Blended *it*

There are some rather clearly substantive uses where *it* serves as an indefinite pronoun with the meaning 'things', 'business', 'idea', etc: *We settled our differences and left it* ('the matter') *at that; How did you fix it* ('things') *so that nobody had to pay?; He faked it* ('the affair') *so that we didn't get caught.* Where a *so that* is explicitly given, as in the last two examples, *it* is grammatically detached from the *that* clause – the two cannot stand in apposition, as they do in all the cases cited thus far. But *that* is frequently used in a result or purpose (unaccomplished result) clause without *so, eg, He gave me enough (so) that I didn't need any more,* and the line between apposition and result fades. If the *it* in both cases is a substantive as I have claimed, then the constructions can easily blend:

[132] How did you manage it (so) that nobody had to pay? ('How did you manage things so that . . .?' or 'How did you accomplish nobody's-having-to-pay?')

[133] Who would want it that you should get into trouble? ('Who would want things to be such that . . .' or 'Who would want your getting into trouble?')

[134] He doped it out (such) that you were to be appointed acting chairman. ('He doped the question out so as to yield the conclusion that . . .' or 'He judged that . . .')

A paraphrase for the first meaning of [134], showing non-appositive *it*, would be *As he figured it (the question) out, you were to be . . .*

It is probably blending over this line that makes clauses with other conjunctions virtual equivalents of clauses with *that:*

[135] I can't help it (the problem) if he is bigger than you are.
[136] I don't like it (the situation) when they're not around.

7 Ambient *it*

In one of the many insightful passages in his *Meaning and the structure of language* (Chafe 1970), Wallace Chafe characterizes sentences like *It's hot,*

It's late, and *It's Tuesday* as referring to 'all-encompassing states'. 'They cover,' he says, 'the total environment, not just some object within it' (101). His treatment, in common with most others – but in his case partly because of the centrality of the verb in his system – denies any value to *it*: 'it need not reflect anything at all in the semantic structure'. I believe that the notion of ambience is correct, though that of totality must be modified; but I think that once again *it* has a referent, in this case precisely the 'environment' that is central to the whole area. There is a hint of this notion in an observation by Arthur Schwartz (1972, 70–1) concerning *it seems*: 'the surface *it* is not really a pronominal substitute for the proposition, but closer to the impersonal situational *it* of *It is cold today* or *It is crowded in here*'.

If ambience is proper to *it*, then it does not belong to the verb (counting as 'the verb' the entire predicate in such a sentence as *It is hot*). Assigning it to the verb creates problems elsewhere than in the interpretation of *it*. To mention just one, parenthetically, there is the meaning of sentences of the type *Tom is hot*, which Chafe paraphrases as 'It's hot with respect to the experience of Tom' (1970, 147). Such a paraphrase, if it means anything, would have to refer to ambient heat which Tom senses, not to Tom's own inner sensation of heat; the paraphrase would need to be paraphrased, something like 'The weather is hot with respect to the experience of Tom' or 'Tom senses or judges that it is hot'. The retention of ambient *it* in the paraphrase confuses the issue. Inner sensations must be handled differently; they are not 'it' constructions. *Tom is hot and thirsty* is a normal conjunction, and *Tom is thirsty* can hardly be paraphrased 'It's thirsty with respect to the experience of Tom'.

Given that *it* is ambient, but not the verb, one would predict that the range of constructions involving ambient *it* would not be restricted by any general property of verbs, specifically, in Chafe's view, that of PROCESS: 'a verb may be specified as ambient if it is a state or an action, but not if it is a process' (102). This, in terms of his system, means that no PATIENT can occur in ambient sentences; one may ask *What's it doing?*, but not *What's it doing* TO *something?* The following show, I believe, that no such restriction applies:

[137] What's it like over there today? – It's holding the same pattern as yesterday. (Two rangers talking by telephone.)

[138] How's it down there? – It's fairly calm. How's it up there? – It's practically ripping the trees out.

[139] It's brewing a tempest; it's threatening a storm.

[140] Do you think it will manage a shower by this afternoon?

[141] What's it going to be like today? – Another sizzler. It's building up quite a temperature already.

[142] Isn't it nice out this afternoon? – You must be crazy. It's so hot that it's giving me a headache.

[143] It's cold enough to freeze the balls on a brass monkey.

Presumably in the last two sentences the *it* that refers to the weather is the same *it* that gives the headache and freezes the balls on the brass monkey.[9]

One thing that creates illusions about ambient *it* is our restricting the vision of it to expressions of weather and time. No line can be drawn between those and others in which it is apparent that patients may occur:

[144] I can't walk. It's oozing oil all over here! Look at my shoes!

[145] Get away from there; it's too dangerous. Look at the way it's shooting sparks.

[146] Come down here in the basement and look at the way it's dripping water from every pipe. You'd swear they were leaks, but it's just condensation.

Expressions without patients are of course even more common:

[147] It's scary in the dark.

[148] It's inspiring here at MIT.

[149] It's all smeared down there on the right hand corner of the page. (Bolinger 1961, 367)

[150] I'm climbing down. It's too exposed up here.

Weather and time do exhibit the trait that Chafe ascribes to ambience: they are all-encompassing. But this is not what determines the nature of ambient *it*. All that the ubiquity of weather and time contributes is obviousness. The following represent the same construction:

[151] It's hot.

[152] It's hot in here.

[153] It's too cold to work and too nice in here not to cuddle up by the fire.

The only difference is that when *it* refers to weather there is no need for further specification. One can say *It's too cold* OUT but the *out* is implied without being specified. If the ambience embraces less than totality, then it often needs to be defined either explicitly or contextually. As the examples I have cited show, the usual way of specifying it is by the addition of an adverb: *out, in here, at MIT, in the dark*, etc. That some such adverbial is involved even when not mentioned can be seen in the last example above and in one like *God, it's hot; I wonder if it's as hot as this in Kansas City*, where *Kansas City* contrasts with unexpressed *here*.

Obvious ambience is not limited to weather and time. It is also to be found in connection with occasion, as manifested by event nouns:

[154] She has to stay in Cambridge because it's her graduation.
[155] Didn't you have your tennis game? – We couldn't get in because it was the annual Moose picnic.

These too may be further specified by time or place:

[156] It's her graduation next week.
[157] It was the annual Moose picnic at the park.

Probably the obviousness is more important than the ambience. The caller on a talk show who said *It seems to me that in the early sixties it was more fun* was inviting his audience to imagine the content of the second *it*. He could have said *things were more fun*, and in either case it would have been impertinent to ask *What was more fun?* We are supposed to know. I would maintain that the same *it* turns up in the following:

[158] Stop it! (what you are obviously doing).
[159] Don't do it! (what you are obviously about to do).
[160] Come off it! (what you are obviously insisting on).

These are cases of *it* without anaphora, *ie* without any necessary previous mention, but having a deixis ad oculos, a reference to the immediate situation. *How goes it? (How are things?)* is both obvious and ambient.

Having an adverbial specification at the end (*It's cold* OUT, *It's late* NOW) is so reminiscent of extraposition that one wonders whether the best treatment might not be to regard *it* as a copy of the adverbial. Certain equivalences, or near-equivalences, appear to justify the idea:

[161] Tomorrow's her graduation.
[162] It's her graduation tomorrow.
[163] Today's our homecoming celebration.
[164] It's our homecoming celebration today.

But this kind of apparent extraposition is possible only with forms that function freely as either noun or adverb; *today, tomorrow, next week*, etc, are typical. In other cases the equivalence is less clear:

[165] California is pleasant.

[166] *In California is pleasant.
[167] It's pleasant in California.
[168] This place is oozing oil.
[169] *Over here is oozing oil.
[170] It's oozing oil over here.

The fact that *it* occurs freely in the above when no extraposition has occurred, *eg:*

[171] Tomorrow it's her graduation.
[172] In California it's pleasant.
[173] Over here it's oozing oil.

suggests that *it* does not actually copy the environmental expression, but is only to some degree specified by it. The conclusion is that the following, despite their similarity in meaning, are distinct constructions:

[161] Tomorrow's her graduation.
[162] It's her graduation tomorrow.
[171] Tomorrow it's her graduation.
[174] Her graduation is tomorrow.

This is then a case where 'different semantic structures . . . converge on a single meaning' (Chafe 1970, 139).[10]

The same arguments apply to another apparent case of extraposition, which is not part of the literary standard but is common enough in colloquial English, as in this example from a radio conversation: *In the Bible it says that* . . . A somewhat more usual order is *It says in the Bible that* . . . Purists insist on *The Bible says that* . . ., which would be justified if *it* merely copied the location. But not all such locations can be copied. We are not apt to hear a sentence like *In John's letter it says that* . . . There is no syntactic reason for this but there is a semantic one: *it* is too general, *letter* is too specific. This is confirmed by the greater freedom of choice when *it* precedes; there is no confinement of *it* by a prior context, and ambience has more play: *It says in today's paper that* . . ., less likely *?In today's paper it says that* . . . The relative vagueness of the *it* construction can be particularized by adding an indefinite locative, changing *In John's will it provides that the local parish is to receive a substantial amount* to *Somewhere in John's will it provides that* . . ., an addition that is somewhat discordant in *John's will somewhere provides that* . . . The two constructions are not the same. (At the same time they are so close semantically that there is some blending syntactically, most conspicuous in the avoidance of *it* for plural locations: *It says in the Bible and in the Koran that . . ., *It says in today's papers that . . . While we can manage a notional singular in It says in the Pentagon Papers that . . ., even that is avoided when the plural would come before the verb: *In the Pentagon Papers it says that . . .)

If ambient it is not, in Chafe's terms, a semantically empty element, and is not, in generative terms, a transformationally introduced particle (therefore also semantically empty), we naturally ask ourselves whether it is really a distinct morpheme or just another manifestation of the same it that we have already characterized as an abstract nominal with the meaning 'definite'. I would maintain that if the two are not the same they are at least connected by a gradient too smooth for separation to be anything but arbitrary.

To gain more flexibility in the choice of examples I offer first some evidence that it needs to be cited in other roles than that of subject:

[175] It's hot down here.
[176] The furnace is making it hot down here.
[177] It's nice in California.
[178] I like it in California.
[179] It's hard to study.
[180] The noise makes it hard to study.
[181] It's snowing.
[182] I like it snowing.
[183] It was raining.
[184] When we got there we found it raining.
[185] Now that you've been here a couple of months, how do you like it? – I don't. It's too intellectual around here.

Assuming that the same it is involved in:

[186] It's unpleasant there.
[187] They're making it unpleasant there.

and that both represent ambient it, and assuming also that It's tough to get anything accomplished represents the same construction as It's hard to study, we can make the following combination:

[188] You mean they're making it unpleasant there? – Not unpleasant, exactly; just tough to get anything accomplished.

I have no sensation of zeugma here. The same it that is construed with unpleasant in the ambient sense in the question is understood with both *unpleasant* and *tough* in the answer. The fact that *tough* has an 'extraposed infinitive' makes no difference; it combines with *unpleasant* without clashing. This could hardly happen if *it* were a copy of the infinitive phrase. Another combined example:

[189] How is it at the Pentagon? – It's pretty rough there these days, rough even to do the routine things.

In simpler terms, an ambient *it* in a question may be answered by an *it* with infinitive, where the 'normal' SV order would be unacceptable:

[190] How is it in your room? – It's hard to study.
[191] How is it in your room? – *To study is hard.

(Compare the combination *It's noisy and hard to study there*.) The same problem occurs with *-ing*:

[192] How is it in your room? – It's hard studying there.
[193] How is it in your room? – *Studying there is hard.

Even a weather expression may combine without zeugma:

[194] How was it this afternoon? – It was hot and just about impossible to get anything done.[11]
[195] What caused the accident? – It was dark and also raining and consequently impossible for the driver to see the road.

Further evidence that *it* does not copy extraposed nominals is to be found in the variety of elements that can supposedly be extraposed, all converging on pretty much the same meaning:

[196] It's hard to do a job like that.
[197] It's hard doing a job like that.
[198] It's hard when you try to do a job like that.
[199] It's hard if you try to do a job like that.
[200] It's hard where you try to do a job like that.
[201] It's hard once you try to do a job like that.

The relationship of the adverb clauses to *it* appears to be the same as we find with other adverbials, as for instance in *It's a total mess after a flood* or *It's eight miles from here to Brighton* or the purpose clause in *I worked it so they would agree*. The main thing that suggests that they might be some sort of displaced subject of the main verb (even though not all can occur in that position: *From here to Brighton is eight miles* but not *When you try to do a job like that is hard*, *After a flood is a total mess*) is the resemblance to the infinitive and *-ing* constructions and to parenthetical additions in sentences like *It's terrible, what he has to put up with;* but this is turning the argument the wrong way around: it is more likely that we should look to the constructions with the adverbials for proof of the independ-ence of *it.* If there is blending between *that* clauses and adverbial *if* and *when* clauses as claimed above, there may well be blending between the latter – along with other adverbials – and infinitives and gerunds. With the *-ing* the potential for independence is fairly easy to see. In the follow-ing build-up it is apparent that the *-ing* is a circumstance paralleling the locative, not a subject:

[202] It's nice here.
[203] It's nice playing chess.
[204] It's nice here playing chess.

Adverbial specification is not unknown with other pronouns, where we would not think of regarding the adverb as a displaced subject. Non-standard *this here* and *that there* parallel non-existent *it here and *it there, but also parallel the standard postpositions in *That's pretty good there!* (where *there* as well as *that* points to the referent) and *It's nice here.* Perhaps the best examples are those of *there* as specification of *you*, as in the follow-ing:

[205] Hey there!
[206] Stop it there! (*there* with parenthetical accent)
[207] You there, stop it!
[208] You're looking tired there, my lad.

These uses of *there* are only special cases of a usage that ranges from barely more than repeating the element specified to encompassing its whole setting. The pronoun too has a kind of adverbial spread sometimes. In a sentence like *You're smoking in your left rear brake there* both *you* and *there* have more than a personal reference. We can no more separate a 'pro-nominal' *there* from an adverbial *there* than we can dissect *it.*

The notion of ambience has led us by a different route to the same conclusion regarding the nature of *it:* that it is a 'definite' nominal with almost the greatest possible generality of meaning, limited only in the sense that it is 'neuter'. Other neuters can often replace it, as we have seen; for example, *things:*

[209] They're making it unpleasant for him.
[210] They're making things unpleasant for him.

[211] It's tough when you have to work all day.
[212] Things are tough when you have to work all day.

Similarly for *it* followed by *all* and *thing* preceded by *every*:

[213] He knows it all.
[214] He knows everything.
[215] It's all finished between us.
[216] Everything is finished between us.

But *it* is more general than *things*. It embraces weather, time, circumstance, whatever is obvious by the nature of reality or the implications of context. If someone says out of the blue, *It's over; he's dead and I'm free*, the hearer infers 'that person's concerns' as the referent of *it*. Similarly he infers 'the state of his health' on hearing the response in *He looks like a ghost – Yes, it's terrible, but there's no remedy for it*. Our mistake has been to confuse generality of meaning with lack of meaning.

Saying that *it* is meaningful is not to deny that there are syntactic problems connected with its use, but only to say that syntax should not be the exclusive focus. There is a gradient at one extreme of which *it* is a relatively independent lexical item, and at the other approaches a rather tightly controlled element of syntax. The free end exhibits *it* alternating with a demonstrative:

[217] It's (this is) nice, isn't it? – What's nice? – Sitting around and talking.

One gets the same impression of an independent *it* whenever there is such a break as this, suggesting that the specification comes as an afterthought, for instance *It's nice, sitting around and talking*. But as soon as the structure is tightened up, the specification is felt not to be an afterthought, hence to be more necessary, and this suggests that it is grammatically prescribed: *It's nice sitting around and talking*. The same is true with adverb clauses:

[218] It's not much fun, when you have to work all the time.
[219] It's not much fun when you have to work all the time.

The last sentence is somewhere in the middle of the gradient. At the farther extreme is the infinitive, where the specification rarely comes as an afterthought and if it does the speaker seems to be correcting an oversight:

[220] It's tough to make him understand.
[221] ?It's tough, to make him understand.
[222] It takes a week for the mail to arrive.
[223] ?It takes a week, for the mail to arrive.

(In the following, the comma break is virtually obligatory after the demonstrative, which is relatively more independent:

> [224] It [this] is so nice of you[,] to visit us today.
> [225] It [that] was so nice of him [,] to have us over last night.)

In these cases the specification is so necessary that *it* seems to be redundant, and it is almost correct to view it as nothing more than a grammatical device whereby a certain syntactic order may be achieved. But even here the anaphora that has been with us all along still lurks in the background. The sentence *To study is hard* is possible though stilted, but as examples [190] and [191] showed, it cannot occur in a context requiring anaphora:

> [190] How is it in your room? – It's hard to study.
> [191] How is it in your room? – *To study is hard.

Ultimately the infinitive constructions, like those with *that* in the discussion of blends, are probably akin to expressions of purpose: *It's hard to work* is related more than superficially to *It's too hot (in order) to work*. We could paraphrase the first as 'General circumstances are difficult for working'. The same interpretation fits the following: *I've got to help them. – No. It's too late and too risky*. The first half is clearly purposive. One could not say *To help them is too late*. But the second half could be taken as *To help them is too risky*. Taken together, they paraphrase satisfactorily as 'Conditions are inopportune and risky for the purpose of helping them'. Purpose seems to be blended with extrapositions such as we find in

> [226] It was nice that he could come and to have had an opportunity to visit with him.
> [227] It's tough to have to give in all the time, and when nobody pays attention to your feelings.

I have deliberately used conjunctions that show the spread of *it*. Cases like [194] show the ease with which weather and purpose come together – similarly *It's too hot to play tennis and utterly out of the question to do anything else*. So we are not surprised when we find a sentence like *I'm going to make it as hot for him and as tough for him to accomplish anything as I can*, where one and only one *it* serves for the general circumstances surrounding his comfort and his power to attain an end – the latter half is equivalent to *It will be tough for him to accomplish anything*, straddling 'Circumstances will be tough for his purpose of accomplishment' and the appositional 'It for him to accomplish anything will be tough'. The ties can be seen in the requirements of anaphora and in the comparative freedom to combine without zeugma.

The generality of *it* is what makes it appropriate for specification by circumstantial complements, which are adverbial, and it is the relationship of these to *it* and other indefinite nominals that needs to be studied before any further pronouncements about the syntactic status of *it* can be made. In sentences like the following,

> [228] I hate it when she acts like that.
> [229] What I hate is when she acts like that.
> [230] The thing I hate is when she acts like that.
> [231] I would hate it if she acted like that.
> [232] What I would hate is if she were to act like that.

we find both *it* and *what*, with adverbials in apposition or serving as complements. Under the narrowest contextual conditions, the adverbial provides most if not all the content of the nominal. Thus *I hate it when she acts like that* is able to serve instead of the ungrammatical **I hate when she acts like that*. But the narrowest conditions are only special cases. In the sentence *I can't stand it when Joe's not around* the narrow interpretation is 'I can't stand Joe's not being around'; his not being around is the only thing said about the environment, embodied in *it*. But the same sentence in answer to *Why are you leaving?* may refer to other elements of the setting 'I can't stand it here (I can't stand this place) when Joe's not around'. It is the same sentence, and the only difference is that the context expands or contracts the reference of *it*.

Whatever the answer to the wider syntactic questions, I would say that all the uses of *it* stem from a common semantic base.

Notes

1 Based on the content of two papers, with an excerpt from a third. The first half is a fairly extensive revision of 'The Lexical Value of *It*', *Working Papers in Linguistics* (University of Hawaii) 2:8 (1970) 57–76, which has benefited from the criticism of Robert Hetzron. It already contained a paragraph from 'A Look at Equations and Cleft Sentences', in Evelyn Scherabon Firchow *et al*, eds, *Studies for Einar Haugen, Presented by Friends and Colleagues* (The Hague and Paris: Mouton, 1972) 96–114. The second half subsumes 'Ambient *It* is Meaningful Too', *Journal of Linguistics* 9 (1973) 261–70.

2 Hypothetical complements with these verbs use the infinitive or the gerund: *I love to hear them sing; We welcome your moving in with us.*

3 This is not to say that *it* is wrong with *be sorry*. Nevertheless, the *about* on top of

the *it* is rather awkward, and while *I'm sorry about it that all those things went wrong* is not unacceptable we would tend to choose another verb (*I hate it that*) or omit *about it*.

4 'Tense' here meaning perfective. If the verb is past but imperfective, no *it* is required: *To assist you was a pleasure – I always looked forward to it.*

5 An instance where the infinitive is not the topic is the greeting *Hello, Jackie. It's nice to see you.*

6 The normal thing in [97] and [99] is the infinitive: *It would be inexcusable for them to run away.*

7 There are of course other idioms in which the *it* is quite impervious, in meaning as well as form. *It behooves you to try harder* has no counterpart **To try harder behooves you.* *It seems to me that you've had enough* is nonsense as **That you've had enough seems to me.* And *It makes no difference what he said* means something like 'I don't care', whereas *What he said makes no difference* means 'It is irrelevant'.

8 The fact that there is shared knowledge is shown by the falling intonation curve that is normal with *take it that*, which contrasts with a newly formed inference such as might be introduced with *guess that*:

```
        take
            it
              that
[i] I             you want     some        el
                         ed        thing      se.
```

```
                          el
[ii] I  guess want   some    thing
            you   ed              se.
```

Though the *it* here is meaningful, it does not follow that *it* is required to get the effect of knownness. The verb *to gather* includes knownness within its own meaning: *I gather that you wanted something else* means the same as [i] and prefers the same intonation.

9 Sentences like *It's pouring rain, It's blowing a gale, It's raining drops as big as your fist* appear to fit Chafe's notion of COMPLEMENT rather than PATIENT. 'Blow' implies 'wind' as 'sing' implies 'song', and 'gale' specifies 'blow' more narrowly than 'wind', just as 'Star Spangled Banner' specifies 'sing' more narrowly than 'song' (*cf* Chafe 1970, 157). I am sceptical of the distinction between complement and patient. A complement is only a patient that duplicates more of the semantic traits of the verb and gives fewer other traits. But the argument here is not affected. Chafe does not deal with complements in relation to ambience.

10 At least two additional problems suggest themselves here, though I believe they are tangential. One is the comparative status of the two types *Tomorrow's her graduation* and *Her graduation is tomorrow*. The first seems to mean the same as *Tomorrow is when she graduates*. The event noun is used to define *tomorrow* functioning as a noun, the *when* clause to define it functioning as an adverb, with no practical difference in meaning. (Compare *At the office is where I work* and *The office is where I work.*) On the other hand, *Her graduation is tomorrow* I believe has *tomorrow* as an adverb (compare *Her graduation was in the auditorium*), and *be* is not a copula but an event verb: 'Her graduation takes place tomorrow'. But *Tomorrow's her graduation* can also be interpreted as having *be* as an event verb:

'Tomorrow comes her graduation.' This interpretation is easier with a sentence like *Today's the big event!* 'Today comes the big event!'

The other problem is the status of a sentence like *At the park was the annual Moose picnic*, which appears to be a counter-example to the unacceptability of *In California is pleasant*. But it does not represent the same construction. It is closely allied to *At the park there was the annual Moose picnic*, a type that is more frequent with indefinites:

Over here is a drinking fountain if you're thirsty.
There's a drinking fountain over here if you're thirsty.

If there are grounds for speaking of extraposition and copying here, they do not involve *it* but *there*. But see Chapter 5.

11 The doubtfulness of this sentence without *just about* reflects the coupling of *hot* with *impossible*, not the simultaneous coupling of *it* with *hot* and with *impossible*. The same thing can be accomplished with a comma as with *just about* – the separation of *hot* and *impossible*:

*It was hot and impossible to get anything done.
It was hot, and impossible to get anything done.

Chapter 5

There

Generative and traditional grammar alike have carried on the notion of the essential meaninglessness of English unstressed *there* in constructions like *There was nobody around, There comes a time when you've got to take a stand.* The current manifestation is to speak of '*there* insertion', whereby a *there* is added to a structure which is semantically complete without it.[1] The conditions affecting *there* insertion are seen as purely syntactic.

There is no disputing the fact that when *there* occurs, certain syntactic conditions obtain. Mostly these involve presenting *there* as a kind of subject pronoun. The real subject becomes a complement:

[1] There is *money* in the drawer.
[2] There became visible *a faint discoloration* just below the surface.

Like other pronouns, *there* inverts with the verb in negations, conditions, and questions (including tags):

[3] Never did there arise the slightest suspicion about his character.
[4] Had there occurred one more accident, the policy would have been canceled.
[5] Is there time?
[6] There's time, isn't there?

There is excluded from certain types of verbs, a semantic fact that will be dealt with later:

[7] A steady stream of new recruits offered (tried, wanted, agreed) to join the movement.
[8] *There offered to join the movement a steady stream of new recruits.
[9] A steady stream of new recruits continued (began, happened) to join the movement.

[10] There continued to join the movement a steady stream of new recruits.

Finally, *there* is alleged not to occur with definite subjects:

[11] *There are they in the room. (Bresnan 1970, 123)
[12] There are some in the room.
[13] *There are all three in the room.
[14] There are three in the room.

But this too is a syntactic fact that turns out to be a semantic one, as we shall see. Definite subjects occur rather freely, and we can learn as much about what indefiniteness means in the light of *there* constructions as about what *there* means in the light of indefiniteness.

Meaninglessness and automaticity are the burden of almost all the traditional treatments of 'existential' *there*, as it has commonly been called – not in reference to any meaning of *there* itself but to the construction in which *there* is used. Brown (1884, 666) cites Murray, Webster, and Priestly to the effect that *there* is meaningless, and as recent a grammar as Quirk *et al* (1972, 961) calls it a 'dummy element' and says that in a sentence with an initial adverbial such as

[15] In front of the carriage there rode two men in magnificent uniforms.

'there can be freely omitted'. This is also the position of Kuno (1971, 361–4), who sees existential sentences as having, in their basic order, an initial locative, which when displaced has *there* inserted for it, with a later transformation permitting the movement of the locative back into initial position; or, to use the example just cited, roughly the following:

[16] In front of the carriage rode two men ⇒ There rode two men in front of the carriage ⇒ In front of the carriage there rode two men.

There can often be freely omitted, or freely inserted, of course; but is this a freedom without sense? We have learned enough recently about lexical invariance, and especially about subscript pairs such as any_1 and any_2, $that_1$ and $that_2$, $which_1$ and $which_2$, where typically one member of the pair is stressless, to make us look with suspicion on any distinction between a meaningful $there_1$ and a meaningless $there_2$. Whether $there_2$ is meaningless ENOUGH to force a distinction depends on one's sense of proportion, but my intention is to show that 'existential' *there* is an extension of locative *there*, with a meaning that refers to a generalized 'location' in the same abstract way that the anaphoric *it* refers to a generalized 'identity' in *It was John who said that*.[2] I use the loose term *extension* in order not to claim that *there* and *there* are the 'same word' in the fullest sense of sameness. Breivik 1976 concludes that the present major functions of *there* have existed throughout the history of English. We may never be able to reconstruct existential *there* from a demonstrative locative referring to physical space. No matter. As I view it, it is still locative.

Among the traditional grammarians I have consulted, only Brown seems to have realized this. After chiding his predecessors for their notion of meaninglessness, he adds (1884, 666):

> The noun *place* itself is just as loose and variable in its meaning as the adverb *there*. For example; '*There* is never any difference'; *ie*, 'No difference ever takes *place*.' Shall we say that '*place*,' in this sense, is not a noun of place? To *take place*, is, to occur *somewhere*, or anywhere; and the unemphatic word *there* is but as indefinite in respect to place, as these other adverbs of place, or as the noun itself.

Later I shall try to show that Brown's comparison with *take place* is a useful test for the appropriateness of *there*. To add one comment here: he could have strengthened his argument by noting the stressless anaphoric use of *place* as an alternative to *there* in reference to locations that do not admit to the usual anaphoric *it* or *them*:

[17] *Miami is nice but I wouldn't care to líve in it.
[18] Miami is nice but I wouldn't care to líve there.
[19] Miami is nice but I wouldn't care to líve in the place.

The meaning of *there* can be approached through the meaning that almost no one has denied to the construction in which *there* occurs. It is 'existential' for almost every grammarian, including Jespersen (1909–49, but not 1933, where the non-committal 'preparatory' is substituted). The problem with this term is that it covers too much. Quirk *et al* use it for *have* constructions such as *The porter had a taxi ready*, and the unadorned verb *be* is existential in *Can such things be?* In fact, with the *there* construction itself the existential meaning is more a function of the verb than of *there*, especially in the most frequent combination of all (and almost the only colloquial one), *there* plus *be*.

In place of 'existential' I shall adopt a modification of the description that was first suggested by Joseph Silverman for Spanish *hay*, whose function is identical to that of English *there is*. Silverman said that *hay* 'brings something into existence'.[3] I alter this to 'brings something into awareness', where 'brings into' is the contribution of the position of *there* and other locational adverbs, and 'awareness' is the contribution of *there* itself; specifically, awareness is the abstract location to which I referred above.

1 *There* and its absence

To tease out the true sense of *there* we shall have to find contrasts in which the 'bring into' or (to borrow a term from Hetzron 1971 and 1975) presentative function of the CONSTRUCTION is present, but the meaning of abstract awareness is absent. This calls for finding, if possible, a minimal contrast between a sentence with *there* and one without – which of course is a direct test both of *there*'s deletability and of its mechanical insertability.[4]

The physical absence of *there* does not always contrast with its physical presence. Under very special circumstances – especially in certain questions – a *there* seems to underlie a zero. Whereas the question *Who's in the next room?* may receive the answer *John and Mary are* (the presence of the persons there has already been noted, and the question concerns their identity), the question *What's for supper tonight?* cannot be answered by **Bread and beans are*. It has not been established that there is anything for supper, and that must be attended to first: *There's bread and beans*, or simply *Bread and beans*. Other examples: *What's to be done about it?* (*?Nothing is to be done about it; There's nothing to be done about it*); *What's to stop us?* (**Nothing is to stop us; There's nothing to stop us*); *I don't know what's to prevent you. What is there to* with its succession of dentals is an ideal spot for dissimilation, and that may be what has happened to *there* in these cases. (The *What's for supper?* type may actually be vague as between *there* and *it*. Compare *What's for supper tonight? – It's bread and beans again* versus *What's to stop us? – *It's a storm coming up;* and also the question form *What's it going to be for supper tonight?*)

Elsewhere it is not difficult to single out a contrast. I shall use the term PRESENTATIVE CONSTRUCTION for both of the following, where a locative, or *there*, or both, precedes the verb:

[20] Across the street is a grocery.
[21] Across the street there's a grocery.[5]

The question is, do these two presentatives mean the same? At first blush they look identical. Yet if we assume that the first presents something on the immediate stage (brings something literally or figuratively BEFORE OUR PRESENCE) whereas the second presents something to our minds (brings a piece of knowledge into consciousness) we have an explanation for the following:

[22] *As I recall, across the street is a grocery.
[23] As I recall, across the street there's a grocery.
[24] As you can see, across the street is a grocery.
[25] *I can see that across the street is a grocery.
[26] I can see that across the street there's a grocery.

Examples [23] and [26] deal with a piece of information, whereas [24] is deictic; *see that*, like *tell that*, is factive.

Atkinson 1973 notes exactly the same distinction in French, conveyed by the presence or absence of *il:*

A: Vint un homme.
B: Il vint un homme.

Type A refers to 'staged activity': 'those portions of a novelistic discourse that purport to describe sensuous phenomena taking place "on stage", as though directly perceptible to a reader, in the course of a narrative' (5). He adds that 'the reader has the impression, not of being informed by the author of what is happening, but rather of being "on stage" himself, receiving directly the impressions of the moment' (15). Type B involves mental operations, whereas type A never represents 'an explanation, illustration, correction, objection, corroboration, deduction, conclusion, or personal appreciation of what has just been mentioned . . . but only the phenomenon itself' (68–9).[6]

Without *there*, the presentative construction brings something on a physical stage. Not always literally: *From the past come echoes and memories* or *In that year occurred three more eruptions* pictures time as if it were space; but the contrast is still apparent: *From the past there come echoes and memories* or *In that year there occurred three more eruptions* does not so much picture the events as acquaint our minds with them. A similar contrast can be seen in *Yesterday was the Elks' convention and today is the Masons'* and *Yesterday there was the Elks' convention and today there's the Masons'*.[7] A reasonable context for *there* could be one in which the event is introduced within a situation where no preparation has been made for it. If we were speaking of the history of the Hawaiian Islands we might mix together references to royal successions, agricultural problems, and volcanic eruptions:

[27] In the first year of Kamehameha II's reign there occurred an eruption of Mauna Loa, fortunately for the later condition of the soil
which was depleted from overcropping.

Just *occurred an eruption* would not be likely. On the other hand, if eruptions or disasters were already the general topic and one more occurred, it
would not be necessary to say, in effect, 'I invite you to consider this':

[28] Mauna Loa erupted in 1856 but things remained more or less quiet
until 1862; in that year occurred two eruptions of Kilauea, destroy-
ing several villages.

The construction *in that year occurred* PRESENTS the eruptions, but without
there it does not imply that we need to adjust our sights to them.

The more vividly on the stage an action is, the less appropriate *there* becomes, as can be seen in the following gradient:

[29] Out of nowhere appeared a mysterious figure.
[30] Out of nowhere there appeared a mysterious figure.
[31] Down the mountain leaped and thundered a foaming stream.
[32] ?Down the mountain there leaped and thundered a foaming
stream.
[33] Out flew a funny bird.
[34] *Out there flew a funny bird.

We are more apt to use *there* when something is out of sight, and so are
unlikely to accompany it with a pointing gesture:

[35] Over on the other side a little to the left (pointing at the object) is a
millinery shop (?there is a millinery shop).
[36] ?About a mile from here is a police station.
[37] Staring me right in the eye (?there) was a horrible apparition.
[38] Leaning against a lamppost (there) was a lonely figure of a man.

If I have a pencil in my open palm extended forward and an eraser in my
clenched fist held behind my back, I will say, for the respective hands,

[39] In my right hand is a pencil, and in my left there's an eraser.

for the same reason that if I OFFER you something I say *Here is*, not *Here
there is*. If something is out of sight and out of mind, as with a perfect
tense, *there* is appropriate to bring it into awareness; but if the scene is
before us, as with a narrative tense, *there* is unnecessary:

[40] Nearby was (?had been) a fight in full progress.
[41] Nearby there was (had been) a fight in full progress.

The less vividly on stage an action is, the more necessary *there* becomes. This puts a premium on concreteness. Two examples from Breivik 1975 illustrate this: *In the house was no sign of life; *On the table is probably a book (75). Abstractions make poor actors in this drama; and the POSSIBILITY of something being there is rather less than vivid. The same difficulty affects -*ing:* *At the party was dancing.

2 Relevance of the verb

The verb *be* is the locational and existential verb par excellence. It accounts for very nearly all of the colloquial uses of *there:*

[42] There's a bug on your collar.
[43] For there to be that kind of cooperation, you have to work among friends.

The locative sense of *there* accordingly is clearest with *be*. In fact, the 'other' *there* can be used in a similar abstract sense in a sentence analogous to [43]:

[44] The kind of cooperation we needed just wasn't there (wasn't to be had, wasn't in existence).

Charnley 1973 gives a number of examples of this kind of abstract use of locative *there* (he approaches the problem of common ground from the other end – the existentialness of the locative, whereas I am trying to look at the locativeness of the existential):

[45] No use, even in a story, trying to make it credible. It just happens. It simply is there.

The strain on *there* as a locative grows more severe as we move away from verbs that do not themselves embody a locative sense – that are not 'verbs of emergence', as Hetzron (1975, 354) calls them. Dependence increases on other locative cues. Following are examples without *there* to test the locativeness of certain verbs:

[46] Exhumed were at least a dozen corpses.
[47] ?Embalmed were at least a dozen corpses.
[48] Materializing was a mass of ectoplasm.
[49] ?Dissolving was a mass of ectoplasm.
[50] Slowly dissolving was a mass of ectoplasm.
[51] Approaching was a weird procession.

[52] ?Departing was a weird procession.
[53] All built was the house of our dreams.
[54] ?All painted was the house of our dreams.

The acts of exhuming, of materializing, of approaching, and of building all establish the thing in question on the scene. If the verb alone does not accomplish this, then it has to be fortified, as in [50], where slow motion holds the action on the stage. Fairly common is the use of a verb that represents a normal or customary action of a thing to suggest that the thing is there:

[55] Waving gaily was a bright flag.
[56] ?Burning merrily was an enemy flag.
[57] Blowing fatefully was a wind so strong that nothing could withstand it.
[58] ?Subsiding gradually was a wind that had caused untold damage.

With verbs embodying an on-the-sceneness, *there* can readily be used:

[59] There were exhumed at least a dozen corpses.
[60] ?There were embalmed at least a dozen corpses.
[61] There materialized a mass of ectoplasm.
[62] ?There dissolved a mass of ectoplasm.
[63] There slowly dissolved a mass of ectoplasm.
[64] There was approaching a weird procession.
[65] ?There was departing a weird procession.
[66] There waved a flag.
[67] ?There burned a flag.
[68] There ruled a king.
[69] *There complained a king.
[70] There were just coming through several important messages.
[71] ?There were just going out several important messages.
[72] There blew a wind.
[73] ?There subsided a wind.

I have queried examples instead of starring them because it is possible to rig contexts that justify them. The point of this demonstration is only to show that the verb alone, or with very little assistance, can convey enough locativeness to facilitate the use of *there*. Certainly *There blew a wind* is a commonplace way of saying that there WAS a wind on the scene. The importance of context can be seen in the following pair:

[74] There is just being decoded an important message.
[75] ?There is just being encoded an important message.

The decoding presents the message to our understanding. Encoding it does not; but if we add a bit,

[76] There is just being encoded a message that you are supposed to pick up and deliver.

then the encoding does present the object to be acted on.

Phrasal verbs are at the opposite extreme. Of all potential presentatives, they restrict the use of *there* most severely. We have already noted that when the adverbial particle is placed first, it is most unusual to have a *there* (**Out there flew a bird*).[8] The emphasis is on concreteness, which excludes initial position for an adverb that is not literally locative:[9]

[77] John stood up, Up stood John.
[78] John gave up, *Up gave John.
[79] The tree fell down, Down fell the tree.
[80] The car broke down, *Down broke the car.

The locative must not only be literal, but vivid:

[81] *Apart came the toy.
[82] *Aside stood the soldier.
[83] ?Back stepped the doorman.

In fact, the criterion seems to be 'How does this HIT the viewer?' Particles which are relatively undramatic can be improved by repetition:

[84] ?Over flopped the dolphin.
[85] Over and over flopped the dolphin.
[86] ?Around turned the carousel.
[87] Around and around turned the carousel.

Or – for more impact – a towardness (threatening the viewer by approaching him) or other dramatic motion may be added:

[88] ?Over flew the kite.
[89] Over and on and out of sight flew the kite.
[90] Over flew the frisbee.

A kite's flying over is a matter of position; a frisbee's adds an approach. It is apparent now why *there* is unsuitable: abstract location is devoid of sensory impact. By the same token, the perfect tenses are not well suited unless somehow compensated for – they envision an action peripherally rather than frontally:

[91] *Down has fallen the tree.
[92] *Away had sailed the ship.
[93] Down, down have come all my hopes.

The simple tenses, past and present, virtually monopolize the field, though the future is possible:

[94] Then in will come John and say . . .
[95] Then out will step a clown brandishing a torch.

Vividness is also disclosed in the way inverted phrasal verbs are affected by definiteness:

[96] ?Away sailed a ship.
[97] Away sailed an enormous ship.
[98] In sailed a ship.
[99] Away sailed the ship.

By adding towardness or size, we can give an unidentified and hence vague ship enough impact to justify the inversion; but with a known ship, one already in focus on the scene, that is not necessary. Here we see inverted phrasal verbs and *there* presentatives at opposite extremes, for if *there*'s function is to bring something into awareness, it is a bit unusual for it to be needed for something that has already been identified:

[100] There sailed in a ship.
[101] *There sailed in the ship.

3 Relevance of the locative expression

Something can be brought into awareness by relating it to a concrete scene or to an abstract one (existence). Location and existence are the two extremes, but there is no dividing line between them. Whether we say *Is there a God?* or *Is there a God in the universe?* we are expressing the same locative. To exist, a thing has to be somewhere – Thorne (1973, 863) cites the pre-Socratic dictum 'Whatever is is somewhere, whatever is nowhere is nothing' – and if the somewhere is not expressed it can be inferred:

[102] There is too much unhappiness (in this life).
[103] There comes (into the picture) a time when one must take a stand.
[104] There's no time (in the present emergency) to do it.

Given the possibility of a locative expression, a verb which in itself is not locative enough can be fixed up to allow a *there*:

[105] There rose a flag.
[106] *There smoldered a flag.
[107] In a corner of the wall there smoldered a flag that some angry patriot had torn down and ignited.

Smoldering, as a physical act, can occur anywhere, and needs only to be given a location. Other examples:

[108] There appeared (emerged) ship after ship.
[109] *There disappeared (went down) ship after ship.
[110] In this vortex there disappeared (went down) ship after ship.
[111] There grew a tree.
[112] *There quivered a tree.
[113] Looking up at these giant redwoods, you think to yourself, if ever there were to quiver a single tree, the whole place would break apart.

The position of the locative expression makes a difference:

[114] ?There smoldered a flag in the corner of the wall.
[115] ?There went down ship after ship in this vortex.
[116] ?If ever there were to quiver a single tree, you think as you look up at these giant redwoods, the whole place would break apart.

It may seem strange to consider a locative as topic of the sentence, yet that may be what accounts for the acceptability of [107], [110], and [113] and the unacceptability of [114–116]. In [110], for example, the sentence from *there* on tells us something about the vortex. Similarly in the following:

[117] In this building there exploded one of the most powerful bombs.
[118] *In this sink there broke one of my best plates.

A building can be remembered as the site of an explosion; a sink is hardly memorable as the site of breaking a plate. The place is too trivial to be worth characterizing (compare the effect of transforming *There's a bug on your collar* to *?On your collar there's a bug*), and the action is not one that has any locative repercussions. Here we can apply Brown's test:

[119] In this building took place the explosion of one of the most powerful bombs.
[120] *In this sink took place the breaking of one of my best plates.

The notion of 'locative repercussions' can also be tested against the behavior of the verbs *occur* and *happen*. The breaking of a plate is a happening; an explosion is an occurrence:

[121] When did the explosion occur?
[122] ?When did the explosion happen?
[123] ?When did the breaking of the plate occur?
[124] When did the breaking of the plate happen?

An occurrence is at least partly locative, a happening is purely eventual. The latter can be seen in the unacceptability of this verb in a presentative construction without *there*; it is not sufficiently locative in its own right for a temporal adverb to serve:

[125] *At that moment happened one of those strange coincidences.
[126] At that moment occurred one of those strange coincidences.

Although the explicit locative *there* eases the difficulty somewhat with *happen*, the result is still apt to be unsatisfactory:

[127] ?At that moment there happened one of those strange coincidences.
[128] If ever again there happens an accident like that, we'll have only ourselves to blame.
[129] At this corner there occurred (*happened) an accident last night.

In the last example, if instead of the purely eventual *last night* we use a modifier that signifies some lasting effect – and consequently leaves its mark on the topic *this corner* – the result is normal:

[130] At this corner there happened an accident that was to be remembered for years.

Similarly in the following, where merely increasing the scope of the action changes the result:

[131] ?At this table there was eaten a piglet.
[132] At this table there was eaten many a piglet.

The same effect is observed when the action serves as a restrictive modifier of the topic, *table*:

[133] At this table there was eaten a piglet, at that one a lamb.

The rest of the sentence must not only have enough spatial impact to mark the locative topic, it must be appropriate to it:

[134] ?In this auditorium, in 1956, there failed one entire freshman class of 140 students.

[135] In this exam room, in 1956, there failed one entire freshman class of 140 students.

[136] At least 40 per cent are bound to fail in the second semester.

[137] *In the second semester there are bound to fail at least 40 per cent.

[138] At least 40 per cent are bound to fail in the final exam.

[139] In the final exam there are bound to fail at least 40 per cent.

We can describe an exam, but not a semester, in terms of the percentage of failures.

Difficult as the generic definite article is with *there* (*There screamed the panther*), even it becomes possible with an appropriate setting which can be described by the action:

[140] In this alternate world, millions of years ago, there screamed the panther – there laughed the hyena – there howled the baboon – all was as if in our own sphere.

4 Relevance of the passive

There is a notably low percentage of active transitive expressions in presentative constructions. If the transitive verb is part of a phrase that is a kind of semantically analytic intransitive, that is, one that amounts to a single verb, its appearance here is normal enough so long as the sense is appropriate:

[141] In that realm (there) held sway (= ruled) a hated despot.

[142] There was slowly making its way toward (= was approaching) us a figure in black.

[143] Near here (there) have taken place (= occurred) some of the most striking events in the state's history.

[144] In the tower there strikes the hour a clock of many chimes.

But elsewhere the transitives seem to involve too many entities, and to violate the loose constraint against saying more than one thing at a time. Some examples contrasting intransitive and transitive verbs:

[145] In the roundhouse (there) was puffing away an old-time locomotive.

[146] *In the roundhouse (there) was letting off steam an old-time locomotive.

[147] From the ridge above was descending upon us a horde of savages.

[148] *From the ridge above was menacing us a horde of savages.

[149] From this pulpit (there) preached no less a person than Cotton Mather.

[150] *From this pulpit (there) preached his weekly sermon no less a person than Cotton Mather.

The passive makes it possible to use transitive verbs in a presentative construction by avoiding the problem of too many arguments. The agent is simply deleted. If it is named, it is apt to appear as an afterthought:

[151] ?In the afternoon there were brought in by the porters some half dozen cases of wine.

[152] In the afternoon there were brought in, by the porters, some half dozen cases of wine.

[153] ?There were shown to us by the diggers several interesting specimens.

[154] There were shown to us, by the diggers, several interesting specimens.

Passive verbs are no different from active in the requirement of a real or implied locative meaning, if they are not to need some other reinforcement to accommodate *there*; in fact, a number of the examples cited previously have been passive. In the following we see that a verb referring only to the action without any spatial import, such as *lose*, does not serve very well by comparison with *purloin* and *steal* (*They stole away*), both of which involve distance. Similarly the actions of *torturing* and *maiming* lack the spatial sense of 'disposing of, eliminating from the scene' that is conveyed by *beheading* or *hanging*:

[155] There were stolen (purloined, spirited away, hijacked, taken, ?grabbed, *snatched, ?pilfered, ?lost) quite a number of very valuable jewels.

[156] There were jailed (incarcerated, locked up, ?detained, ?arrested, ?apprehended) fifteen or so drunks and junkies.

[157] There was carted away (?loaded up) a heap of trash.

[158] There was laid aside (reserved, saved, stored, kept, retained, housed, sheltered, ?protected, ?guarded) enough for another occasion.

[159] A few days after that there were beheaded (hanged, ?tortured, ?maimed) at least a dozen felons.

[160] There were evicted (thrown out, expelled, ?inconvenienced, ?abused) so many tenants that the state authorities had to step in.

[161] There have been destroyed (?damaged) any number of historic landmarks.

But the passive is significant in a more subtle way – through a kind of double function of the verb *be*. It is customary to think of a construction such as *was sold* as a straightforward verb, with *be* simply an auxiliary of passiveness. Yet we know that the passive was originally a combination of copula and modifier, and we still have an 'apparent passive' in expressions like *They were exhausted*. (In similar vein, Langacker and Munro 1975 argue for an underlying unity in existential senses of *be*, among which they include its use as a passive auxiliary.) If passives are in some sense – where *there* constructions are concerned – a combination of *be* plus modifier, then it might be worth while to look first at combinations of *be* plus adjective, for possible clues to the adjectival function of the past participle. And such adjective combinations are indeed significant, at least in their own way. We find that an adjective which establishes something on the scene, such as *valid*, can be used with *there*, whereas one that merely describes and has no 'being there' about it, cannot – *good*, for example:

[162] For there to be valid (*good) even one of these propositions, it first has to be proved that they were arrived at inductively.

[163] There being true (*persuasive) some fundamental part of the argument makes the rest easier to accept.[10]

Other adjectives whose locativeness is a little more obvious are those that refer to what can be reached physically or through the senses. They are virtually adverbs in meaning and in tendency to non-preadjunct position:

[164] There were present and voting about fifty persons.

[165] There were about fifty persons present (=there).

[166] There were missing almost half of the most vital documents.

[167] There were almost half of the most vital documents missing (=not there).

[168] There were available several more.

[169] There were several more available (=within reach).

[170] There were visible only a few stars.

[171] There were only a few stars visible (=within view).

So for *audible*,[11] *obtainable, accessible,* etc.

In one position at least the verb *be* pretty clearly stands in double function in the passive, as the following examples show:

[172] X found all those people.
[173] There were found all those people.
[174] There were all those people found.
[175] X blamed all those people.
[176] *There were blamed all those people.
[177] There were all those people blamed.

Find is a presentative verb in its own right, so that [173] creates no problem; but *blame* is not, which makes [176] nearly if not quite impossible. But [177], where *were* seems to take the noun directly as its complement, obviates the problem. A similar set:

[178] X ate away still more of it.
[179] The next time we looked, there had been eaten away still more of it.
[180] The next time we looked, there had been still more of it eaten away.
[181] X ate still more of it.
[182] ?The next time we looked, there had been eaten still more of it.
[183] The next time we looked, there had been still more of it eaten.

To eat away (cause to disappear by eating) has spatial overtones that *eat* lacks; but in [183] the noun complement is presented directly by *had been*. The same effect can be seen in a somewhat archaic context if we contrast the old *be* perfect with the modern *have* perfect:

[184] Several new ones had come to judgment.
[185] Several new ones were come to judgment.
[186] There had come to judgment several new ones.
[187] There were come to judgment several new ones.
[188] *There had several new ones come to judgment.
[189] There were several new ones come to judgment.

come to judgment is a normal locative expression, so that [186] and [187] are both good; but *had* is not locative – a handicap that does not afflict *were* in its split function in [189].

But even without the shift of position it is possible to find passive sentences not involving specifically locative verbs which nevertheless have a locative impact by virtue of doing what was noted earlier in connection with such a verb as *explode* – namely, producing a kind of lasting effect. We can speak of 'resultant-condition verbs', a category that is motivated in other ways than the one outlined here.[12] So, even though we would not be likely to say *?There were cleaned several floors*, since *clean* is not in itself locative, nevertheless *to clean* has the resultant condition *clean(ed)* in a way that *to wash* does not have a resultant condition *washed*, and this makes a difference in *Wh* questions:

[190] ?What floors have there been washed?
[191] What floors have there been cleaned?[13]

(The distinction that we make between *cleaned* and *washed* can also be seen in *How thoroughly cleaned it looks!* versus *?How thoroughly washed it looks!*)[14] Other examples:

[192] ?What jewels were there weighed?
[193] What jewels were there inscribed?
[194] ?How many jokes were there laughed at?
[195] How many jokes were there written?
[196] ?How many wafers were there tasted?
[197] How many wafers were there bitten into?

One could almost paraphrase *How many jokes got into that written state-location?*, which would be absurd with **How many jokes got into that laughed-at state-location? Written* leaves a mark, *laughed at* does not. Of course, looking at the last pair, it could be argued that *How many wafers were there bitten into?* is acceptable because it is a transformation of *There were several wafers bitten into* rather than of **There were bitten into several wafers.* But that does not explain why *?How many wafers were there tasted?* is doubtful in spite of the acceptability of *There were several wafers tasted.* The meaning of the verb still has to be reckoned with.

Kruisinga–Erades (1953, § 56.1) were conscious of the 'lasting effect' or resultant-condition factor of locativeness, though they put the rule too strongly: 'the verb expresses a state or an occurrence, never an activity'. As we have seen, it may express an activity if there are locative consequences. A test for state as against activity is the use of a modifier that refers to an event:

[198] Rudely (painfully) shaken were several of the passengers.
[199] ?Abruptly (suddenly) shaken were several of the passengers.

– *rudely* and *painfully* describe the visible effects of the shake-up; *abruptly* and *suddenly* give the timing or extent of the happening. But the contrast is equally noticeable in the meaning of the verb:

[200] ?Tempted by Satan were many of the aspirants to heaven.
[201] Marked by Satan were many of the aspirants to heaven.
[202] ?Fought by all the other parties were the Social Democrats.
[203] Opposed by all the other parties were the Social Democrats. (The others were *in opposition*.)
[204] ?Forced to yield were all of the palace guard.
[205] Forced to kneel (hence, in a kneeling position) were all of the palace guard.

All that has been said in this section points to the impossibility of drawing a line between state (resultant condition, 'apparent passive') uses of the past participle, and 'true passive' uses. The dual function of *to be*, which straddles taking the participle as a complement and joining with it as an auxiliary, the ease with which participles are adjectivized, the meanings of certain verbs which incline the balance one way or the other, and the reshuffling of apparent constituents in *Wh* questions, all result in a gradient extending from pure activity to pure state, with – in addition – many lexical adverbs and lexical adjectives at the state end. State at its purest is location (etymologically the word means 'stand'), and it has not been amiss to extend the meaning of 'locative' to those cases that are most amenable to the presentative construction.[15] In the following contrasts we see the locative overtones of the acceptable examples, from literal location to being-in-a-state:

[206] Told to wait (hence on the scene, waiting) were a dozen or so schoolchildren.
[207] *Told to behave were a dozen or so schoolchildren.
[208] Neatly filed (hence in their place) were half a dozen folders.
[209] *Well educated were half a dozen persons.
[210] Garishly displayed (laid out on the scene) was a row of guns.
[211] Carefully aimed (pointing in a direction) was a row of guns.
[212] *Carefully oiled was a row of guns.
[213] Painted clearly (hence visible, on the scene) was a warning sign in Dutch.
[214] *Painted red was a warning sign in Dutch.
[215] Flaunted were a number of charges that would be hard to refute.
[216] *Fabricated were a number of charges that would be hard to refute.

[217] Remembered (lodged in memory) were all the happy days we spent together.

[218] ?Recalled were all the happy days we spent together.

[219] Commemorated (celebrated; hence established) were most of the important anniversaries.

[220] ?Observed were most of the important anniversaries.

The more visible the effect of an action, the more we sense the resultant state over and above the action itself. Sheer IMPACT may improve the acceptability of a sentence – a fact noted earlier in connection with the particles of phrasal verbs:

[221] Ruined are the ideals we stood for.

[222] ?Weakened are the ideals we stood for.

[223] Gone (lost, vanished) are all the friends we once had.

[224] ?Gone away are all the friends we once had.

[225] Completely charred was one of the grandest of the old redwoods.

[226] ?Slightly charred was one of the grandest of the old redwoods.

[227] Heavily damaged were two Vermeers.

[228] ?Lightly damaged were two Vermeers.

[229] Thoroughly mangled were most of the first class passengers.

[230] ?Somewhat shaken up were most of the first class passengers.

[231] Resented (keenly felt) were all the insults they had had to endure.

[232] ?Perceived were all the insults they had had to endure.

[233] Shamefully abused were hundreds of children.

[234] ?Abused were hundreds of children.

Impact and high visibility may be shown by adjectives as readily as by participles:

[235] Noticeable were two dark-clad figures in the background.

[236] Visible were many traces of their occupancy.

[237] Discernible to any eye were the ravages of time on her face.

Some contrasts with adjectives:

[238] Plainly detectible were the disfigurements left by smallpox.

[239] ?Detectible were the disfigurements left by smallpox.

[240] Rather obvious was the lack of precautions.

[241] ?Rather suspicious was the lack of precautions.

[242] Especially interesting is the belief in ghosts.

[243] ?Essentially uninteresting is the belief in ghosts.

[244] Quite colorful is the custom of the nines.

[245] ?Quite colorless is the custom of the nines.
[246] Intent on winning the race were two very small boys.
[247] ?Indifferent to winning the race were two very small boys.
[248] Rather widespread (general, common, frequent) is the belief in witchcraft.
[249] ?Rather parochial is the belief in witchcraft.

As we noted earlier with phrasal verbs, the perfect tenses view the action peripherally and this undermines the impact:

[250] ?Rather widespread has been the belief in witchcraft.
[251] *Shamefully abused had been hundreds of children.

The presentative construction is not the only instance of complement fronting in declarative sentences. It is also found in highly charged speech:

[252] A million dollars that blunder cost me!
[253] Crazy is the word for your friend!

What is uppermost in mind comes out first. It is very likely that presentatives – especially to the extent that impact rather than mere locativeness is important – trade on this same principle. The fact is that impact has a prosodic as well as a semantic side. In a number of the preceding examples it was necessary to inflate the complement with extra modification; for the most part the added material increased the semantic force, but in one or two instances – for example in [240], it did not.[16] The same is true of the following:

[254] Fairly clear is the argument that refunds will have to be made.
[255] ?Clear is the argument that refunds will have to be made.

Adjectives may be accumulated, thus gaining semantically as well as prosodically:

[256] Rich and deep were the tones of her voice.
[257] ?Rich were the tones of her voice.
[258] Completely good and true were all the sentiments they expressed.
[259] ?Completely good were all the sentiments they expressed.

An example such as [257] is normal of course in poetry. In fact, the lyrical effect of fronting transcends presentatives:

[260] Good and true they were in all they did.

I conclude the treatment of the passive by disposing of an irrelevancy, the passive of the information verbs *know, believe, say, assert, estimate,* etc. These are the verbs that can be freely postposed, much like adverbs:[17]

[261] They're crazy, she said (*she doubted).
[262] It's about ten feet, I would estimate (*I would deny).
[263] It's impossible, I fear (*I regret).
[264] More could be done, it was proved (*disproved).

The passives of these verbs are like auxiliaries in that they can be inserted after *there* without affecting the locative criterion of the verb to which they are attached:

[265] There might (could, should, was to) arise some other objection.[18]
[266] There are said (*doubted) to have been discovered on this very spot the remains of an ancient civilization.
[267] There was asserted (*denied) to be more.
[268] There was shown (*disproved) to have developed a rather strong opposition.
[269] There were feared (*regretted) to be more difficulties than had been imagined.
[270] There were remembered (*forgotten) to be a few like that.

Adjectives that have the same assertive function as the information verbs (*sure, certain, likely,* but not *possible, impossible, uncertain*) belong in the same class with the passives of those verbs:

[271] There was certain (*uncertain) to be brought to light all the rancor that had built up.
[272] There was likely (*possible, *impossible) to be an outbreak.[19]

When *there* and its verb are extraposed, the corresponding passives and adjectives are normal:

[273] It was denied that there were more.
[274] It was impossible for there to be an outbreak.

5 Relevance of prior context

In presentatives without *there,* the stage is a link to what has gone before; it is in a sense topicalized. We saw this in examples [27] and [28]. But if the presentative initiates a line of thought, *there* must be added. Someone lecturing on the brain would not stand up and say, as an opener,

[275] *In the left hemisphere of the brain are centers that control the production of speech.

But if the matter of lateralization has already come up – for example, if the functions of the right hemisphere have been mentioned – this sentence can follow naturally. Similarly one would not begin a story with

[276] *In Xanadu lived a prince of the blood.

– a *there* would be required. On the other hand, a *there*-less presentative is normal in second position:

[277] In Xanadu there lived a prince of the blood. Near him lived a beautiful princess whose name was Divinapreciosa.
[278] What lives in Xanadu? – In Xanadu live all manner of crawly creatures.

Journalism exploits the link with prior context – provided by *there*-less presentatives – to create a kind of artificial continuity in news stories. Though good journalism will not neglect impact – the presentative expression should be striking enough to bring the new actor in with a flourish – the emphasis is on maintaining the contextual stage and the range of choice for presentative expressions is widened to include anything with a hint of resultant condition. The act of recording the event is itself the means of arresting it on stage, a journalistic trick rather than a colloquial one. Comparing the two following sentences,

[279] Blamed for the failures was Turner's chief assistant, R. Dunaway.
[280] ?Blamed for his failures was Turner's chief assistant, R. Dunaway.

we sense the correct tie-in with previous context provided by anaphoric *the*. And *blamed* has the requisite degree of impact. Similarly:

[281] Still alive were three of the trapped victims.
[282] ?Alive were three of the trapped victims.
[283] As good as ever are the parts you will find at Mickey's.
[284] ?As good as new are the parts you will find at Mickey's.
[285] Green with envy at his good fortune were most of his companions.
[286] ?Green with envy were most of his companions.

– *still, as ever,* and *his good fortune* imply matters already on the record. The informational balance reveals itself intonationally when the syntax is in the normal order. The usual pitch curves for the uninverted versions of [281] and [282] would be

[287] Three o f the t r a p p e d victims were still a l i v e .

[288] Three of the trapped vic tims were a li v e .

What is more or less taken for granted has a lower pitch, but fronting it – topicalizing it, as in [281] – enables the speaker to give it prominence.

Some examples of the usual newspaper fare:

[289] Booked were several prostitutes and a few of their clients.
[290] Caught in the act of entering were two youths aged 16 and 18.
[291] Fully accepted are the provisions that have to do with taxation.
[292] Known to enjoy the prince's confidence are two or three of the younger correspondents.
[293] Even more excited and happy were all the children in the audience.
[294] Made up to look like a clown was Abner's grandson. (in the setting of a junior circus)

6 Relevance of the position of *there*

The last two sections give an idea of the scope of the presentative expression when no *there* is used. It reaches from literal location through state to mere location in the text (topicalized prior context):

[295] In a cage was a talkative parrot.
[296] Utterly blighted were the last of our hopes.
[297] Supporting this idea are the following facts.

But when *there* is introduced, only a literal locative can stand to the left of it as part of the presentative expression. Re-using a few examples that were normal without *there*, and adding a few more, we have:

[298] ★Booked there were several prostitutes and a few of their clients.
[299] ★Fully accepted there are the provisions that have to do with taxa-tion.
[300] ?Told to wait there were a dozen or so schoolchildren.

[301] *Green with envy at his good fortune there were several of his companions.
[302] Still extant were a few copies of the first edition.
[303] ?Still extant there were a few copies of the first edition.
[304] Strewn about the stones were the remnants of a campfire.
[305] Strewn about the stones there were the remnants of a campfire.
[306] Written on the wall were some indecipherable characters.
[307] Written on the wall there were some indecipherable characters.

But when the rest of the presentative expression FOLLOWS *there*, a suggestion of locativeness is enough:

[308] ?There were booked several prostitutes and a few of their clients.
[309] *There are fully accepted the provisions that have to do with taxation.
[310] There were left to die a number of wounded.
[311] *There were green with envy at his good fortune several of his companions.
[312] There were still extant a few copies of the first edition.

Some contrasting pairs:

[313] ?Neatly filed there were about a dozen folders.
[314] There were neatly filed about a dozen folders.
[315] *Garishly displayed there were a number of costumes.
[316] There were garishly displayed a number of costumes.
[317] *Rather widespread there is a belief in witchcraft.
[318] There is rather widespread a belief in witchcraft.
[319] *Painted clearly there was a warning sign in Dutch.
[320] There was painted clearly a warning sign in Dutch.

What happens when the rest of the presentative expression is in no sense locative can be seen in the examples of the section on relevance of the verb.

7 Relevance of definiteness

The first task at this point is to relate the notion of definiteness to that of staging. The second is to look at the history – and fundamental irrelevance – of the supposed relationship between presentatives and GRAMMATICAL definites.

'On stage' can be seen as no more than a graphic way of describing demonstrativeness. The clue lies in the two uses of *that, those:* in one, a deixis ad oculos – *that lamppost* (over there); in the other, anaphora, that is, contextual deixis – *that lamppost* (that I mentioned in my last paragraph). Exactly these two kinds of staging have developed as the basis for presentatives without *there*. In *Here is the money you asked for*, the deixis is to the physical setting. In *Beyond the hill was a sanitarium* it is again to a physical setting, though in a narrative sense; but it is also to the linguistic context, since *the hill* bespeaks something already known. Here we have a blend of literal and figurative deixis. In *Arrested were the following persons* there is purely textual anaphora: the sentence will not be put this way unless *arrested* ties in with a narrative scene in which an arrest was a natural consequence; the implication is 'arrested on that occasion' or 'arrested as a result of that fracas' or whatever. This is the 'relevance to context' that Givón regards as 'an important feature of presentative devices' (1976, 155).

Now we can appreciate our sensation of 'being there', on the scene, whenever we encounter a *there*-less presentative with an outright locative. And also our sensation of being carried along with the conceptual scene when a writer uses *there*-less presentatives anaphorically. The fact of putting the presentative expression first, of topicalizing it, if we can extend this term a bit, is the linguistic cue to a kind of deixis that in other situations is carried by an explicit demonstrative. A reader accepts contextual deixis on broad and fairly uncritical terms because the links between one part of a narrative and the next are so numerous. But more is demanded of a literal or figurative deixis ad oculos: *Carefully aimed was a row of guns* is acceptable because aiming is directional, hence locative; *Carefully oiled was a row of guns* is unacceptable because *oiled* is not locative (and oiling would be hard to conceive as a link to anything preceding).

The two deictic-demonstrative schemes are also the clue to the use of *there*. If a party of would-be picnickers parks at a roadside and looks vaguely around, a ranger would not greet them with *Ten miles down the road are some picnic tables* (though this would do very well after some preliminary remark to set a CONTEXTUAL stage), but would add *there*. On the other hand, *Across the road are some tables* would be normal, out of the blue, if the tables could be pointed to. Second, when we narrate, if no stage has been set we must use *there* to orient the hearer to our scene, but once the scene is established no *there* is required:

[321] In Kansas there lived many colonies of New Englanders.
[322] . . . Near them in Missouri lived a good many Southerners.

One step beyond this are the journalistic presentatives that are purely contextual.

The connection between definiteness and indefiniteness and the use and omission of *there* should now be obvious. The first mention of an entity is normally indefinite: *He bought a house* (second mention, *The house was green*). So to the extent that bringing something into awareness, creating an abstract stage when the concrete one or the contextual one is missing, is an occasion for *there*, it is also an occasion for indefiniteness:

[323] ?In a house on a hill lived a ghost.
[324] In a house on a hill there lived a ghost.
[325] In the house on the hill lived a ghost.
[326] In the house on the hill there lived a ghost.
[327] In the house on the hill lived the ghost.
[328] ?In the house on the hill there lived the ghost.

The last sentence is odd because with everything marked by a definite article it appears that all the introductions have been made. But suppose our interlocutor has forgotten someone or something that must then be REINTRODUCED:

[329] I'm surprised she hasn't left him long before this. – There are the children – remember?

There can bring something BACK into awareness as well as make us aware of it for the first time.

It is only recently that grammarians seem to have been talking about the unacceptability of *there* with grammatically definite subjects. No such restriction is noted in any of the older comprehensive handbooks. In fact, all have a scattering of definites, on the order of five per cent or so of the examples cited. Following are a few:

[330] From the total of this rental there has ... been previously deducted the expenditure upon repairs (Kruisinga 1932, § 2176).
[331] There is always the possibility ... of being All (Curme 1931, 10).
[332] Then there shot through Philip's mind the recollection of the money he had seized (Poutsma 1928, 401).
[333] There can be only Bingley and yourself more dear to me (Jespersen 1909–49, 3.17.7.2).

Of the more recent handbooks we find no restriction mentioned in Long 1971, who cites the following:

[334] There's always George.

Though I have made no thorough investigation of it, the first reference to definiteness of which I am aware was made by Bull 1943 in connection with Spanish *hay* (*haber*). Bull was aware that instances of definite subjects are found with *haber* (He cites *Hay, pues, primero la necesidad de conocer para vivir* . . .; *sin éste no hay aquél* 'There is, first, the need to know in order to live . . .; without the latter there is not the former'), but he was satisfied with the statistical percentages in order to 'formulate practical rules' (123). But with the theoretical rather than practical sufficiency that today's linguist demands, the exceptions must either be ignored or given a special rule. Wasow 1975 and Bresnan 1970 ignore them. Quirk–Greenbaum 1973 (and also Fries 1952) make them a special case: 'The rule that existential sentences should have an indefinite noun phrase as "notional subject" prevents the derivation of sentences like *There is the money in the box* from *The money is in the box*. This limitation can be waived, however, in answer to existential questions (actual or implied):

A: Is there anyone coming to dinner?
B: Yes, there's Harry and there's also Mrs Jones.' (419)

As so often happens, the need for a special rule is an artifact of a false main rule. The handbook citations given above suggest that definites can be found in other contexts than answers to existential questions. Existential questions themselves may have definite subjects:

[335] Is there God?[20]

For Bresnan 1970 and Wasow 1975 the interesting fact about the putative indefiniteness rule is that it excludes personal pronouns as subjects. At first glance it does seem that anything like Bresnan's *There are they in the room* or Wasow's *Some burglars shot a man who discovered that there were they* (*them*) *in his house* must be impossible. Nevertheless, pronouns are normal provided they do not violate the proper rule for *there*:[21]

[336] *Mr* A: Who of all our friends can we trust? *Mr* B: There's only John, I'm afraid. *Mr* C: Not so. Because if there were only him, you'd be denying the essential goodness of human nature.

[337] *Ms* A: How many can we get for our group? *Mr* B: Well, there's Tom, and Gladys, and Lucille . . . *Ms* A: Let's not forget Bill. *Mr* B: Oh, yes, there's him – and there's you and me – that ought to make up the number we need.

Bresnan's example is impossible because it is a bald introduction of a *they* which clearly has to refer to something already on the scene. Similarly, and more explicitly, with Wasow's: the sentence has *some burglars* on the scene at the very outset; to use a *there* later is redundant. The counterpart sentence *A man who discovered that there were some burglars in his house was shot by them* is normal because the introduction is placed where introductions belong.

The problem with pronouns of course is that they relate by definition to something already mentioned, hence presumably on the scene (Unless a deixis ad oculos is involved: *Who will do it? – Well, there's him* [pointing].) My examples are acceptable because they involve reprises: *if there were only him* repeats the whole introduction made by the previous speaker; *there's him* repeats the implied *there's Bill* in *Let's not forget Bill.* If an introduction can be made it can be repeated. The only striking fact is that the repetition permits pronominalization; the meaning relationships are preserved.

Not only are definites possible with *there* plus *be;* they are just as normal with other presentative verbs:

[338] When we ask ourselves who are the likeliest candidates, there come to mind the following: Arthur Lovelace, Perry Amador, Mark Arsuaga, and Lucius Neale.

[339] When I asked myself what was most likely to interest them, there occurred to me the parable of the loaves and fishes.

[340] Which copies had there been stolen?

The need to distinguish between semantic definiteness (knownness) and grammatical definiteness can be detected in what at first sight appears to be a prosodic rule:

[341] *Behold! There stands before you Christ!

[342] Behold! There stands before you the Son of God!

This looks like a case of 'longest element last' as in *We discussed at great length Henry* versus *We discussed at great length Henry and his brothers*, but it probably answers instead to meaning. In [342] there is an additional unknown – besides 'who is he?' there is a 'what is he?': underlying the sentence is *There stands before you he who is the Son of God*.[22] (*Christ* could be changed to *Jesus Christ* and the preferences would remain the same.) A similar pair:

[343] ?Behold! There stands before you the king!

[344] Behold! There stands before you the king himself!

The prosody has changed, but so has the meaning: the added intensification suggests a situation where the identity is in doubt. Some more comparisons in which one member of each pair is semantically less known and more in need of an introduction, though both members are grammatically definite:

[345] *In Africa there dwells the lion.
[346] On the plains of Berimabu there dwells the mythical beast known as the Unicorn, who consorts with his fellows, the Hippogriff and the Wampus.
[347] *On this hill there will arise the city.
[348] On this hill there will arise the city of the future.
[349] *Suddenly there appeared the solution.
[350] In that instant, in a blinding flash, there appeared the Solution! No more would I have to grope, blindly, for faith.

All the same, prosody may well be a factor in a case like the following:

[351] If there stood before us now either Solomon or Socrates, I doubt that we could draw the answer to this problem.
[352] *If there stood before us now Solomon, . . .

It is hard to disentangle the fact of syllabic weight from that of the inherent indefiniteness of plurality.

Another problem with definiteness is anaphora (as in *The desk is too big*) versus cataphora (as in *The desk you are seated at is too big*). Anaphoric definites are known. Cataphoric definites, which need modifiers to pin them down, are being presented:

[353] There has long existed the suspicion that cancer may be a viral disease.
[354] There will soon appear the definitive edition of the *Scottish National Dictionary*.
[355] There is nowhere to be found the kind of treason that his mind has conjured up.

Conditional clauses add an extra dimension of uncertainty:

[356] Were there still living today those patriarchs of old, we should have little lack of wisdom.
[357] If there is ever to be written the true history of that science, it will have to be through the cooperation of every one of its sub-disciplines.

How definite is definite? In a descending semantic scale of definiteness the grammatical definites fall more or less like this:

1 Third-person anaphoric pronouns. The referent is agreed upon by both speaker and hearer and must already have been mentioned in the context.
2 Personal names and anaphoric nouns. The speaker assumes that his hearer will be able to make the connection with the referent immediately, though mention within the context is not essential.
3 Cataphoric nouns with *the*. Something needs to be added to delimit the noun.
4 Cataphoric demonstratives. The determiner does no more than point to a clause as something designating a thing that is known to exist but about which nothing is presupposed: *that which, those who*.
5 The indefinite superlative, called by Quirk–Greenbaum 'the indefinite exclamatory *the*', as in *There's the oddest-looking man standing at the front door!* (419). (This probably stems from the cataphoric *the oddest-looking man you ever saw*.)

This is an increasing scale for the use of *there*, which is perfectly commonplace at the bottom end. Where Quirk–Greenbaum characterize (5) as 'indefinite', Poutsma 1916 does the same for (4) – *there are those who* he says is roughly equivalent to *there are some who* (921). Even in (3) there are situations where the definite article may be more usual than the indefinite. Such are the instances with *means* and its synonyms:

[358] The board vetoed the school lunch program alleging that 'there just weren't the means (*there just weren't means, *there just weren't any means) for it'.
[359] We'll start the project next month if possible. – Are there (the) funds (resources) for it? (Is there the money necessary for it?)

'Reminders' have already been mentioned; expressions of obligation are frequent here, especially involving the verb *to consider* and its synonyms:

[360] I would say let's take our vacation this month, but there's John to consider. And there's the election to keep in mind – I don't want to skip voting this time. And also there's the supervisor's proposal to think over – it might mean missing out on that deal.
[361] I'd like to go with you, but there's all this work to do! And there's my mother-in-law who's got to be taken to the airport.
[362] We're all booked up. There's yesterday's accident still to be investigated, and the holdup that just got reported. No time for anything.

Obligation is of special interest because it has been syntactically formalized for 'existential *have*' but not for 'existential *there*' (to use the Quirk *et al* terms):

[363] I have these (some) papers to file.
[364] I have to file these (some) papers.
[365] There are these (some) papers to file.
[366] *There are to file these (some) papers.[23]

Obligations are typical of things already known of which someone may need to be reminded.

8 Conclusion

If the discussion in this chapter seems to have turned more on questions of style than of grammar, it is because the meaning of *there* is too abstract to discover through some rough commutation test with a few words in a few hackneyed contexts. Most of the confusion about *there* has been due to a failure to see its underlying constancy in the welter of its associations. When a meaning is tenuous our impulse is to try to firm it up with features borrowed from incidental contexts. 'Awareness' is tenuous and abstract, but not vague. The common thread in all the uses of *there* is its original locative meaning – locative in the broadest sense of whatever in space and time can be seen as something 'out there' and more than an ephemeral event, but so strongly adhering at one end of the spectrum to the literally locative (as in *There's a cake on the shelf*) that we can feel a reasonable confidence in regarding the rest of the range as an abstraction and metaphorical extension. As Kruisinga–Erades put it – despite their earlier claim of meaninglessness – 'the association between particle . . . and the adverb of place is not completely lost, in spite of their phonetic divergence' (1953 § 56.1).

I leave open the question of whether to split *there* into two lexical entries. *There* is not like *it*, where no sharp line can be drawn between the abstract and the concrete meanings. It is more like *that*, where the relative has split off from the demonstrative, though – if we are to understand it as distinct from *which* and from zero – still requiring us to regard it as semantically demonstrative. There is nothing unusual about having a word with two meanings related at their base but discontinuous with each other. Every established metaphor is an instance of it.

As for the universal tendency to put presentative expressions first, I suspect it is an example of 'natural' word order, as uncomplicated as the temporal sequencing in *She* (1) *came in and* (2) *sat down.* I would relate it to the natural order vocative+locative+spectacle, as in *Look! On your leg! A tarantula!*

Notes

This chapter was presented in summary form as a lecture at Georgetown University Round Table 1976, 11 March 1976.

1 For example, Wasow 1975. 'Meaninglessness' can be taken in either of two senses, 'empty' or 'redundant' (*eg*, recapitulatory). The latter is the one adopted by those transformationalists – Kuno 1971 and Thorne 1973 among them (and by Hetzron 1971, 98–9, at least for the history of *there*) – for whom *there* is a kind of pronominal copy of a locative; in this sense *there* is not vacuous but has certain features of the locative for which it stands, just as *he* embraces some of the features of *John*. Taken either way, *there* contributes nothing to the semantic content of the sentence in which it occurs, and to that extent is meaningless. My purpose is to show that *there* is neither empty nor redundant, but is a fully functional word that contrasts with its absence.

2 See this volume *pp* 74–6.

3 Private conversation.

4 The transformational-generative treatments are even cruder than this critique suggests, for they do not make the elemental distinction between a sentence that assumes the presence of an entity and a sentence that presents the entity. All three of the following are regarded as equivalent: *A mad dog was roaming the streets; Roaming the streets was a mad dog; There was a mad dog roaming the streets.* See Long 1968.

5 These do not exhaust the possibilities of presentative constructions. There is at least one other type whose affinity is obvious: *A man just came in who has two ears* contrasts with *A man who has two ears just came in*, and with *?A man just left who has two ears*; it uses *come in* presentatively and is roughly equivalent to 'Behold a two-eared man'. This is briefly discussed in Ziv 1976, *p* 48 fn 12, but will not be dealt with here.

6 Type B appears to be freer in English. In French it 'is not allowed to predicate about Animate Beings Seen or to contain transitive verb material, active or passive' (51), which if it were true of English would eliminate a sentence like *There were seen many strange peoples in many strange lands.*

7 The adverbial *yesterday* in these last two examples is not to be confused with the nominal *yesterday* in *Yesterday was my birthday*, which lacks the counterpart *Yesterday there was my birthday.*

8 With *Back and forth there flew a flock of shuttlecocks* we have the sensation of standing back from the scene.

9 See Palmer 1965, 186 and Bolinger 1971*b*, 116–17.

10 Here we encounter one of those peculiar restrictions of the verb *be* that permit *be*, *been*, and *being* but exclude *is*, *are*, *was*, and *were*:

*There was valid (true) at least one of those propositions.
There seemed to be (might have been) valid at least . . .

Compare:

> In order to be it you have to seem it.
> *Since he is it it is easier for him to seem it.
> If it hadn't been for you I'd have died.
> *Since it was for you I didn't die.

The adverb-like adjectives are not affected by this restriction, as the following examples in the text show.

11 These are a subset of 'temporary' adjectives, but do not comprise the whole set. One would not be apt to say, for example, *There were weary several persons – the adjective is in no sense locative.

12 See references in Bolinger 1972b.

13 There seems again to be dual function here. The corresponding declaratives There were these floors washed and There were these floors cleaned are both normal, so that whatever makes [190] doubtful while [191] remains acceptable must be due to the apparent reassortment of constituents in the Wh question. Since with the change of order these floors is no longer an apparent complement of were – the passive been washed and been cleaned pulls be more tightly into the verb – acceptability depends on the nature of the verb, and cleaned, being more resultant-condition, especially in the perfect, gets by.

14 Causatives such as to clean are by nature resultant-condition. To clean is 'to cause to become clean', whereas to wash is not *'to cause to become washed'.

15 Thorne too recognizes the relationship between state and location (Thorne 1973, 868–74, esp 872–3), but for him it is the justification of there as a pronominal copy of a predicate noun phrase (to be replaced by there, a predicate noun phrase needs to be in some sense locative; so NPs are analysed as 'being in a state'). For me, the presence of there is independently motivated and locativeness belongs not in the noun but in the presentative expression, with which there has to be consonant.

16 In [229], although thoroughly does not add much if anything to the force of mangled, it probably promotes the state rather than the action sense of the verb.

17 See Bolinger 1968b.

18 Like auxiliaries also are a number of active verbs. We note in the following that it is the GOVERNED verb that determines the acceptability of there:

> There presumed (affected, pretended, dared, managed) to join the movement several unfrocked anarchists.
> *There presumed (etc) to complain about the tactics several . . .

What seems to characterize these verbs is that they are attitudinal: want is among them, but demand and hurry (*There demanded to join the movement . . .) are not.

19 Whereas *There is uncertain to be more is clearly unacceptable, I find There is unlikely to be more acceptable. Unlikely tends toward categorical negation and can be intensified qua negative (most unlikely); uncertain stresses chance, and when intensified does not approach absolute negation (It is most uncertain). Unlikely resembles not likely more than uncertain resembles not certain:

> 'Will he come?' – 'Unlikely' (?uncertain).

– and negatives of information expressions are normal: There was not asserted (remembered, said, certain, etc) to be more. A similar case of categorical negation is the verb to fail: There failed to appear (there did not appear) the very one we needed most.

20 Lawrence Sanders, *The first deadly sin* (Berkeley Medallion Book, G. P. Putnam's Sons: 1973), 173.

21 In my counter-examples I disregard *you*, *me*, and *us* because they are deictic rather than referential and examples are too easy to find. Jespersen cites two instances of *There's you* (1909–49, 2.6.82).

22 I am here claiming that some NPs are predicative, others not. Thorne (1973, 874) adopts the proposal of Bach that ALL NPs are predicative, *ie*, *a man* is derived from something approximating *one who is a man*. If I am right, this is an overstatement, as it would destroy the basis of the distinction between [341] and [342]. There are other distinctions as well that depend on not regarding all NPs as predicative: see Bolinger 1972*b*, references sv predicative degree noun.

23 Spanish fills the empty hole in this pattern; [363–366] have the following equivalents:

> Tengo estos (unos) papeles que archivar.
> Tengo que archivar estos (unos) papeles.
> Hay estos (unos) papeles que archivar.
> Hay que archivar estos (unos) papeles 'It is necessary to file these (some) papers'.

Spanish presentatives have the same principal characteristics as those of English:

> En el patio está una mesa 'In the patio is (stands) a table'.
> En el patio hay una mesa 'In the patio there is a table'.

– the first is 'on stage', the second informs, brings into awareness. With or without this particular contrast, presentative constructions, as Hetzron 1975 makes clear, are a linguistic universal.

Chapter 6

Apparent constituents in surface structure

When a violin string is set vibrating, it vibrates as a whole and also in fractions.[1] This is what gives depth to most musical sounds – we hear not only a fundamental, but higher and higher overtones that correspond to smaller and smaller parts of the source.

Does a sentence, too, give off overtones that correspond to some part of its length rather than to the whole? A sentence is a string of parts, *abcde* ... The function of syntax is to determine how those parts are joined to form constituents – say [a(bc)] [de]. But from the standpoint of sheer linear arrangement, there is no reason why [ab] should not be a constituent at the same time that [a(bc)] is, with its more complex internal structure. And if [ab] makes some kind of sense, the form-to-meaning principle to which this volume is devoted may well lead to our taking it at face value, especially if the value of the part – like the overtone in music – is harmonically related to the meaning of the sentence as a whole. 'Apparent constituents' are the evidence that such things do happen.

The writing here is within the transformational paradigm. That is because the most important theoretical question that apparent constituents raise is a transformational one: Do transformations change meaning? Are there aspects of the meaning of a sentence that cannot be determined until the final 'surface' form of the sentence is arrived at (and we know exactly what stands next to what)?

It would be hard to say how much influence the earlier published version of this article may have had in rescuing surface structure from its semantic low estate, but we do know that in the past few years transformationalists have conceded that some semantic interpretation has to be done 'at the surface'.

The assumed equivalence that makes this chapter relevant to the book as a whole is the one that is found between certain infinitive phrases and certain *that* clauses. There are probably many more reasons than the one given here for not believing that the two are the same, but the difference that can be attributed to 'apparent constituents' in the infinitive construction is interesting in its own right.

When generativists began to turn to the concept of deep structure as input to the transformational rules that produce 'surface' sentences, it came to be generally accepted that transformations do not add meaning (though they might affect something vaguely thought of as 'style') and that consequently whatever semantic interpreting is done must be done before transformations apply. Surface structure was denied any effect, direct or indirect, on interpretation. This view has still not been completely abandoned.

Challenging the direct effects was to challenge the theory of deep structure. But it ought to have been obvious long since that even if the main outlines of deep structure were accepted, room would have to be made for some interpretation at the surface. This is because of restrictions that take effect only after the transformations have applied and the surface sentence has been arrived at. A congeries results that forms an apparent constituent with a deep structure of its own, plus a semantic interpretation that may or may not coincide with that of the deep structure in question. If it does, the result is accepted; if not, it is rejected or tends to be avoided.

This differs from the usual situation with regard to ambiguity. *Flying planes can be dangerous* has more than one deep structure, but they may be said to be irrelevant to each other. Speakers unhesitatingly produce this surface structure regardless of its source; the surface does not affect the acceptability ordering of the result. In the evidence to be cited, however, the surface result itself is a factor in the degree of acceptability.

I start with examples using the English verb *believe*. When it takes an infinitive complement, this verb, together with *know*, *suspect*, *think*, and a few others, represents an embedding whose underlying structure, according to the usual notions, is the same as that of similar sentences with *that* clauses. Thus

[1] I believe John to be a man of integrity.
[2] I believe that John is a man of integrity.

are paraphrases of each other and do not differ in their deep structure.

But if we examine sentences that make perfectly good clauses, as in

[3] I believe (that) the rain is falling.

[4] I believe (that) the word has already come.

[5] I believe (that) you think I am lying.

we find that the acceptability ordering of the corresponding infinitives goes from bad to impossible:

[6] ?I believe the rain to be falling.

[7] ??I believe the word to have already come.

[8] *I believe you to think I am lying.

When these are compared with instances that do match, such as (to cite only the infinitives),

[9–11] I believe the report to be true (the man to be honest, their intentions to be honorable).

a sort of pattern emerges, which is that if the string *believe*+NP when taken as a constituent in its own right has a meaning compatible with that of the sentence as a whole and more or less suggesting it, this becomes a factor in improving the degree of acceptability:

[12] I believe the report=The report is true.
I believe the report to be true.

[13] I believe the man=The man is honest.
I believe the man to be honest.

[14] I believe (in) their intentions=Their intentions are honorable.
I believe their intentions to be honorable.

(There are other factors that will be mentioned later, but this is the one relevant to surface interpretation.) Once the compatibility is lost, the sentence drops in acceptability:

[15] I believe the lights≠The lights are on.
?I believe the lights to be on.

[16] I believe George≠George is ready.
?I believe George to be ready.

We find two conditions under which surface incompatibility spoils the result. One is irrelevance:

[17] I believe the report to have been found accurate.

[18] ?I believe the report to have been held up by a telegraph strike.

The other is contradiction:

[19] I believe the report to have been proved beyond a doubt.

[20] ?I believe the report to have been disproved.

[21] I believe John to be telling the truth.
[22] ?I believe John to be telling a lie.

But acceptability is a matter of degree. In

[23] We believe that man to be sane.
[24] ?We believe that man to be demented.

the first yields a better setting for belief than the second.[2] Similarly

[25] I believe this decision to be right.
[26] ?I believe this decision to be wrong.
[27] We believe these facts to be true and relevant.
[28] ?We believe these facts to be true but irrelevant.
[29] We believe these views to be important.
[30] ?We believe these views to be unimportant.

Believe+infinitive seems to be a receding construction. It may be typical of such constructions that they maintain themselves only under the most favorable circumstances and are uncommonly sensitive to environmental effects. Besides the degree of compatibility there are two other factors in the acceptability ordering of *believe:* the nature of the nominal and the predicate (it is most favorable when these refer to information: nouns like *claim, report, opinion, theory, accusation,* adjectives such as *true, genuine, self-evident, accurate*), and the speech level (it should be relatively formal). If the sentence uses information nouns and is more or less formal, it will get by even if there is some incompatibility. Thus

[31–34] I believe these claims to be unwarranted (doubts to be justified, accusations to be false, suppositions to be unfounded).

are passable, with their formal, legalistic flavor. But if the predicate does not refer to information, then it needs to make up for this by being compatible. So

[35] We believe these ideas to be constructive and helpful.

is compatible with *We believe (in) these ideas;* but

[36] ?We believe these ideas to be destructive and worthless.

is not. Similarly when neither the noun nor the adjective refers to information:

[37] I believe their rights to be inviolable (=I believe [in] their rights).
[38] ?I believe their rights to be insignificant.

Similarly with personal nominals:

[39] Everybody believes him to be incorruptible.
[40] ?Everybody believes him to be dishonorable.

Finally, if the level is informal the result is not good even though all the rest may be favorable:

[41] I believe these facts to have proved accurate.
[42] ?I believe these facts to have checked out 100 per cent.
[43] I believe these ideas to hold true generally.
[44] ?I believe these ideas to hold up generally.[3]

Believe, of course, is not unique. *Suspect* and *know* show much the same restrictions:

[45] I suspect that man to be a liar (=I suspect that man).
[46] ?I suspect those observations to be relevant to the case.
[47] I know the facts to be true.
[48] ?I know John to be the person you are looking for.

Similarly *understand*. The infinitive construction is normal only if what is referred to is correct and intellectually ascertainable, and *understand* plus the noun is compatible:

[49] I understood that to be the reason.
[50] I understood that explanation to be the right one.
[51] *I understood that explanation to be the wrong one.
[52] *I understood the natives to be unfriendly.
[53] I understand this solution to be the simplest.
[54] *I undertand this solution to be the most complicated.

Understanding a person, as in [52], is obviously incompatible because it brings in a non-intellectual meaning of the verb. And intellectual understanding goes with what is understandable (simple, right, rational), not with its opposite. Yet all these sentences are normal with *that* clauses (*I understood that the natives were friendly*).

The verb *to consider* deserves attention as a foil to the other verbs because it does not have an interfering sense. Both infinitive phrases and *that* clauses are permissible so long as they conform to one meaning – they must express an opinion about the nature of something:

[55] I consider John to be a churchgoer (that John is . . .).
[56] *I consider John to go to church (*that John goes . . .).

[57] I consider him to be saying exactly the opposite (that he is saying
. . .). (Refers to the nature of an action).

[58] I consider John to be a first-rate salesman (that John is . . .).

[59] *I consider John to be a salesman on the third floor (*that John is
. . .).

[60] I consider the trip to have benefited her greatly (that the trip benefited . . .).

[61] *I consider the clock to have struck (*that the clock has . . .).

The interferences we have noted apply only to the active voice. Though
most verbs in English use the passive less than the active, verbs of the
believe, think, suppose, consider, suspect, etc class are an exception – particularly
in the highly formal usage represented by infinitive complements. The
reason is probably to be found in Stanley's 'exploitation' theory (Stanley
1972). These verbs express opinions and viewpoints concerning which the
speaker, when he wants to sound impressive, would rather shift responsibility to some unnamed – and hence remote and powerful – agent.
John is believed to be a thief implies a generality of belief that is absent in *I
(he, somebody) believe John to be a thief.* The passive is accordingly not a
receding construction and maintains itself against the apparent constituents
that interfere with the active, even to the point of allowing verbs that are
not used at all in the active:

[62] *They say John to be the prime suspect.

[63] John is said to be the prime suspect.

and allowing the simple present tense of verbs other than *be* and *have:*

[64] *They believe that judge to accept bribes.

[65] That judge is believed to accept bribes.

Some examples whose active counterparts [18], [48], [51] were doubtful
or unacceptable:

[66] The report was believed to have been held up by a telegraph strike.

[67] John is known to be the person you are looking for.

[68] That explanation is understood to be the wrong one.

The one restriction that remains, predictably, is the one against too high
a degree of informality:

[69] ?These facts are believed to have checked out 100 per cent.

[70] ?Mary is thought to have gotten sore at him.

So much for *believe* and its sister verbs. What of similar interferences elsewhere? I offer three more examples, with less elaboration. Two are in Spanish, one in English.

Normally, Spanish infinitives are comparatively free to take pronoun subjects in the nominative case:

[71] Démelo ahora para dárselo yo esta tarde 'Give it to me now in order for me (I) to give it to him this afternoon'.

But this does not work when the infinitive is a required complement of the verb:

[72] *Vino para verla yo 'She came for me to see her'.

[73] *Quiero hacerlo usted 'I want you to do it'.

The same applies to infinitive phrases that are subjects but stand in normal complement position:

[74] *Sería imposible hacerlo él 'It would be impossible for him to do it'.

In all these conditions a clause with a verb in the subjunctive is required. But when the infinitive phrase stands in normal SUBJECT position, speakers are sometimes willing to accept the infinitive with nominative subject, sometimes not. A sentence like

[75] Hacerlo él sería imposible 'For him to do it would be impossible'.

is judged superior to one like

[76] *Hacerlo él sería posible 'For him to do it would be possible'.

This seems to pose a fairly routine problem of negative constraints, and it would not be difficult to write a transformation to take care of it. But that would not explain why negation should operate in such an unexpected way. For an answer we can look to the apparent constituents in the surface structure, and seek confirmation in other sentences where negation-affirmation is absent or at least attenuated.

There is a great deal about the surface structure of declarative sentences in Spanish that suggests an analogy with a question-and answer series. *Juan no viene* normally has rising intonation on *Juan*, falling on *no viene*, as if the speaker were saying *¿Juan?–no viene* '[You want to know about] John?–he isn't coming'. A symptom of this isolation of the subject is the punctuation of writings before typographers get hold of them: *Juan, no viene* – subject and predicate are often separated by a comma. The English parallel is, of course, the *John, he isn't coming* type, which our schools have virtually succeeded in educating out of us.

Now a sentence like [75] is particularly subject to this sort of interpretation: *Hacerlo él sería imposible* = *¿Hacerlo él?–sería imposible* 'He do it? – it would be impossible'. In Spanish there is no problem with a redundant subject *it* since such a subject would never be expressed anyway; this abets the analogy. It becomes clear why negatives allow the full infinitive phrase with independent nominative subject and affirmatives do not: one who says *¿Hacerlo él?* would ordinarily be asking something he finds hard to believe, and the stage is set for acceptability when what follows is an assertion of the disbelief.[4]

If this is true, the formal presence of negation should be irrelevant. What is to the point is that the infinitive phrase, which starts off the sentence, suggests a kind of surprised question and the rest of the sentence is a sort of comment on it, generally denying or disapproving. As predicted, at least some speakers are willing to accept the sentence

[77] Decir eso yo parecería una ofensa 'For me to say that would seem offensive'.

which resembles *¿Decir eso yo? – parecería una ofensa* 'I say that? – it would seem offensive'.

The second Spanish example involves the position of the with-verb pronouns. A sentence like

[78] La oí venir 'I heard her come'.

is normal. But when the infinitive is a transitive verb with an expressed object, many speakers require that the first pronoun be dative rather than accusative: in place of

[79] La oí cantarla 'I heard her sing it'.

(which other speakers accept) we find

[80] Le oí cantarla.

And in any case, when the second pronoun is shifted to join the first one, as is normal with most dependent infinitives, the first one must become dative:

[81] Se la oí cantar.

Since the verbs of perception normally take accusative pronouns as subject of their dependent infinitives, why this switch to dative? The two cases are constituents that ordinarily give different interpretations: *Le hablo* 'I speak to her', *Lo hablo* 'I speak it'. The probable reason is that

Spanish does not admit two accusative pronouns side by side – *La la oí cantar* is impossible – so that to get the pronoun into that position at all requires that it be made dative. But since [79] is a perfectly good construction, the more obvious solution would be simply to eliminate [81], blocking the transformation that moves the pronoun before the verb. What makes the shift possible, and facilitates the change to the dative, is probably the apparent constituent *Se la oí* 'I heard it from her', like *Se la compré* 'I bought it from her'. Thus

[82] La Simonelli estaba cantando el aria de *Othello*. ¿Se la oíste? (¿Se la oíste cantar?) 'Simonelli was singing the aria from *Othello*. Did you hear it from her? (Did you hear her sing it? or Did you hear the singing of it from her?)'

are both possible, and compatible.

My last example involves one, and possibly two, apparent constituents. It was suggested by the sentence

[83] These [exams] I'm planning to take place in May.

overheard at a linguistics department meeting. It is one which at least sometimes (and maybe all the time by some speakers) would be given the form

[84] These I'm planning to have take place in May.

to avoid the apparent constituent

[85] *I'm planning to take place in May.

ie, the absurd suggestion that *I* is the subject of the infinitive, which is hard to avoid because of the high frequency of *I plan to*. The other apparent constituent can be observed more easily in the usual order without the displacement of the subject of the infinitive:

[86] I'm planning these exams to take place in May.

If we regard *these exams* as purely the subject of the infinitive, with nothing to do with the main verb, *ie*, if we ignore the apparent constituent

[87] I'm planning these exams.

on the theory that underlying [86] is something corresponding to the following,

[88] I'm planning to have these exams take place in May.

[89] I'm planning for these exams to take place in May.
[90] I'm planning that these exams shall take place in May.

then we have no way of accounting for the ungrammaticality of

[91] *I'm planning John to go out by himself.[5]

– a peculiar ungrammaticality in that the supposedly underlying structure is represented in a perfectly grammatical way by

[92] I'm planning to have John go out by himself.
[93] I'm planning for John to go out by himself.
[94] I'm planning that John shall go out by himself.

But if we heed the apparent constituent in [87], which here gives

[95] *I'm planning John.

we have the clue to the ungrammaticality of [91]: one does not plan people. But in this case I suspect that it is more than an APPARENT constituent. Instead, one might regard [86] as a blend, corresponding not to [88–90] but to

[96] I'm planning these exams to have them take place in May.
[97] I'm planning these exams for them to take place in May.

In other words, BOTH the exams and the happening are being planned.[6]

Before drawing the obvious conclusion, a warning is in order. The claim that A influences B is invalid if A and B are not in fact distinct phenomena. Suppose that topics in Spanish really are, at some fundamental level, questions – that is, that as we understand questions better we will find it necessary to include the topics of declarative sentences as a subtype. Questions then could not be said to 'influence' the way a topic behaves.

The conclusion – barring the handicap just mentioned – is that the meaning of a sentence cannot be described in terms of deep structure alone.

Notes

1 Based on a paper in *Word* 23 (1967) 47–56. I gratefully acknowledge the suggestions made by George Lakoff and J. R. Ross, who read an early draft.

2 These examples are similar to but not quite the same as Zellig Harris's zeroable X_{ap} ('Transformational theory', *Language*, 41 [1965], 390). Harris cites *When do you expect him to come?* → *When do you expect him?* In the examples I cite, compatibility

does not reach to redundancy. One may prefer *He guessed the answer to be right* to *He guessed the answer to be wrong* on the basis of the higher degree of compatibility of the first with *He guessed the answer;* but this does not mean that *He guessed the answer to be right → He guessed the answer.*

3 Ross and Lakoff point out (personal communication) that some of the doubtful examples become less so if *I* is replaced by a third-person subject. Perhaps this is because one affirms one's own beliefs but reports another's. The former would produce more apparent contradictions.

4 An affirmative answer is conceivable, eg, *John dislike his brother? – it's possible,* but there is more likely to be a pause before it, and, more importantly, the intonation changes: it tends to lose the conclusive terminal fall that characterizes the full statement: *For John to dislike his brother is possible.*

5 Example suggested by Ross.

6 If [97] is taken as the source instead of [89], the problem can be solved transformationally by regarding [86] as a sentence containing a purpose clause with deleted subject: *I'm planning (scheduling) these exams [in order for these exams] to take place in May.* This blocks [91] through the selectional restrictions on the verb *plan.* Compare also *I'm planning this house [in order for this house] to be finished by September 1.* Regardless of this solution, the tendency to avoid [83] is still due to [85].

Chapter 7

Ergative *of* and infinitives of specification

In this chapter I return to a bit of unfinished business in an old controversy with Robert B. Lees about the status of what Jespersen calls – lumping them all together – 'infinitives of specification'. Lees 1960*b* had tried to disentangle them by assigning separate transformational origins up to eight in number. I advocated (Bolinger 1961) a less rigid treatment that would allow for contamination between one type and another. But one argument of his I did not take on then, which was that a sentence like *He is noble to suffer* has the same transformational origin as one like *It is noble of him to suffer* (Lees 1960, 220). That is a clear challenge to the theme of this volume, and I now engage it, adding some observations on infinitives in general, especially with adjectives.

The following three types of infinitive construction bear obvious re-semblances to one another:

[1] It was foolish for Mary to go there.
[2] It was foolish of Mary to go there.
[3] Mary was foolish to go there.

It is easy to imagine a situation where the three might serve indifferently. But this is a pragmatic sameness, and we must look for possible differences beneath the apparent synonymy.

The question is, what does the adjective *foolish* modify? – not as an inference, for in all three cases we infer that Mary was foolish, but grammatically. In [1], *foolish* would appear to modify the abstract pro-position *it* (*for Mary to go there*), and in [3], if the form of *Mary was foolish* is to be trusted, it would appear to modify *Mary*. But [2] has the earmarks of a hybrid: *it was foolish* and *foolish of Mary;* we seem to be condemning both her and her deed at the same time.

Other sentences identical to [1] in their syntax make it clear that Mary's folly is not stated but inferred. This can be seen more easily if the infinitive is fronted:

[4] For Mary to go there was foolish (on Mary's part).
[5] For Mary to go there would be lucky for us.
[6] For Mary to go there would be beneficial to the commonwealth.

Our inference was evidently based on the meaning of the adjective: a foolish action is one performed by a foolish person, whereas a beneficial action is not one performed by a beneficial person. The syntax of type [1] is therefore the following:

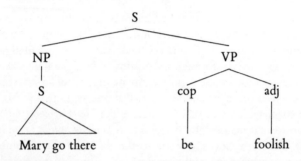

The appropriateness of this analysis for type [1], and its inappropriateness for [2] and [3], can be shown by a careful selection of adjectives. If there are adjectives that can describe actions but not persons, they ought to work for [1], but not for [2] or [3], assuming that in these it is the noun and not the action that is modified. Two such adjectives are *imperative* and *mandatory:*

[7] It was imperative for Mary to go there.
[8] *It was imperative of Mary to go there.
[9] *Mary was imperative to go there.

(and so for *mandatory*).

Leaving aside type [2] for the moment and comparing only [1] and [3], we find obvious differences between adjectives that can modify persons [10], [11] and adjectives that normally modify only actions [12], [13]:

[10] Mary was clever (sensible, unwise) to go there.
[11] It was clever (sensible, unwise) for Mary to go there.
[12] *Mary was questionable (gratuitous, uncalled-for, preposterous) to go there.
[13] It was questionable (etc) for Mary to go there.

Predicate nouns – personal and non-personal – point the same way:

[14] Mary was a fool to go there.
[15] *It was a fool for Mary to go there.
[16] *Mary was a mistake to go there.
[17] It was a mistake for Mary to go there.

There can be little doubt that type [1] is an impersonal construction and type [3] a personal one.

1 *It was foolish of Mary:* the *of* construction

Before applying any syntactic tests to the *of* construction (type [2]), a look at the pragmatic side. It seems to have the effect, by comparison with type [3], of toning down the impact of the adjective. Speakers must be careful when they call people names; the thrust can be parried by seeming to aim the adjective at the action rather than at the person – the *of* construction is euphemistic:

[18] It was unkind of you to do that.
[19] It was rash of them to move so quickly.

This is less harsh than saying

[20] You were unkind to do that.
[21] They were rash to move so quickly.

By the same token a compliment can be made less gushing:

[22] It was splendid of them to be so attentive.
[23] They were splendid to be so attentive.

If the impression that the *of* construction is a kind of hybrid is accurate, the downtoning effect comes as no surprise.

On the syntactic side, adjectives can again be used to test the putative hybridness of the construction. Suppose there are adjectives that have one meaning when applied to an action and another when applied to a person; with the *of* construction they might be expected to behave oddly. This appears to be the case with certain adjectives that refer to the LOOK of persons and of actions – for example, *handsome* and *attractive*. *Handsome* applied to an action means 'generous', but applied to a person it means 'good-looking':

[24] It was handsome of John to share the prize.
[25] *John was handsome to share the prize.

But

[26] It was generous of John to share the prize.
[27] John was generous to share the prize.

From examples [24], [25] we are drawn to the conclusion that the adjective in the *of* construction primarily modifies the action, since that is the sense that prevails. Yet [24] and [26] are so much alike (and so like [27]) that one feels the person to be modified too. This impression can be made more definite by using one of the adjectives in example [12]. I choose *gratuitous* because of its close synonymy with *unnecessary*. In [28–31] it is important to observe the effect of switching tenses as well as that of switching adjectives:

[28] It was gratuitous of Mary to say that.
[29] ?It was unnecessary of Mary to say that.
[30] It is gratuitous of Mary to have said that.
[31] *It is unnecessary of Mary to have said that.

In [28] and [30] we have an adjective that contains, as part of its meaning, a double modification. It refers to an unnecessary action but also describes the agent as knowing that the action is uncalled-for and wilfully doing it anyway. We do not as a rule go quite so far as to say *?a gratuitous person*, but the semantic package nevertheless enables us to chide the person a bit at the same time that we berate the action. The reason for the shift in tense should be obvious. In [30] the fact that Mary is still that kind of person now explains why she acted as she did earlier (like *It* is *true that it* WAS *raining*). The *of someone* can be omitted and the preferences remain the same:

[32] It is gratuitous to have said that.
[33] ?It is unnecessary to have said that.

– the disparity in time does not harm *gratuitous*, which describes something more than just the transitory action, something that lingers on, a personal responsibility for bad judgment, hence the person responsible. *Unnecessary* looks only to the requirements and appropriateness of the action at the time.

There are other pairs with the same peculiarity as that of *gratuitous* and *unnecessary;* for example, *surprising* and *unexpected:*

[34] It was surprising of John to say that.
[35] ?It was unexpected of John to say that.
[36] It is surprising of John to have said that.
[37] *It is unexpected of John to have said that.

John can be a surprising person; he is not an unexpected person in that sense of *unexpected.* If *unexpected* gets by at all, it is where the tense tips the balance away from absolute dependence on the noun: in [35] the action WAS unexpected.

Another pair is *wrong* and *mistaken:*

[38] It was wrong of John to say that.
[39] ?It was mistaken of John to say that.
[40] It is wrong of John to have said that.
[41] *It is mistaken of John to have said that.

Apparently *mistaken* can describe a person only in the light of something related to the action at the time, whereas *wrong,* even though it modifies the action, to a certain extent modifies the noun independently. The disparity in time can be made quite explicit:

[42] A hundred years from now it will still be wrong of John to have said that.
[43] *A hundred years from now it will still be mistaken of John to have said that.

To summarize: The adjective test demonstrates the in-between status of the *of* construction. First, since the person is described, an adjective that cannot serve in that capacity is anomalous:

[44] ?It was only temporary for Mary to feel ill.
[45] *It was only temporary of Mary to feel ill.

Second, since the action is also described, an adjective that cannot serve in that capacity is likewise anomalous:

[46] You are strong to have convinced them.
[47] *It is strong of you to have convinced them.
[48] The Eskimos are hardy to survive such winters.
[49] *It is hardy of the Eskimos to survive such winters.

Third, if an adjective has a meaning that readily applies to both an action and a person, it will serve in the *of* construction. This includes meanings, such as *handsome* 'generous', that may apply to persons even though the adjective is not normally predicated of persons in that particular sense. So for *outrageous:*

[50] It was outrageous of them to make such a claim.
[51] ?They were outrageous to make such a claim.

The adjective in the *of* construction is Janus-faced. It joins the ranks of other such elements, for example adverbs: *He wisely tore it up* says that both he and his action were wise (see Greenbaum 1969, especially 153 *ff*).

A still unsettled question is where the *of* of the *of* construction comes from. For [52] below, there are two likely paraphrases, [53] and [54]:

[52] It was tiresome of the Commission to insist.
[53] It was tiresome, coming from the Commission, to insist.
[54] It was tiresome on the Commission's part to insist.

But there are problems with all three in playing the deep-structure game, that is, in assuming that they are identical at some level. First, the acceptability ratings differ when they are tested with adjectives:

[55] *It was unnecessary of the Commission to insist.
[56] It was unnecessary, coming from the Commission, to insist.
[57] It was unnecessary on the Commission's part to insist.
[58] *It was mandatory of the Commission to insist.
[59] ?It was mandatory, coming from the Commission, to insist.
[60] It was mandatory on the Commission's part to insist.

In both paraphrases the adjective is unrestricted by the requirement that it be able to modify the noun. Second, the *of* construction cannot easily express contrastivity, whereas both paraphrases can:

[61] ?It would be odd of Parliament to raise that issue, but not of the Prime Minister.
[62] It would be odd, coming from Parliament, to raise that issue, but not coming from the Prime Minister.
[63] It would be odd on Parliament's part to raise that issue, but not on the part of the Prime Minister.

It appears that both paraphrases are in some sense looser constructions. The relative looseness can be seen in the freedom of the prepositional phrase to move elsewhere in the sentence:

[64] *Of the Commission, it was tiresome to insist.

[65] *It was tiresome to insist, of the Commission.
[66] Coming from the Commission, it was tiresome to insist.
[67] It was tiresome to insist, coming from the Commission.
[68] On the Commission's part, it was tiresome to insist.
[69] It was tiresome to insist, on the Commission's part.

It would seem that the tightness of the *of* construction reflects the attachment of the adjective at one and the same time to both the noun and the action.

But though neither paraphrase is perfect, the one with *from* is suggestive in a way that entitles it to a further look. There is another construction with *of* that is relevant here, that of the 'subjective' *of* in the following, which I pair off with starred examples to show that something other than subjectivity is involved:

[70] The glowing of the sun is essential to life on earth.
[71] *The existing of the sun is essential to life on earth.
[72] The falling of the wall was disastrous.
[73] *The leaning of the wall was at an extreme angle.
[74] The babbling (metabolizing, bed-wetting) of the infant was interrupted.
[75] *The sleeping of the infant was interrupted.
[76] The departing of the guests was welcome.
[77] *The staying of the guests was welcome.
[78] The gushing of water is noisy.
[79] *The evaporating of water is silent.

It appears that the role of the noun in this construction is not to name the subject but the agent – which is all the more remarkable in that the corresponding possessives are all perfectly normal, whether or not the noun represents an agent:

[80] The sun's existing is essential to life on earth.
[81] The infant's sleeping was interrupted.

Predictably, passive subjects are excluded, though there is no problem with the objective genitive; and again, the possessive is normal:

[82] *The being (getting) caught of the criminals was bad for them.
[83] The catching of the criminals was easy.
[84] Their being caught was bad for them.

We conclude that *of* is used for an action originating in or proceeding FROM an agent – a kind of ergative case relationship.

By the criterion of agentiveness, the same *of* appears in our infinitive construction with adjectives. In the sentence

[85] It was nice of them to accept.

both the niceness and the action proceed FROM *them* as agent. In a pair such as

[86] It was confusing of John to mix up the explanations.
[87] *It was confusing of the text to mix up the explanations.

our objection to [87] is due to the difficulty of conceiving the text as an agent. A sentence like

[88] It was nice of the rain to come today.

is obviously a figure of speech, as is

[89] It is wonderful of you just to exist, my love.

where the *you* is figuratively cast as having the power to decide.

If my ergative theory is correct, the passive should be excluded here as it was from example [82]. But the passive suffers doubly. Besides the problem of the agent, it is rare for the passive to be predicated of an infinitive. One can devise an example such as *It would be misunderstood for you to do that*, where the inclusion of a subject reduces the hypotheticalness of the infinitive by a degree or two, but without a subject the passive is all but impossible:

[90] ?It would be misunderstood to do that.
[91] ?To do that would be misunderstood.[1]

(Compare the more 'concrete' *-ing: Doing that would be misunderstood*.) About the best we can do is look for past participles that function as verbs rather than as adjectives, to see the extent of the 'agent' requirement. A promising set for comparison is *misguided, misled*, and *deceived. Misguided* is very nearly pure resultant condition and hence quite adjectival. It can modify both action and person: *That act was misguided; That person was misguided*. It is normal in the *of* construction, where it allows the interpretation that the person either has a hand in the action or is in a position to do something about it:

[92] It is misguided of you to think that.

Misled is exactly the opposite. It can hardly be anything but verbal: we would never say *★a misled fool,* whereas *a deceived fool* is at least possible and *a misguided fool* is normal. It is unusual even in a type [3] sentence,

[93] ?You are misled to think that.

and quite impossible in the *of* construction:

[94] ★It is misled of you to think that.

Our best opportunity is with *deceived.* It is normal in type [3]:

[95] You are deceived to think that.

At the same time, it is still half passive. We use *deceived* to let the person off the hook, to suggest that someone is deceiving him, that it is not his fault. And this passiveness I assume is what rules out the *of* construction:

[96] ★It is deceived of you to think that.

It remains to show that the 'agent' requirement does not apply to type [3], but is exclusive to the *of* construction. Thus we might perhaps say

[97] Your music is unpleasant to demand such close attention.

but hardly

[98] ★It is unpleasant of your music to demand such close attention.

even though

[99] It is unpleasant of you to demand such close attention.

is a normal sentence.

2 *Mary was foolish to go there*

About the rival construction *Mary was foolish to go there,* type [3], I have already made some observations (in Bolinger 1961), and my reviving the question here is by way of trying to see the whole problem of specifying infinitives in a broader perspective.

The examples cited thus far have been chosen to illustrate the uses of type [3] that are closest to the *of* construction – they focus on the relationship of the infinitive to the adjective. With the *of* construction the adjective explicitly modifies the action as well as the person. In type [3] it only inferentially modifies the action; grammatically the relationships are reversed – the infinitive modifies the main proposition, which is to say that *Mary was foolish to go there* tells us the respect in which *Mary was foolish* is asserted. If *foolish* seems to modify the action it is because pragmatically a foolish person commits foolish acts. The readiness with which we draw such conclusions points to this construction as one of the conduits through which so many adjectives that basically modify persons come to be used with actions as well: *You were wise to do it* enables us to say *That was wise*, even though it is hard to see how an action can be either wise or unwise. Not all adjectives lend themselves to the inference. In

[100] Mary was angelic to say that.

it is stretching things a bit to claim that the saying was angelic. But the best proof of what the predicate modifier modifies is the fact that it embraces nouns as well as adjectives; I repeat [14] and add [101]:

[14] Mary was a fool to go there. (*To go there was a fool.)
[101] Mary was an angel to say that. (*To say that was an angel.)

The question that concerns us now is one of macro- rather than microsyntax: what is the relationship between the main proposition (*Mary was foolish*) and the infinitive (*to go there*)? Or, to use a rather different kind of example, between the main proposition and the infinitive in

[102] You must be new around here to be asking such a question.

I hypothesize that type [3] manifests two polar constructions with a gradient between. The two constructions embrace non-subject infinitives in general, and are not limited to governing expressions using adjectives. One, at its extreme, covers infinitives that are clearly felt as complements, where the *to* of the infinitive has its basic meaning of 'goal':

[103] She wants to run.
[104] They get to eat and I don't.
[105] I'm in a hurry to catch the train.

The other, at its extreme, covers infinitives that are not felt as complements. Underlyingly they represent a separate proposition expressing some kind of contingency relationship with the main proposition – an 'if', a 'when', a 'given that', etc, on the basis of which the main proposition is true or is asserted. The prosody – at the extreme end of the gradient – shows this generally looser connection by optionally inserting a pause:

[106] You wouldn't think so(,) to look at him. ('Given the look of him, on the basis of looking at him.')
[107] She's got to be kidding(,) to say that! ('If she says that.')

The pause of course implies the possibility of inverting the clauses, and there are instances ([110] is one) where the inversion is the normal order:

[108]   To look at him(,) you wouldn't think so.
[109]   To say that(,) she's got to be kidding.
[110]   Not to put too serious a face on the matter, I would say that he was merely envious.

Adjectives have long assimilated themselves to the complement construction, probably by way of past participles that originally contained some features of 'goal', and were in time adjectivized. *Wont* in *They are wont to complain* is an example. (Compare the still visibly verbal *inclined* in *They are inclined to complain*.) So *eager*, which has no verbal base, when appearing alone as predicate of *be* comes to be used almost exclusively with infinitives:[2]

[111]   ?John is eager.
[112]   John is eager to speak up.

But since adjectives take complements only to the extent that they come to resemble verbs, they fit the non-complement construction just as naturally, as in [102] and in

[113]   Most of the ingredients are poisonous, to give just one reason for wanting to ban the stuff.

So adjectives are subject to a tug of war. Depending on a number of factors – the meaning of the individual adjective, the position of the infinitive (to be a complement it must follow), the closeness of the juncture, and, of course, the intent of the speaker (which determines the other factors and makes a full listing impossible) – the adjective is pulled toward one extreme or the other. An adjective pair where meaning is a principal factor is *glad* and *joyous* – *glad* is quite verb-like (we would never say simply **I am very glad this morning*), *joyous* is less so:

[114]   They were glad to learn that they had been chosen. ('They welcomed it.')
[115]   They were joyous to learn that they had been chosen. ('On the basis of the knowledge they became joyous.')

A comma disjuncture may make the difference with the single adjective *nice*:

[116]   You are nice to say those things! ('I appreciate your saying them.')
[117]   You are nice, to say those things. ('On the basis of your saying those things I assert that you are nice.')

The meaning of the infinitive may decide the question:

[118] I was puzzled to know what they meant. ('I was curious, I wanted to find out.')
[119] I was puzzled to learn that they had left. ('Their leaving occasioned my puzzlement.')

The complement (goal) extreme of the gradient has the tendency to produce auxiliaries – the bond between the main verb and the infinitive is so tight that the two amalgamate syntactically and semantically. This of course is the history of the *to*-less infinitive, giving such things as *will go, does go, need go, make (him) go, let (him) go*, etc. But it is gradiently true of the other combinations. *I'm happy to do it* expresses more than satisfaction: it is a willingness to proceed to the doing. This is the basis of inceptives – *start to, plan to, try to* – but also to some degree of adjective combinations like *be ready (likely) to* (compare *tend to*), *be quick to*, and, at a farther remove, *be sorry to* (compare *regret to*), *be afraid to (fear to)*, and *be thankful to*. An important measure of tightness is the possibility of 'anaphoric *to*', that is, of deleting the verb proper:

[120] Was he glad to hear about it? – No, he wasn't glad to, he was sorry to.
[121] No, he wasn't glad to hear about it, he was mad to hear about it.
[122] No, he wasn't glad to, *he was mad to.

Be mad has not achieved the status of a collocation in the sense *be angry* (any more than *be angry* itself: *He was angry to*),[3] but it has in the sense *be crazy*, whether referring to insanity or eagerness:

[123] Should I try to swim the Channel? – You'd be mad to.
[124] Would you like to meet her? – I'm simply mad to.

I have referred to a gradient between the two poles of complement and non-complement – goal and contingency – and that implies a vague middle ground. But there are instances that make one wonder whether the middle ground is not one of ambiguity rather than vagueness:

[125] John must have been furious to have had a stroke. ('He must have been furious at the event'; 'He must have been furious judging by the event'.)
[126] They were crazy to be on that boat. ('They wanted to be there'; 'Their being there makes me doubt their sanity'.)

Yet a closer look suggests that the ambiguity belongs to the adjective. *Furious* and *crazy* divide rather sharply between a physical or mental condition and an attitudinal stance. The glandular state of a furious person may cause a stroke. But *furious* (*at, to*) also means 'disapproving to the point of fury', as *crazy* (*for, to*) means 'eager to the point of madness'. An attitude is directed TOWARD something – goal; a condition comes about on the basis of something – contingency.

The vagueness comes clear when we note the position of attitudinals on the gradient by comparison with instances that are purely contingent. Although [126] has as its second gloss the contingent 'Their being there makes me doubt their sanity', that is, 'On the basis of their being there I assert that they are crazy', it nevertheless expresses an attitude of disapproval ON THE PART OF THE SPEAKER, and hence is not purely contingent. In fact, it is the impurity that makes the construction in this form possible. To find what happens with pure contingency we must choose an adjective that is attitudinally neutral; and then we discover that the result is not acceptable unless something is added (a modal or an explicit performative) to show that a judgment is emanating from the speaker. *Nervous* is such an adjective:

[127] *He was nervous to behave that way.
[128] He must have been nervous to behave that way.
[129] I think he was nervous to have behaved that way.[4]

Nervous is not used to express either the speaker's attitude (as *crazy* expresses his disapproval) or the subject's attitude. An instance of the latter, more or less synonymous with *nervous*, is *worried:*

[130] He was worried to hear the news.

He did not LIKE hearing the news – subject's attitude; hearing the news caused him to be worried – contingency. *Worried* draws from both ends of the gradient. Other adjectives likewise fall somewhere in the middle. *I'm grateful to be alive* is more attitudinal (my gratitude is directed toward my being alive) than contingent (my being alive inspires gratitude in me). In *This shirt is annoying to have to button up so tight* the speaker's annoyance is about equally provoked and projected. *Right* is almost purely attitudinal, expressing the speaker's approval:

[131] You were right to do that.
[132] ?You must have been right to do that.

Wise is very close – it is mostly approval, but can, at a stretch, suggest inferring wisdom FROM the action:

[133] You were wise (well advised) to do that.
[134] He must have been wise to make such a sound decision.

Clever alters the proportions – we are now a bit over on the contingency side, though still expressing some approval:

[135] You were clever (cunning, smart) to do that.
[136] To do that, you must have been (*you were) clever.

As a number of examples have shown, with both goal and contingency (that is, RELATIVE goal and RELATIVE contingency) there is the possibility of orienting either toward the subject or toward the speaker. *She was happy to do it* expresses the subject's attitude; *She was right to do it* expresses the speaker's attitude. Similarly *They were overjoyed to have won* represents an effect (state of joy) that terminates in the subject, whereas *They were foolish to have left* represents an effect (an opinion) that terminates in the speaker; both are contingent: 'based on their winning', 'based on their leaving'. The goal-contingency polarity thus seems to embrace without distinction both locutionary and illocutionary expressions.

But there is the difference with attitude that on the speaker's side only approval and disapproval are involved; there is not the variety – reluctance, eagerness, willingness, haste, ability, etc – that is found with a subject's inclination toward an action. Since the subject is the one that gets bent to or from the action, there is little that the speaker can do to further the process except to signal 'go' or 'stop'. For that reason, the adjectives that are suitable must not only be degree adjectives, they must also fall on one or the other side of the line that divides good from bad. Non-degree adjectives are doubly excluded (except, as before, when dressed up with a modal or a performative):

[137] *The music was orchestral to achieve such a peak of volume.
[138] The music had to be orchestral, to achieve such a peak of volume.

A degree adjective is excluded if it is not good-bad. For example, we can call someone (*rather*) *vocal* without either approving or disapproving; but (*rather*) *gabby* disapproves, hence

[139] ?She was rather vocal to say those things. (OK She had to be vocal to say those things.)
[140] She was rather gabby to say those things.

Example [140] is of course midway on the goal-contingency gradient: we infer her gabbiness from her words, but what makes it possible to use this construction, without disjuncture, is the disapproving attitude of the speaker as expressed by *gabby*. (It is difficult to find degree words that are neutral as regards good-bad. Particularly if one uses such an adjective in a construction that requires a good-bad interpretation, the tendency is to give the construction the benefit of the doubt – not to reject, but to twist the meaning of the adjective a bit to make it fit. Hence the query rather than the star on [139].) The approval-disapproval has to be on the part of the speaker. Adjectives like *popular* and *famous*, which suggest the approval of others, will not serve:

[141] *Mary was popular to do those things.

Nor will adjectives, even degree adjectives, expressing physical traits unless they contain a value judgment:

[142] *John was tall to be so impressive.[5]
[143] John was ugly to say that.

The contingency element manifests itself in what happens with 'permanent' and 'temporary' adjectives. The adjective *impertinent* may describe a person in the light of what he does at the moment, or of the way he naturally is. The adjective *fresh* is ordinarily momentary. So if we are to conclude something 'on the basis of', the temporary adjective is best keyed to what is being done at the moment, whereas the permanent one (I choose *headstrong* to fit, more or less, with *fresh* and *impertinent*) is better keyed to what has been established – using, say, a perfect tense – and the permanent-or-temporary one may go either way:

[144] You were fresh to say that.
[145] ?You are fresh to have said that.
[146] ?You were pretty headstrong to do that.
[147] You are pretty headstrong to have done that.
[148] You were impertinent to say that.
[149] You are impertinent to have said that.[6]

To conclude the observations on the goal-contingency duality, we note that unlike the infinitive, the *that* clause now has only the goal relationship; that is, a *that* clause is only a complement (except where it is obviously a subject). While it may be that such sentences as

[150] I am glad that you are here.

[151] I rejoice that they were acquitted.
[152] I am worried that she has not shown up yet.

were originally expressions of EMOTIONS CAUSED ('Her not showing up worries me'), they are now expressions of EMOTIONS PROJECTED. One sign of this is the impossibility of inversion: *That she has not shown up yet I am worried. With the infinitive the inversion is frequently possible: To have done that you are wise. (And such cases encourage the unnecessarily specific interpretation 'in order to' for the infinitive.)

I believe that the crossover between goal and contingency, between final and efficient cause, reflects a congenital defect in human psychology, the inability, much of the time, to separate cause and effect. Spanish does a pretty good job of spelling out case and transitive relationships with prepositions, as the following show:

[153] Vino a verme 'He came to see me'. (literal or figurative motion toward)
[154] Vive para comer 'He lives to eat'. (conceived goal)
[155] Tiene mucho que hacer 'He has a lot to do'. (obligation)
[156] Es fácil de hacer 'It's easy to do'. (in-respect-of)
[157] Fue el primero en llegar 'He was the first to arrive'. (position)

yet the same preposition is used for both efficient and final cause:

[158] Lucha por salvar a sus hijos 'She struggles to save her children'.
[159] Está desconsolada por no haber conseguido el premio 'She's unhappy because of not having got the prize'.

And of course English for likewise: He works for money – 'to get', goal; He works for love of money – 'motivated by', efficient cause. Is a woman who works for her children motivated by them or is she directing her efforts toward them? A good part of the time the distinctions are not very clearcut. To take a type [3] example, I am disgusted to hear that is close to efficient cause: it is a little strange to say I would be disgusted to hear that meaning that I oppose hearing it, a meaning that can easily be got from I would be extremely annoyed to hear that.

I have tried to explain not what makes infinitives different from one another but what makes them so much alike. The interesting question grammatically may be why three such sentences as

[160] John would be nice to give that job. (John, dative)
[161] John would be nice to fill that job. (John, nominative)
[162] John would be nice to have around. (John, accusative)

should be so different in the cases implied; but the interesting question semantically is what they have in common that leads us to express them all in the same way. An infinitive is, stretching the etymology a bit, 'unfinished'. When it is more or less unattached it is up in the air, contingent, iffy. (This hypotheticalness extends to subject infinitives.) When it is attached it links up tightly as a complement, as something toward which an action tends. English has generalized the goal function, and the process is still going on, as can be seen in such innovations as *They convinced him to do it* and *They forbade him from doing it*.

Notes

1 But compare

> *To go there now would be condemned.
> To go there now would be deemed the height of folly.
> To go there now would be the height of folly.

The passive *would be deemed* is a kind of illocutionary verb that does not affect the acceptable non-passive modifier *the height of folly*.

2 In other combinations *eager* is not so restricted: *Don't look so eager; She's an eager sort of person.*

3 I regard the *to* of *angry enough to* as dependent on *enough* rather than on *angry*. It can be expressed separately:

> He was angry. – Enough to commit murder?

4 See Bolinger 1973 for discussion.

5 *John was too tall to get through the door* is not relevant to speaker's opinion. The goal relationship obtains between subject and action.

6 The line between temporary and permanent is erratic. There are very few adjectives that fall clearly on one side or the other. *Fresh* describes a person in the light of his actions: this is especially true of the simple predication *Mary was fresh* (she behaved in a fresh manner), where *was* is point action. We are not apt to say, simply, *?Mary is fresh*, since without further elaboration *is* tends to be 'habitual', though *Mary is being fresh* is normal. On the other hand, when an intensifier is added, *fresh* is no longer quite so clearly temporary: *Mary is pretty fresh* suggests not a momentary action but a tendency to behave habitually in a fresh manner. So *Mary is pretty fresh to have said that* is better than *?Mary is fresh to have said that*. It is also better because there is no question about the 'disapproval' – which may itself be the 'permanent' feature that has been added.

Chapter 8

Is the imperative an infinitive?

Two themes here accord with the design of this book.[1] The chief one is the difference in meaning between the FORM that has traditionally been recognized as 'imperative' (*Buy that stock*) and the distinct form of various roughly equivalent constructions (for example, *You will buy that stock*). The second is the equivalence in meaning – once contextual factors are filtered out – between this imperative and other constructions using the SAME FORM of the verb, which is simply the bare infinitive (for example, *John be a liar? – Impossible*).

1 The generative 'source'

The imperative was the one type of supposedly elliptical sentence which the first decade of generative grammar was willing to accord the status of an independent construction. It lacked the auxiliary, and could also lack a subject, but it was too conspicuous a feature of the landscape to ignore. The problem was how to clothe it to keep company with the arbiter of fashion, the full declarative. A favored recourse was to assume that an imperative such as *Eat the meat* was the same as *You will eat the meat*, with obligatory deletion of *will* and optional deletion of *you*. The justifications, as set forth by Katz and Postal, were as follows:

1 *Yourself* is the only reflexive pronoun that can occur in imperative sentences: *Wash yourself*, not *Wash himself*. To harmonize this with the description of reflexives requires that *you* be assumed as the subject.
2 While *Eat the meat, will you?* is normal, 'we find no sentences like *Eat the meat, will she (he, they)*' (P 254). To harmonize this with the description of tags again requires that *you* be assumed as the subject.
3 *Will* 'is the only permitted auxiliary form' in tags following imperatives (P 254): *Eat the meat, will you?* but not *Eat the meat, can he?*, etc.

4 Assuming an underlying *will* 'provides an explanation of why we understand that imperative sentences refer to the future' (P 254).

The test that I want to apply is suggested by two points of generative
doctrine: (1) that the intuitions of the native speaker are the guide to
grammaticality, and (2) that a grammar must account for sentences that
have never been heard before. These tenets put a premium on inventive-
ness. They require the grammarian to sit down and assiduously concoct
sentences to the limit of his capacity, to try to see everything that CAN be
done with the resources of his language in the linguistic area in question.
It is not enough to skim a few examples from the handbooks, and add a
few more invented on the spur of the moment. One must improvise
situations, imagine conversations for them, judge, and finally accept or
discard; then reinvent, and repeat the whole process many times. Only by
going in this way as far as ingenuity will carry one is it possible to discover
what the real boundaries of a construction are – and to justify the appeal
to intuition and originality, which I believe is profoundly correct.

In this part of the discussion I shall omit the kinds of imperatives that we
can assume K-P did not intend to treat: conditions (*Scratch a Russian and
find a Tartar*), advice (*Go west, young man*), and wishes or hopes (*God help
us*) – imperatives that are not commands. I do not believe that we can
really categorize all these separately in a convincing manner and will return to them later, but for the time being it is best to keep to the middle of
the road. Also it is necessary to give K-P the benefit of the doubt regarding
certain statements that are probably more sweeping than they were
intended to be. When Postal says 'we find no sentences like **Eat the meat,
will she (he, they)*' (P 254), he must mean 'no imperative sentences', because a question of the type *Eat the meat, will she? – I'll fix her!* is normal.

Here is what one diligent native speaker finds to be true of the four
propositions:

1 Other reflexive pronouns than *yourself* (*-selves*) readily occur. The
imperative repeated in an echo question, *eg, Don't kill yourself. –
Don't kill myself! Why should I?*, should be laid aside because it is the
result of a further transformation. But other examples are relevant. An
announcement at a square dance: *Whoever wants to dance get himself a
partner and let's begin.* An unceremonious host might say to a group of
guests waiting to go to a buffet table, *Somebody help himself quick, before
all this food gets cold.* A lawyer might advise a group of clients just before
a hearing by an investigative committee, *Nobody (don't anybody) say a
word about himself – stand on the Fifth if you have to.* A *yourself* in either

of these examples would be ungrammatical. In certain other contexts there is a choice. A doctor tending an accident victim says to the by-standers, *One of you lend a hand and make himself (yourself) useful here; let's get this man to where he'll be more comfortable.*

This is simply to say that there is an indefinite imperative with subjects on the order of *somebody, everybody, anybody, nobody, whoever* clauses, numerals, demonstratives and *all* and other quantitative pronouns (*some, a few*, etc), used when the speaker is addressing without any precise *you* in mind, with which third-person reflexives are compatible. I think there is one restriction: the subject must be expressed and must stand in the normal position before the verb: *Don't anybody say a word about himself, Don't say a word about yourself anybody, ★Don't say a word about himself anybody.*

Probably as a result of blending, we can even find a *myself*, motivated by a tendency to regard *myself* as less intimate than *I* or *me* (*John and myself have reached an agreement; It was up to John and myself*), or to a desire to avoid a decision between *I* and *me*, or to both. So starting with the following,

[1] Take me, for example.
[2] Take me, as an example.
[3] I take (offer) myself as an example.
[4] ★I take (offer) myself, for example.

and combining the second and third, we can get the nearest approxima-tion to the first, which is the most usual form, that will allow a *myself: Take myself, as an example.* It sounds a little less egotistical and avoids the too obvious clash of persons that would be found in *?Take myself, for example*, which lacks the echo of the fully acceptable *I take myself as an example.*

2 As far as I can ascertain, it is true that *you* is the only pronoun occurring in tags following an imperative. In other words, although an indefinite *someone* and a reflexive *himself* are possible, a following *will he?* is not. (In everyday conversation a tag often picks up a subordinate verb, with the result that we find not only a different auxiliary but sometimes a different subject and even a different verb. The switch is generally found in questions: *That looks like an ice plant, isn't it?* But it can happen with imperatives: *Have them come by a little later, could they?*)

3 Other auxiliaries than *will* occur in tags of this type. Curme cites (434) *Come down quietly, can't you?*, and Jespersen *Be quiet, can't you?* (5.24.2.1).[1] Furthermore, a tagged *will* is restricted to commands that cajole. It is

not apt to be used (except metaphorically, and here voice qualifiers betray it) in commands that insist. Negative commands are relatively more insistent than affirmative ones, and a tagged *will* is less likely with them, though a sentence like *Don't let them know my part in this, will you please?* is possible. But when a non-contrastive *you* is added after *don't*, or in the normal vocative position in affirmative commands, tagged *will* becomes extremely unlikely; commands of this sort are highly insistent: *Don't you let them know my part in this, will you please?* The vocative in *Come here, John, will you?* is normal; that in *Come here, you, will you?* is not. Affirmative *do* cajoles, and tagged *will* is common: *Do come over tomorrow, won't you?* The insistent *you* is as incompatible with the cajoling *do* as with the cajoling *will you:* *Do attend to this, you.*

But the question is not so much whether other auxiliaries than *will* may be used under these circumstances, but whether the use of *will* itself is significant. *You'll do it will you?* can be spoken without a break. *Do it, will you?* and *Do it, won't you?* demand an intonational disjuncture that suggests a deeper constituent cleavage.[2] If *will* is more closely tied to what it is attached to than are the tags in the examples that follow, it is only a matter of degree: *Be nice to him, would you?; Be more careful, can't you?; Let me help you, may I?* Perhaps the most tag-like of all, in view of its intonation (it is laid out on the same terminal line as an adverbial, vocative, or parenthesis, and does not involve altering the normal intonation of the imperative) is a form containing *do*[3] or *can:*

[5] Come o_ve_r t_omor row why don't you.

[6] Look it up yo_ur se lf why can't you.

Compare

[7] Come o_ve_r t_o mor row then.

The best argument for a *will* in the imperative would be something to confirm the analogy with other repeated auxiliaries. In the negative there appears to be a close parallel; one can agree with a negative question, statement, or command by repeating the negated auxiliary: *He didn't go, did he? – No, he didn't; It wasn't too late. – You're right, it wasn't; Don't look now. – I won't.* But agreeing in the affirmative is troublesome. Not only is *yes* a poor response to a command (whereas *no* is a good one), but the repeated auxiliary, which does well with questions and statements (*Are you ready? – I am; He has already gone. – So he has*), is almost as bad: *Come in! – ?I will; Hand me that screwdriver. – ?I will.* Normal responses are *OK, all right, sure thing, right-o;* but in an exchange like *Come with me. – OK, I will* the *will* seems to be an expression of will after a fleeting moment of deliberation: 'OK, I'll just do that little thing.' Refusal is equally awkward using *will* to respond to an imperative: *I can't* is actually better than *I won't.* Compare *Take me along. – No, not this time* with *Take me along. – ?I won't, not this time. I won't* is a structurally independent – and rather rude – expression of will.

4 The futurity of the imperative raises two questions: whether the imperative is necessarily future, and, if it is, whether *will* has any bearing on the matter.

The first question is a pseudo-question within the framework of the K-P imperatives as I am assuming it. If a command is an order that is to be carried out, it is necessarily understood as referring to the future – futurity is part of the definition of 'command'. From this standpoint, K-P's emphasis on *will* becomes not a desire to prove that commands refer to the future but simply an interest in detecting the underlying linguistic correlate of futurity. For the traditional grammarians the futurity of imperatives had a larger relevance, and I shall return to it later when we are able to step out of the straitjacket of strict commands.

But the second question is pertinent. The motive for raising it, from the generative standpoint, seems to be that since Tense is a necessary part of Aux, something needs to be done to involve the imperative in a tense, and *will* is the answer. But K-P are careful to show that a sentence like *You will go home* is ambiguous, and to account for the imperative interpretation they posit an Imperative morpheme. Thus presumably *will* in the imperative carries the basic notion of futurity and Imperative is added to it.

For more than one reason, this is not very satisfying. In the first place, if the *you will* in the imperative interpretation of *You will go home* already is accompanied by the Imperative morpheme, then so is both the *you will* and the *he will* in the imperative interpretation of *You will sit here and he will sit there*, and we have the makings of a third-person imperative. In the second place, *will* often is not future. *Accept the job, if you will*, and *I asked him to accept the job, if he would*, clearly relate to *Accept the job, will you?*; and yet in *I asked him to accept the job, if he would, but he wouldn't, then or later*, the *wouldn't* is not necessarily future to the past time axis; it means 'He refused'. The confusion on this point is occasioned not only by the ubiquitous tense associations of *will* but also by reading too much importance into action verbs. In *I keep telling him she's stepping out on him but he won't do anything about it* one has the illusion of futurity because in the nature of action verbs there has to be a time span between the telling and the acting. But in *I keep telling him she's stepping out on him but he absolutely won't believe it* the meaning is that he absolutely refuses, now, at the time of the telling. The reference is to willingness, and whatever futurity one infers is just as readily to be inferred if *will you* is replaced by *do you agree, do you so incline*, etc. *Will you* is an appeal to willingness. Its function is to cajole, like that of *please*, as we have already noted. *Help me, will you?* means *Help me, are you willing to? Talk back to me, will you!* refers to the interlocutor's wilfulness.[4]

If this is true, then the imperative *will* is not a future *will* plus an Imperative, but is a homonym of the future *will*. It follows that we do not interpret the imperative to refer to the future because of the implied presence of *will*, since even if that implied presence is conceded, it is the wrong *will*. WHEN we interpret the imperative to refer to the future we do so because that is in the nature of the stimulus-response relationship.[5] The same relationship and the same interpretation, with no assistance from any *will*, is present in the following examples:

[8] Where are you going? – I'm going on a picnic, and *you're going along*.

[9] What are you having there? – We're having some ice cream, and *you're having some with us*.

2 Other imperatives, real or apparent

Going along with what I suppose K-P had in mind, up to this point I have narrowed the field to imperatives that were obviously commands. It is time now to consider whether there was a justification for this.

1 *Conditions*

The commonest non-command use of the imperative is in *if-then* sequences like the following: *Spare the rod and spoil the child; Cut ourselves off from that source of income and we're ruined; Break that vase and I'll break your neck.* It is obvious that these are no more commands than *Can I have a nickel?* is an inquiry about one's ability to own five cents. What is less obvious is that they are not imperatives.

To exclude them from imperatives, or try to distinguish a pure set of imperatives that are commands and nothing else, may simplify the analysis of commands but it complicates that of conditions. Consider the following coordinations:

[10] A fellow gets a few gray hairs and they think he's ready for the ash-heap.

[11] A telegram comes and you're sure it's bad news.

[12] Macy's advertises a sale and the whole town goes crazy.

or adjective clauses:

[13] Any man tries to talk back to his wife usually catches it.

[14] The employee who presumes to advise his boss risks losing his job.

or especially adverb clauses of time:

[15] When you accept I'll accept.

[16] Once you see the effect of those hard words, you'll want to speak more softly.

To the last example one might add the explicitly conditional *if* to counter-balance the *once* clause: *but if you don't, I guess I'll have to resign myself to your continuing to be rude.* It seems that cause-effect and condition-consequence are not limited to specific structures. It would seem easier to call the structures what we have traditionally called them, and assign their conditional uses to figures of speech within discourse. The speaker who says *A telegram comes and you're sure it's bad news* is saying in effect *A telegram comes – just imagine this; then imagine what comes next – you're sure it's bad news.* This is exactly the type of discourse that includes all phases of story-telling: 'just imagine.' And we don't on that account categorize story-telling statements separately from fact-reporting ones.

But there is a bit more to the question of imperative conditions. We can trace it by starting with sentences containing impersonal *you*, which are especially common:

[17] You try to please somebody and all you get is a kick in the pants.

[18] You have half a degree of temperature and they put you to bed; you look a little pale around the gills and they act like it's time to call a priest.

[19] You tell him anything and he just looks at you blankly.

These are all normal without the *and*, as in the following from a popular magazine: '*Don't get too conscientious,*' Keely said. '*You get like that, you become a nuisance.*'6 This suggests that the *and* may well be parasitic. If we so regard it, then all barriers between *if* conditions, coordinations, and imperatives are virtually flattened:

[20] ([If] you) tell him anything, (and) he just looks at you blankly.

The fact that *anything* rather than *something* can be used in any one of these three telescoped conditions is significant (see *p* 28). Now compare these with the well-known aphetic questions:

[21] ([Do] you) like it?
[22] ([Would] you) care to come along?
[23] ([Can] you) tell any difference?

I suggest that the same thing has happened with conditions, and that in at least some cases there has been an aphesis of the initial *if* or *if you*, which produces something with all the appearance of an imperative and accounts for those supposed conditional imperatives that least resemble commands.

The process of aphesis explains some conditional 'imperatives' without the subject *you*:

[24] ([If] I) give you a nice present, (and) you don't appreciate it.
[25] ([If] they) expect any kind of sensible answer from him, they don't get it.
[26] ([If] I) buy myself a few pretty clothes, (and) you act like you'd been robbed.
[27] ([If] they) give themselves the least advantage, (and) the rest of the gang hollers unfair.

It also explains the ungrammaticality of certain coordinations of two apparent imperatives:

[28] ([If] we) take our medicine (and) we get well.
[29] *Take our medicine and get well.7
[30] Take your medicine and get well.

Since no aphesis is possible in the second verb, only genuine imperatives will get by. Aphesis appears to occur pretty freely with all subjects except third singular:

[31] If she buys herself a few pretty clothes, her husband acts like he'd been robbed.

[32] She buys herself a few pretty clothes, (and) her husband acts like he'd been robbed.

[33] *Buys herself a few pretty clothes, (and) her husband acts like he'd been robbed.

Nor do matters seem to be helped if, on the assumption that this may not be aphesis after all, we use the plain verb stem instead of the inflected form:

[34] ?Buy herself a few pretty clothes, (and) her husband acts like he'd been robbed.[8]

[35] Buy myself a new suit, (and) my wife raises the roof.

There seems to be no similar aphesis of preterite forms:

[36] ([If] you) sell at too low a price, (and) you make no profit.

[37] *Sold at too low a price, (and) you made no profit.

The only thing that seems to work consistently well is aphesis of a subject whose verb is identical in form to the plain infinitive – an oddity paralleling what we find with the 'auxiliary' *go*.[9] The other way of looking at it, which is to assume that this is the plain infinitive attached to various subjects including third person, does not seem inviting because of the exclusion of third-singular subjects; I give some more examples of the latter:

[38] ?Shake down too many people, (and) he gets caught.

[39] Shake down too many people, (and) they get caught.

[40] ?Tell herself that it's true, (and) she ends up believing it.

[41] Tell myself that it's true, (and) I end up believing it.

[42] ?Get careless, (and) he gets hurt.

[43] Get careless, and you get hurt.

The best, of course, is *you*, but the acceptability of the others is improved by having a verb form that resembles the one with *you*.

Of course, *you* and its verb form are the same as for the true imperative, and we must now see what the latter's impact may be. It is most dramatic with the verb *to be*:

[44] If I'm critical, my friends hate me.

[45] I'm critical, (and) my friends hate me.

[46] *Am critical, (and) my friends hate me.
[47] *Be critical, (and) my friends hate me.
[48] If they're scoundrels, people admire them.
[49] They're scoundrels, (and) people admire them.
[50] *Are scoundrels, (and) people admire them.
[51] *Be scoundrels, (and) people admire them.
[52] If you're a scoundrel, people admire you.
[53] You're a scoundrel, (and) people admire you.
[54] *Are a scoundrel, (and) people admire you.
[55] Be a scoundrel, (and) people admire you.
[56] If they're left behind, nobody will pity them.
[57] *Be left behind, (and) nobody will pity them.
[58] Be left behind, (and) nobody will pity you.
[59] If we're as good as our word, others will trust us.
[60] Be as good as our word, and others will trust us.

All constructions with the verb *to be*, including the passive voice, appear to exclude all subjects other than *you* and inclusive *we*. The plain infinitive stem of *to be* is *be*. No subject, including *you*, is compatible with this form. But *you* is compatible with it in the imperative, and the effect extends to inclusive *we*. So it develops that with this one verb the imperative becomes decisive. It seems that the so-called conditional imperatives are a confluence of two streams: one from aphesis of subject (and possibly *if*) from non-third-singular verbs, the other from the imperative. The fact that the non-third-singular is the same in form as the imperative makes it difficult to tell where the water is from once the two streams have met.

There are two restrictions that partially clarify this, one on the use of *any* and the other on the use of statives.[10]

The restrictions on *any* shape up as follows:

[61] If you find any tickets, we'll go to the movies.
[62] *Find any tickets and we'll go to the movies.
[63] If you write any letters I'll mail them for you.
[64] *Write any letters and I'll mail them for you.
[65] If you make any soft cereal for tomorrow's breakfast I'll feed some to the baby.
[66] *Make any soft cereal for tomorrow's breakfast and I'll feed some to the baby.[11]
[67] If you meet John, he wants you to go home with him.
[68] *Meet John, and he wants you to go home with him.

The incongruousness of the last example, which has no *any*, exposes the nature of the restriction, which is less obvious in the others: 'imperative' conditions must be true conditions, that is, conditions of intrinsic consequence. The use of an explicit *if* makes it possible to form outlandish pseudo-conditions like *There's a man in your office, if you want to see him* ('*If you want to see a man you can, because* . . .'). 'Imperative' conditions are limited to those whose consequences are the automatic result of the condition. In **Write any letters and I'll mail them for you* the willingness to do a favor is not consequent upon the writing of the letters. The *any* forces the clause to be a condition, and it is the wrong kind of condition because the consequence is not automatic (a *some* would make the sentence a command, and the problem does not arise: *Write some letters and I'll mail them for you*). On the other hand, if John is such a friendly fellow that he no sooner sees you than he invites you to his house, then *Meet John, and he wants you to go home with him* becomes grammatical. Other examples:

[69] Pay any attention to people like that and they never let you rest.
[70] Invent anything new and the public goes wild about you.

This is the reason why conditions with IMPERSONAL *you*, like these last two examples, are so common. They are the sort of generalizations about the consequences of virtue and folly, mostly the latter, that make up a large part of folk philosophy. But particular conditions are perfectly grammatical if the consequence is intrinsic:

[71] Try any harder and you'll bust a gut.
[72] Find any proofs and I'll believe you.

We are now in a position to ask what the relevance of *any* is to conditions versus commands. We have seen that there are conditions that exclude *any*, and exclude it qua conditions, not qua commands. On the other hand, we would expect imperatives that are commands also to exclude *any*, in the light of obviously ungrammatical examples like

[73] *Let me have any of your time tonight, will you?
[74] *Please go with anybody to church tomorrow.
[75] *Write anybody a letter of condolence.[12]

Nevertheless there are some apparent commands that admit *any:*

[76] All right then. Put up your fists. Let me hear you call me any of those names. Go ahead. Just try it.
[77] If you're real brave, try *him* with any of those wild ideas.

These are dares with unnamed consequences. The consequence, when named, is a threat: the speaker wants to present it as inevitable. The result is a condition with an intrinsic consequence. Conditions that would not get by otherwise do if they contain threats. The sentence *Make any soft cereal for tomorrow's breakfast and I'll feed some to the baby* could be said by a person who dislikes soft cereal and threatens to upset the household by feeding it to the baby, who will kick up a fuss. The sentence *Break one of your teeth and your face will be ugly* is a normal condition; the sentence *Break one of your teeth and I'll take you to the dentist* is either a silly invitation to break a tooth (and hence probably a command, as in *Break these pieces of candy and I'll take them in to the guests*) or it is a condition containing a threat, the dentist being the punishment. The above examples can be completed:

[78] Let me hear you call me any of those names and I'll show you what's what.
[79] Try *him* with any of those wild ideas and see what happens.

Such vague consequences are frequently omitted. Threats are interesting in that they are often rigged to sound like commands – this is the nature of a dare:

[80] Just you make any of those smart-aleck remarks of yours and you're going to get slapped down.

Aside from the cases cited, I believe that *any* is a serviceable test for commands versus conditions.

With statives, we find that intrinsic consequences are again significant:

[81] If you like her I'll introduce you to her.
[82] *Like her and I'll introduce you to her.
[83] If you like her her friends will love you.
[84] Like her and her friends will love you.
[85] If you own this property I'll buy it from you.
[86] *Own this property and I'll buy it from you.
[87] If you own a piece of property you get taxed unmercifully.
[88] Own a piece of property and you get taxed unmercifully.
[89] If you understand Chinese I need you for a teacher.
[90] *Understand Chinese and I need you for a teacher.
[91] If you understand Chinese you can get any of these jobs.
[92] Understand Chinese and you can get any of these jobs.
[93] If you are John Smith this message is for you.

[94] *Be John Smith and this message is for you.
[95] If you are sick they put you to bed.
[96] Be sick and they put you to bed.
[97] If it's six o'clock I'm going home.
[98] *Let it be six o'clock and I'm going home.
[99] If it's six o'clock all the workmen rush for home.
[100] Let it be six o'clock and all the workmen rush for home.

Statives thus appear to be a test. If they can be readily used the construction is a condition with intrinsic consequence. Taking *any* and the statives together, it seems a safe generalization that straight conditions (conditions with no admixture of commands) using the simple verb stem must be conditions of this intrinsic consequence type.

There are of course many straight conditions to which neither of the two tests applies. If commanding the action would be absurd, it is usually safe to assume a straight condition:

[101] Eat too much candy and you get a stomach ache.
[102] Be overly polite and people will be suspicious.
[103] Disobey your parents and you'll get punished.
[104] Dynamite the White House and you'll get arrested.

But in other examples without context it is impossible to tell whether condition or command is intended:

[105] Eat your spinach and you'll be strong.
[106] Be our candidate for president and we'll win.
[107] Join the Navy and see the world.

In still others the command is obviously uppermost:

[108] Hand me that hammer, will you, and I'll nail this down.
[109] Step this way, please, and the doctor will see you.

Coordinations with *or* are easier to interpret than those with *and*. As conditions, they imply 'if . . . not'. Threats are common:

[110] Eat your spinach or I'll spank you.
[111] Put up more capital or we'll have to close you out.

Even the ones that are not threats look very much like commands that are merely reinforced by reference to some unpleasant consequence:

[112] Take your cane or you may fall.
[113] Clear this stuff out or we won't have room for the new furniture.

Subjects other than *you* are difficult if not impossible:

[114] *Be ready on time or we can't take him.
[115] *Take our pills or we'll risk an attack.

(As ellipses, these of course are normal: *So what must he do? – Be ready on time, or we can't take him.*) And the use of *any*, normal in *and* conditions, seems to be impossible with *or*, which suggests that these are not related to true conditions:

[116] Wear anything (something) lighter, and you'll catch cold.
[117] *Wear anything heavier, or you'll catch cold.
[118] Wear something heavier, or you'll catch cold.
[119] If you don't wear anything (something) heavier, you'll catch cold.

Coordinations with *or* appear to be imperatives, whether or not they can be interpreted as conditions at the same time.

We conclude that if K-P intended to exclude conditions, they were right, though it is now clear that we cannot exclude all apparent imperatives that CONTAIN or IMPLY conditions, for some of them are truly commands.[13]

2 *Wishes, hopes, advice*

We noted earlier that 'futurity' was, for K-P, part of the definition of 'command'. It seems that 'possibility of compliance' is also part of the definition, for they star examples like *Believe the claim, Understand the answer, Want more money, Hope it rains,* and observe (77) that it is 'anomalous to request someone to do something which he cannot wilfully choose to do'. To adhere to this condition results in some curious exclusions. First are sentences to which no traditional grammarian would deny the status of commands, but would recognize as figures of speech:

[120] Go to hell.
[121] Be an angel and hand me that comb.
[122] Tell it to the Marines.

Second are certain sentences with statives:

[123] You be young and I'll be old. The make-up man can manage it.
[124] Remember that name. Some day it will be famous.
[125] Just hope you have the courage when the time comes.
[126] Here. Take the money. Get in through the back door. Leave the bag on the table. And hope that nobody sees you.[14]

[127] Just be very clear on this point. I want no misunderstandings. Are you ready now? May I proceed?

[128] Now hear this.

[129] Hear me out. I have only a few more remarks.

[130] Hear the difference between these two passages. Play them over again, Joe.

Third are wishes of various sorts and facetious advice:

[131] Be happy!

[132] Get well!

[133] Sleep well!

[134] (Psychologist to young man on how to get ahead): Choose the right parents.

[135] (Barry Goldwater, same purpose): Inherit a department store.

That these are felt to be commands is suggested by certain pretty clearly injunctive contexts, *eg*,

[136] Be happy! Look on the bright side!

[137] Get well – that's an order!

[138] Sleep well – mind you, now, I mean it.

[139] Get over that headache, now.

[140] Get busy and inherit a department store.

Another requirement would be a distinction between affirmative and negative commands. For example, *be*-passives are awkward (unlike *get* passives, *eg*, *Get paid off before noon today; I want to leave early*), but not in the negative: *Don't be examined by a chiropractor, go to a real doctor.* Certain statives are better in the negative, others are worse:

[141] I've been thinking of owning a place as soon as my wife and I move. – No, no. Don't own if you have a chance to rent. Owning presents too many responsibilities.

[142] Confess, but don't hope for any forgiveness. He's too hard-hearted.

[143] Don't believe that pack of lies. Can't you see how dishonest he is?

[144] ?Don't hear the difference between these two passages.

[145] Know your lesson.

[146] *Don't know your lesson.[15]

The difficulty with any such criterion as what one can or cannot wilfully do is that it is too hard to tell. One may not wilfully choose an action, but still wilfully choose to resist it or not to resist it. In *Oh, come on; be taken in just once – it isn't going to hurt you; do you think you're perfect?* the command is not to resist (a commoner form of this is *let yourself be*). We have more occasion to command resistance than sufferance, and negative passives are correspondingly more frequent: *Don't be frightened (don't let yourself be frightened) by anything he says.* Most passive commands with *be* are otherwise unacceptable: *George, be taken to church by your sister.*

The regularity with which speakers attribute wilfulness to others argues against any squeamishness about admitting it with imperatives that are impossible to carry out. When someone accidentally commits an injury it is commonplace to hear the protest *Why did you have to go and do that?*, with an explicit formula of intent, *go and.*

So when Canute commands the waves or Jesus says to the man with leprosy, *Be clean*, it is better to think of figures of speech, or of the speakers as deluded or possessed of a higher power, than to try to decide whether what they say is a command or not.[16] I believe that no useful generalizations relevant to the task here can be made about advice or hopes or wishes as distinct from other imperatives, and that it is beside the point to ask whether in an exchange like *They complain that they can't read my letters. – Write more clearly. That way they won't complain*, we have to do with a command, a piece of advice, or a condition (*Write more clearly and they won't complain*). It is true that there are interesting combinatory effects, and there must be countless restrictions with particular verbs or classes of verbs that need to be spelled out, but our business now is to get a perspective on imperatives as a whole.

3 Imperatives in present and past

Possibility of compliance and futurity are fundamentally a single criterion. The present and the past cannot be acted on. The future can. With this requirement laid aside, we can now ask whether imperatives may be past or present. The question is pertinent, for it is raised by traditional grammarians for whom lack of any tense but future was not a criterion but an empirical fact – they just had trouble finding examples.

Jespersen is dogmatic: 'The imperative always refers to the future, often the immediate future' (5.24.1.7). Poutsma gives a way out: 'Uncertainty of fulfillment naturally clings to a command or request' (1926, 162). Such uncertainty can attach to a desire about something present as well as something future. Poutsma gives (329) the example *I hope you're thinking*

about me. Please, be thinking about me, which is probably intended to mean
a hope that something has already started and is going on now. In any
event, such imperatives are normal enough. If a man and his wife are
caught after committing a theft, and the wife is uncertain whether the
husband has the loot on his person or has already disposed of it, she may
say to herself, *Please, don't have that money on you!* A person holding a
lottery ticket not yet examined, and hearing the announcement of the
winning number, might say, before turning the ticket over, *Please be the
right number!* A mother, hearing of some possible danger to her child if he
is still on his way to school, might say the prayer *Please be at school
already!* Someone approaching a fallen and hated enemy might say *Be
dead, damn you!* Of course these are all Irish futures: 'What'll he be thinking of me? It'll be ten o'clock already and I'm still here' – the action is
present and the verification is future. But it can hardly be maintained that
the speaker is thinking about the future if he uses words like *now* and
already.

So much for imperatives referring to present time. What of imperatives referring to the past? The handbooks are almost unanimous in citing
Have done as no more than a curious relic, and on the face of it one might
imagine that a past command is impossible. (*Begone* looks to be a similar
form. Both *have done* and *begone* are forms that seem to exploit pastness
for a purpose in the present: *have done* carries more finality than *stop*, just
as – in reply to *When would you like me to do this?* – the answer *Yesterday!*
carries more finality than *Now!* Imaginary situations are always possible,
as when an actor-impresario in a home-made drama says *I've got it! Be
born in 1898. That will make our time sequence work out.*) Yet it ought to be
possible to express 'what is merely a wish' concerning a past act, if one
has not yet verified whether the act has been carried out.

English has two perfectives which can be used to show relevance of a
past act to the present, which is obviously what is called for here. One has
the form *He has the work done* (*already*), the other the form *He has done
the work.* The first, being superficially a present ('He at this moment has
the work done') would seem to lend itself more readily to an imperative,
in so far as we have seen that imperatives can apply to the present. But the
two perfectives are not interchangeable. The first is limited to transitive
verbs, and is even further restricted to constructions in which the literal
sense of having the thing in such-and-such a condition is uppermost.
Thus *They have planned their dinner* and *They have their dinner* (*all*) *planned*
are both normal; but while *He has discovered the hiding place* is normal,
*He has the hiding place discovered is not. We are accordingly left with two

questions: (1) Does the *have the work done* perfective occur more readily than the *have done the work* perfective, as would appear from our dead reckoning?; and (2) Given a situation where the first of these cannot be said, *ie*, where the *have done the work* type is required, is it still possible to have an imperative?

If the ease of inventing examples is any indication, the answer to the first question is yes. In a telephone conversation, A invites B to come over and share the contents of a bottle. B says *I'm on my way*, and then adds to himself, in an undertone, *Only for God's sake don't have three-fourths of it drunk already*, knowing the condition in which his friend will be once that amount has taken effect. It would be much more difficult to express this as *Don't have drunk three-fourths of it already*.

It is easy to show that the FORM, and not the pastness, is what makes these constructions difficult, for they can be rigged to refer to the future. A guest might say on receiving a sudden invitation by telephone, *Just don't have all those good things eaten before we get there*, which is normal. *Don't have eaten all those good things before we get there* is as difficult referring to future as to past. (For one thing, a perfective referring to action rather than state is unmotivated here, for there is too little contrast between it and a straightforward future: *Don't eat all those good things before we get there*.)

The answer to the second question is also yes, given a situation in which there is a strong wish for a past action that has not been verified. I submitted the following passage to twelve native speakers of English, allowing one minute to read it and two minutes to answer the questions that appear below it, with further reading if necessary:

Aline looked out the window of the taxi which moved by inches toward the next traffic signal and the next and the next. She gave a frightened glance at her watch. Five o'clock! Neale would be leaving the office. If only she had not written that note. That stupid, reckless, incoherent note, scrawled in three minutes and left on the mantelpiece. How cowardly to confess in writing. He would never understand!

The taxi broke free of the chain of traffic and sped along the boulevard. Five-fifteen. He would be home by now.

Her lips formed an agonized wish that was a prayer: Please, Neale, don't have read it yet! Let me be there to explain when you do. Let me tell you what was really in my heart.

They drew up to the curb. She fumbled in her purse, gave the driver a dollar, and stepped out.

If you mark 3, ignore 2

1 The wording of the passage seems normal   ☐.
2 The wording of the passage has one or more places that struck me as unusual, but not un-English   ☐. (Underline them)
3 The wording of the passage has one or more places that struck me as incorrect English   ☐. (Underline them)

Only two persons marked anything as 'incorrect English': one thought that *out* rather than *out of* was wrong, and another questioned *the chain of traffic* and *agonized wish that was a prayer*. All the rest felt that the wording was unusual in spots, but not un-English. Their choices were 'window of the taxi' (1), 'moved by inches' (5), 'and left' (1), one or both halves of 'broke free of the chain of traffic' (4), 'agonized wish that was a prayer' (1), and 'don't have read it yet' (3). In other words, only three of the twelve noticed the imperative at all, and no one regarded it as un-English. A later comment: 'If that is the idea you want to express, how else can you express it?'

The restriction, if there is one, does not relate to time but – I think – to accent. The auxiliary *have* is accented in certain situations, *eg*, as a carrier of affirmation-negation: *Háve you done it?* ('I want to know the truth'); *He hás done it* (contrary to what they have said).[17]

These situations do not include the imperative, which is one reason why we recognize *have done* as a fossil: *have* is stressed. But the imperative needs the accent, which can be attached to a *do* or a *don't. Do* strikes me as more unusual, though I would not find the following impossible: *Please, do have made that call by six o'clock; Please, do have made the effort at least once!; Do have given some thought to the question, once you've decided to discuss it. Don't*, which is more frequent over-all than *do*, gets by more easily. An added and highly acceptable *dare* fits in well here: someone who was looking forward to participating in a job and appears on the scene uncertain whether he still has the chance, might say to his supposed collaborator, *Don't you dare have finished that work yet!;* this is another unverified wish, but is unlike the others in that it can be said directly to the person concerned, and not as a form of absentee apostrophizing. The other perfective is less restricted – the *have* can be accented: *Please, have that work finished for once, so it won't all fall on me; Don't you dare have that work finished yet!* It also admits other complements than past participles: *Have the returns in already. Have the buns hot already.*

4 The imperative as bare infinitive

It was Jespersen who emphasized the futurity of imperatives (4.7.4.1, besides the reference already given), the relevance of tagged *will* (4.15.7.5), and the need, even with an expressed *somebody* as subject, to infer a *you* (5.24.1.6; 1933, 15.4.2). But Jespersen makes two appeals to intuition, and they are not entirely consistent. The first is the appeal to *will*: 'Indeed, it is possible that to the actual speech instinct the imperative is nothing but a kind of abbreviated *will* sentence: *Have an egg* = *Will you have an egg?*' (4.15.7.5). The second is an appeal to the form of the imperative: 'As the imperative is formally identical with the infinitive, it may by the actual speech instinct be felt as such' (5.24.2.1). Curiously, he uses the same evidence a second time: the tag question in *Take a seat, will you?* His two ideas could have been separated more clearly had he used an example like *Have a chocolate. – Oh, may I? Thanks!*

Kruisinga goes farther. He lumps the imperative together with other examples of the 'plain verb stem' used predicatively (§§171-185), including types like *Why refuse to come?* and *Gerry Palliser swim! Of course he can't* (§183), and says 'The predicative plain stem can express a command or entreaty' (§172).

Curme points out another analogy with the infinitive (419): 'In reporting indirectly a command we never employ the imperative, but an optative – the volitive – subjunctive or an infinitive with the force of a volitive subjunctive: (direct) "Come at once". (indirect) "He said *I should come* at once" (or *I was to come* at once), or "He told me *to come* at once".' The kinship is closer than this implies, for the types *He said I should come at once* and *He said I was to come at once* only rather loosely report the meaning, not the form, of the imperative. The direct form of the first is *You should come at once*, of the second *You are to come at once;* it would be as accurate to say that *He pointed out the necessity of my coming at once* reports *Come at once*. The virtually unambiguous reporting of an imperative is with an infinitive: *He told me to come at once, He bade me come at once,* and, with the subject deleted exactly as in the direct command, *He said to come at once.* (This last formula both reports and conveys an imperative. If A is asked *Why are you in such a hurry?* and replies B *said to come at once,* he reports B's command *Come at once.* If A says to B *Tell C to come at once,* B may give the command directly, *Come at once – A's orders,* or indirectly, A *says to come at once.*)

The important thing to note here is that finites (statements and questions) are reported with finites (*It's a nice day, He says [that] it's a nice day; Is it a nice day?, He asks if it is a nice day*), and non-finites (*Come at once*) with non-finites (*He says to come at once*).[18] This analogy between direct and indirect discourse points, I think, to a tie, within direct discourse, between imperatives and infinitives.

So our three traditional grammarians present us with two intuitions as to the kinship of the imperative: one, Jespersen, a kinship with *will* sentences; all three, including Jespersen in a different mood, a kinship with the infinitive. I want to see how far the latter idea can be carried, *ie*, the extent to which the two can be lumped together.

5 The undifferentiated infinitive

If we follow Kruisinga we will recognize a 'plain stem used predicatively' and not fall back on 'ellipsis' to account for things like *Why bother?, How make them understand?, John be rude to anyone?* If the imperative is to be dignified by being recognized as a structure in its own right, these deserve the same attention.

The question then boils down to looking for interrelationships among these formally similar structures, to establish an identity among them. The prima facie evidence favors this: the imperative and the bare infinitive are identical in form. It remains to make a case for such a close relatedness in distribution that the distinction between 'imperative' and 'infinitive' is reduced to the same kind of context that distinguishes *May I have the sugar?* spoken at table and *May I go with you tomorrow?*, where a mere *yes* is a satisfactory answer for the second but not for the first.

1 What Jespersen calls 'characteristic clauses of indifference with a pre-posed verb in the crude (stem) form' (4.15.4.7) would be felt, at one end of the gradient, as imperatives by most native speakers of English, if the subject is *you*. Yet they blend imperceptibly with older instances where the subject is not *you*. In fact, *you* has asserted itself to the point where other subjects would nowadays generally be felt a bit odd. Of Jespersen's two examples *Go whither he will, I'le be none of his followers* and *Look where you will, immeasurable Obscurantism is girdling this fair France*, only the second (after eliminating the other quaint features and reducing the first to *Go where he will* or *Go wherever he pleases* and the second to *Look wherever you please*) would be usual in spoken English today. In the following, the first three are surviving fossils:

[147] Come what may, we shall not fear.

[148] Be that as it may, my argument still stands.
[149] Try as she will, she can't do it.
[150] Say what you will, they won't believe you.
[151] Lie all you want, it can't hurt me.
[152] Go where you please; I don't give a damn.

All it takes to make [150] and [151] unmistakable commands is a conclusive intonation. like that of [152]. But that is all it takes to make the
same change of meaning in *He can eat anything he likes, it won't bother me*
('No matter what he eats, it won't bother me') versus *He can eat anything
he likes; it won't bother me,* and I doubt that we would think of classify-
ing *He can eat anything he likes* in two ways in order to take care of that
semantic contrast. It is hard to insist on any clear-cut separation between
imperatives and non-imperatives in utterances like the ones I have listed.

2 With conditions we have already seen at one extreme a kind of sentence
that could not be a command (*eg,* Kruisinga's example, §182, *Give him
a fact, he loaded you with thanks*), at the other extreme a kind that contained some element of condition but was obviously meant as a command (*Here, take this pill and you'll feel better*), and in between and cover-
ing the extremes a tendency toward mutual accommodation: (i) The
more hypothetical the condition the better (a characteristic, as we shall
see, of the bare infinitive): a preference for indefinite subjects and a
requirement of intrinsic consequence. (ii) A restriction of the verb *to be*
to its bare infinitive form (**Are a scoundrel and people admire you*).
(iii) The inclusion of dares, which are a kind of perverted command, in
the scheme of condition-consequence. The accommodation has reached
the point where a sentence like *Join the Navy and see the world* can be
intended both ways. Usually when two different constructions overlap
(produce homonymy) and are intended both ways, we recognize a pun:
I can drink a Venetian blind. But with command-conditions we do not
sense that any pun was intended. This suggests that there is no pun,
that the structures are felt to be identical, and that the common ground
is the bare infinitive with a meaning of hypothesis.

3 With predisposing context, I find another gradient. I believe that any
speaker would feel that the first examples below contain imperatives,
yet I find identical utterances with merely a change of person perfectly
normal:

[153] How can I convince them? – Tell the truth.
[154] What can I do to smooth things over? – Just be more polite in
the future.

[155] What must I do to get ahead? – Work harder.
[156] What should I do? – Write that letter.
[157] How can she convince them? – Tell them the truth.
[158] What can they do to smooth things over? – Just be more polite
in the future.
[159] What should he do? – Write that letter.

Again, I have no sense of punning when I view the answer in [153] as either *Tell them the truth*, a command, or *You can tell them the truth*, an 'ellipsis'. It happens that all these examples can be viewed as replacements after the auxiliary: *What can I do? – You can be more polite; What must I do? – You must work harder*, etc. Also in *Should they go now? – No, see what happens and if necessary go later* it is possible, but a trifle far-fetched, to insist that there is an ellipsis of *No, they should see what happens and if necessary (they should) go later*. Farther out on the gradient the argument for ellipsis gets weaker. In the example *The poor fellow doesn't know which way to turn, he's got himself in such a complicated mess. – Make a fresh start. That's the only way for him to put himself in the clear* there is no obvious frame.[19]

The word *just* gives incidental support to the imperative interpretation as against the elliptical one. Consider the following as answers to the question *How can they look winsome?*

[160] ?Be six years old, is how.
[161] They can be six years old, is how.
[162] Just be six years old, is how.
[163] ?They can just be six years old, is how.

The fourth answer underpins the elliptical interpretation, and is less acceptable than the third, which if it contrasts with the fourth can only do so on the basis of being an imperative. *Just* has the effect of 'relaxing' a lot of imperatives that would otherwise seem doubtful. K-P's **Hope it rains* becomes normal as *Just hope it rains*. The discourse conditions I think are the following: *Just* implies a comparison, which tends to be with something already discussed or taken for granted or otherwise obvious: (*Don't do thus-and-so,*) *just leave things to me; How can I get ahead? – Plain as can be: just own some real estate*. If the action is pictured as obvious, it becomes apparently easy even if commanding it is logically absurd. For example, if you ask a doctor how to keep strong and in good health, it would sound strange for him to reply *Assimilate what you eat*, but *Just* *assimilate what you eat* is normal, as if implying 'Relax – your body will take care of that if you just allow it to'.

In the first and second of the following examples, the 'imperative' may be blended with indirect discourse (*I'd say, 'Let yourself be arrested'*), but the third is not:

[164] She wants to know the best career for a woman? I'll tell her: get herself a husband.

[165] He's afraid the police are going to hang something on him. – In that case, I'd say let himself be arrested and then sue for false arrest.

[166] Why can't he support his family? – He doesn't earn enough on this job. – Then get himself another one. I don't see why *we* should be expected to support him.

A final predisposing context is alignment with a *you* imperative. In the following example (Poutsma 1926, 201), it is not necessary for George to be within earshot: *No; you get the paper and pencil and the catalogue, and George write down, and I'll do the work.* The speaker might add, *Go call him, will you, and tell him we need him and what he's supposed to do.*

The examples to this point have all been either what would be obvious as conventional imperatives or are so close that the sharpness of the conventional notion is called into question. For a more comprehensive view of the bare infinitive it is necessary to look at forms that lie clearly outside the realm of imperatives or apparent imperatives, and to ask whether there are nevertheless such fundamental resemblances that the differences can be relegated to intersection with some other system, like what happens when the statement *They've left already* is turned into a question *They've left already?* with only a change of intonation.

The evidence is mostly semantic, with certain distributional ties that can be fairly clearly stated. I start with those.

1 Restrictions on tense are the same as with imperatives. The types *Why not go there myself?* (Poutsma 1926, 436), *How make them understand?*, *Where find anyone more agreeable?* occur freely without *have*, but I find **How have done it sooner?* as difficult as the corresponding command, while the other perfective, *How have it done sooner?*, is possible.

2 Restrictions on statives and non-statives resemble those with imperatives. Thus *John be tall?* is doubtful, but in

[167] Your brother practically insulted me. – John be rude to a friend? That's certainly not like him.

non-stative *be rude* is normal. The omission of the copula is normal with statives: *John sick?*, *An American a traitor?*[20]

3 Omission of the subject is largely optional, as with the imperative:

[168] If old Doc Jones doesn't collect some of those bills, he's going to go bankrupt. – (Old Doc Jones) dun his patients? He wouldn't have the heart.

4 The bare infinitive readily occurs in an answer that refers to something unaccomplished, but not so readily otherwise:

[169] What are you going to do? – Make the most of it.
[170] What did you do? – ?Make the most of it.

The one who asks the question, however, may readily combine these: *What did you do, make the most of it?* – here the matter of accomplishment is still up in the air. The same restriction shows up when the response is someone else's proposed future action (in this case we have the borderline with commands again):

[171] If he won't believe them, what do they do to convince him? (= 'What are they supposed to do?'). – Tell him the truth.
[172] I marvel at their always getting him on their side. Just what *do* they do to convince him? – *Tell him the truth.

I have starred the latter, though it could occur as a truncated finite (*cf: Got home early last night, went to bed, didn't wake till ten*). Again, the person asking the question can include the suggested but unconfirmed answer in his question: *What do they do to convince him, tell him the truth?*

In tag questions, the un-Auxed negative may occur when the action is viewed as unconfirmed, but not otherwise. The intonation of course differs also:

[173] Not $^{\text{sell it did h}^{\text{e}^?}}$ ('He failed to sell it, did he?')

[174] *Not $^{\text{sell}}_{\quad\text{it}\ ^{\text{did}}_{\quad\text{he?}}}$

[175] (He) $^{\text{didn't}\ ^{\text{sell}}}_{\qquad\text{it}\ ^{\text{did}}_{\quad\text{he?}}}$

Not is the usual form taken by the negative with hypothetical bare infinitives. It is diagnostic in another way too, which will be looked at later.

Difficulty of the past and unaccomplishment of the action suggest that bare infinitive forms have a semantic element in common: that of hypotheticalness. This is obvious in the type already cited, *Why wait?, Why not call them up now?, How believe in such a fantastic story?* It is also obvious in the imperative, where lack of accomplishment or confirmation was seen to be the common semantic thread. Other common types are the following:

1 *Turn my father against me – that's what she wants to do.* The action is potential. ** Turn my father against me – that's what she tried to do,* for something past, is ungrammatical.

2 *Come over and visit us this evening. – And leave my husband to fix his own supper? I wouldn't dare.* The hypothetical imperative meshes with a hypothetical consequence with no more sense of a grammatical change than would be felt in combining two finites: *She came over to visit us last evening. – And left her husband to fix his own supper, I daresay.*

3 *It seems to me that you could at least be as generous as your predecessors were. – Oh, sure: make you one concession and find ourselves making you another and another; there would be no end to it.* This is an inference, where the infinitive might be introduced by *you mean, that is to say,* etc.

4 *Buy a few shares of Hayden and Smith. The price is right. – Hmm. Buy Hayden and Smith. Not a bad idea.* The action is something to be mulled over.

5 Poutsma's example (1926, 437), *My nephew marry a tragedy queen!* may refer to something that has already happened, but which the speaker figuratively refuses to accept.

English has one verb, *to suppose,* which makes quite explicit the relationship between hypotheticals in general and commands as hypotheses: it is used for both. First, as equivalent to the hypothetical question *what if?*:

[176] I order you to do this. – Suppose I refuse. – Then I'll just have to make you.

Second, in conditions: *Suppose I show you how; will you do it?* (If *suppose* is replaced by *supposing,* the intonational break is reduced.) Third, in proposing a hypothetical line of action: *Suppose I go in while you wait out here.* Sentences like these can be interpreted more and more in the direction of commands, as in the following gradient:

[177] Suppose you go in while I wait out here.

[178] Suppose you take care of it. Right now.
[179] Suppose you go in and ask him, will you?
[180] Now suppose you just let *me* be the judge of that, please.

As with other requests for commands, when the first person is involved the tagged auxiliary is *shall*:

[181] Suppose I go in and ask him, shall I?
[182] Suppose we both try, shall we?

While *suppose* has been stereotyped in this use (and *imagine, assume,* and probably most other verbs would sound strange) it is not exclusive. The same meaning of hypotheticalness is present in the following: *Let's just say you march down there right now. I'm getting a little tired of waiting.*

The infinitive, in this perspective, is a general hypothetical that includes the imperative as its most frequent manifestation. The action of the imperative is hypothetical – the command may or may not be carried out. The rest of the identification comes from the context. The mandatoriness is from the intonation:

[183] Let $_\text{me}$ $^\text{have}$ $_\text{a}$ $_\text{nick}$ $_\text{el}$.

spoken with the normal straight fall, which distinguishes commands from other utterances (any one of which can be made more or less mandatory by using this intonation), *eg,*

[184] How $_\text{about}$ $_\text{a}$ $_\text{little}$ $_\text{light}$ $_\text{over here ?}$[21]

If spoken with a low-pitched accent, a native speaker of English would probably say 'That's a request, not a command':

[185] Let $_\text{me}$ $^\text{have}$ $_\text{a}$ $_\text{nick}$ $^\text{e}$ $^\text{l}$

and might even hesitate about how to punctuate it, a problem which would be settled in favor of a question mark in

[186] Let me have a $_\text{nick}$ $^\text{e}$ $^\text{l}$ $^\text{?}$

which is closest to Jespersen's (not K-P's) notion of the imperative as a 'will' sentence: *Will you let me have a nickel?* As for the subject, it comes from the speaker-hearer situation, where it is commonplace to omit *you: Smell that soup? Going there tomorrow? Like a chocolate?* Other instances of the bare infinitive also leave the subject to the situation: the persons are reversed in *Why pick on me? I haven't done him any harm* and *Why pick on him? – he hasn't done me any harm;* and *Why do that?* can mean 'Why should you, we, anyone do that?'

By limiting their examples to utterances in which there is no preceding verbal context, K-P and others have unwittingly IMPOSED the only element of context which is left, that of A addressing B – the vocativeness is all there is to fall back on. It is no wonder then that utterances like *Go now, Call mama, Read this book, Hand over all you have,* etc lead to the conclusion that everything of this kind has to have a *you* subject and be directed toward compliance. Under the circumstances, nothing else could be read in. Stripping down syntactic samples to minimal sentences in the hope of excluding everything irrelevant may have the effect of creating a vacuum which unexpected irrelevancies rush in to fill.

The bare infinitives constitute a single system that derives its variety from intersections with other systems. They have a relatively invariant meaning that is variously colored in different contexts; but it is the contexts that differ, not the verbs. If we insist on a special derivation for the imperative mode, consistency would require that we do the same with declaratives when they are used as commands: *Nobody moves until I give the word, and that means you; You don't speak first, he does; First they come in and then you tell them what to do; You sit here and he sits over there; Please, I hope you're not going to insist; It's time for your medicine, dear.* Or with questions: *Do you mind stepping to one side?; Why don't you be more careful?; Would you kindly leave me alone?* A similar case would be the insistence on a vocative element in the imperative where again to be consistent it would be necessary to add a vocative to *Does the master wish to sit here?* addressed to the master.

This is not to say that we should no longer talk about the imperative mode. There must be more instances of the bare infinitive used for commands than there are of all other uses combined; for convenience we should call them imperatives. And there is a slight formal difference that will be taken up in the next chapter.

Notes

1 A fresh look at material which appeared in *To honor Roman Jakobson: essays on the occasion of his seventieth birthday* (The Hague and Paris: Mouton, 1967), 335–62. The new insights have benefited from private correspondence with Celia Millward. The derivations that were the target of Bolinger 1967 were those of Katz-Postal (abbreviated K-P) 1964 and Postal (P) 1964. References to Jespersen, unless otherwise noted, are to 1909–49.

2 K-P make just such a use of an intonational break to star *No do not drive the car (77).

3 Pointed out by Householder.

4 Example thanks to Celia Millward.

5 Generating the imperative *will* from the future *will* turns history around, because the imperative came first. Even today there are constructions referring to the future that fail to get by if 'willingness' is excluded. Compare

> If he dies tomorrow, and I hope he does . . . (*he will)
> If he gets caught, and I hope he does . . . (*he will)
> If the door blows shut, and I hope it does . . . (*it will)
> If the road they're going to build goes uphill, and I hope it does . . . (*it will)

with

> If he comes, and I hope he will (or does) . . .
> If she seems acceptable, and I hope she will (or does) . . .
> If he climbs uphill, and I hope he will (or does) . . .

6 *Cosmopolitan*, Feb 1951 pp 30, 145.

7 Grammatical, of course, as a fragmentary answer to the question *What should we do?*

8 As a reprise, third singular can get by, but then has the support of a parallel sentence fragment. Thus I find

> Sooner or later he's got to stop running. – Give himself up and they'll hang him.

a bit strained, but not

> The only thing for him to do is to give himself up. – Give himself up and they'll hang him.

(I have provided two contexts for an example from Randolph Quirk.) On the other hand, *oneself* is normal: *Make oneself a slave to another person and one loses all self respect.* This – given its formality by contrast with impersonal *you* – suggests that perhaps the conditional ties ought to be with the older *if*-clauses with subjunctive: *If one make oneself a slave* etc. So for Jespersen's example (5.24.3.4) *Give you women but rope enough, you'll do your own business*, we may add *if one*. The factor working to preserve *one* but not *he* nor *she* in these conditions is probably its indefiniteness. The more hypothetical the condition the better it suits conditional 'imperatives'.

9 *On Sunday they (we, I you) go get the paper; *On Sunday he (she) goes get the paper.* This was pointed out by Celia Millward in 1967. It is the subject of Shopen 1971.

10 These restrictions were brought to my attention by George Lakoff.

11 It is necessary to peel off irrelevant examples of *any*. An *any* implying 'that there may be' does not count here. Usually such instances carry modifiers, *eg*, *Just go out and bring in anybody who hasn't already signed up, Make a list of any missing items and the police will help*. Sometimes not: *Let us in on any news* (that there may be). The contrast here is not between an indefinite *any* versus an 'any whatsoever' but between an indefinite *any* and an *any=if any:* 'Let us in on the news, if any.'

12 Not even EMPHATIC *any* will work in an imperative of the first instance: **Hey, George! Call anybody on the telephone!; *Well, Mary, tomorrow your vacation begins – go anywhere!; *I want to relax – tell me any story*. But as second instance, they get by: *I want to hear a story – tell me any story; I just can't make up my mind where to go. – Go anywhere! You're a free man!* In *Joe's OK – ask anybody!* we have a concealed condition: *Ask anybody and he will tell you that Joe's OK*.

13 Some further examples of conditions, with *don't*, appear in Section 2 of the next chapter.

14 The K-P example with *hope* must be bad because of some distractor in the situation, not because *hope* rejects the imperative. Millward points out that while **Hope it rains* is doubtful, *Hope for rain* is normal. The form with finite verb is perhaps too definite – it may imply rain at a particular time and place; *Hope for rain* – rain whenever God in His goodness may send it – makes a better farmer's prayer.

15 The *know* pair was suggested by Millward.

16 K-P seem a bit uncertain of their own criterion, for they admit as grammatical the sentence *I request that you forget the whole matter* in spite of the fact that one can hardly turn the memory off at will.

17 Also as a stressed modal and as a stressed tense. See Gleitman 1965, 287.

18 I refer, of course, to the verba dicendi. The verb *to claim* may report with an infinitive (*He claims to be the heir*) but not with the change of subject that causes no trouble with the imperative (**He claims John to be the heir*).

19 One could argue for a blend with *The poor fellow doesn't know what to do . . . – Make a fresh start. That's the only thing for him to do*, where the infinitive can be regarded as a nominalized predicate: 'What to do (the only thing for him to do) is make a fresh start.' I purposely avoided this wording in the example, and chose *way* rather than *thing* to create one obstacle to the nominalization of the bare infinitive: *way*, unlike *thing* or *what*, requires *to* with the infinitive: *The way for him to put himself in the clear is to make a fresh start*. But it really is not necessary, I think, to lean so far backward in order to find a context that is utterly free of a grammatically enveloping frame. When we consider the following set,

> Would you advise me what to do ? – Try harder.
> Would you advise him what to do ? – Try harder.
> Do you know what happened last night ? – The whole East underwent a power failure.
> Would you explain why he doesn't like it there ? – They don't feed him enough.

If *Try harder* is an embedded construction because it fits into the position of the nominal laid for it by what precedes, then so is *They don't feed him enough (is why)*. Any answer that is directly responsive to an interrogative-word question may be regarded as embedded.

20 Otherwise, for example when the reference is to a state rather than to an event,

omission of the copula is more in the nature of a sentence fragment. In the following exchanges,

> I hear that Henry is staying at a hotel and Georgette has gone home to Mother. – Henry and Georgette mad at each other? Well, I can't say that I'm surprised.

> I predict that those two are going to get on each other's nerves in no time at all. I'll bet that within six months Henry will be staying at a hotel and Georgette will be home with Mother. – Henry and Georgette be mad at each other? You're kidding.

the form without *be* might do for the second but the form with *be* will not do for the first. In the first a fragment like *Henry and Georgette fighting?* would be equally normal. In the second, if the copula is omitted one has the sensation of two strings rather than one: *Henry and Georgette? Mad at each other?*

21 The intonational dependence of commands is illustrated in

$$\text{Your } ^{\text{na}}_{\text{me}} \quad \text{versus} \quad \text{Your } ^{\text{na}}\text{m}^{\text{e}\,?}$$

each responded to in the same way, but the first felt as a command and the second a question ('Tell me your name'; 'What is your name?'). The bare infinitive is not the only thing intersecting with intonation and a predisposing context to make a command. Any contextually appropriate noun, adjective, or adverb, especially with quantitative modifiers, is equally suitable: *Easy now; Not so fast; Faster!; Quiet!; More light down here; No monkey business, now; Harder!; Careful!; Arms front; Head back; Forward!; One side!; Up on top!*

Chapter 9

Imperatives are imperatives and *do* is *do*

Generative treatments of the imperative are almost a case study in the will-to-be-born of the performative – the theory of sometimes explicit and sometimes hidden 'higher sentences' in discourse – and of linguists' eventual appropriation of the idea from philosophers, J. L. Austin in particular. If one takes statements as the basic form of sentences, as generativists originally did, and tries to derive commands and questions from them, it is hard to avoid thinking of *I order that* and *I ask whether* as the added ingredients. Of course statements imply something too, and performative verbs came into their own when *I declare that* took its place beside *I order that* and *I ask whether*. I simplify matters here by showing the evolution in three steps: the first, Katz and Postal, already taken; the second, Stockwell *et al* 1968; and the third, Schreiber 1972, with its full-fledged performative outlook and its use of *do* as a test for true imperatives.[1]

1 The later generative treatments

Katz and Postal themselves suggest (1964, 149) an alternative to their *will* analysis that is more in accord with recent treatments of the imperative: to subordinate it to a 'request' verb (*I* Verb request *that you will* Main Verb). This was to avoid assuming an Imperative morpheme, which becomes unnecessary since *request* supposedly has the same restrictions. Stockwell *et al* 1968 point out the disadvantages of 'request' and opt for the Imperative morpheme, but make it an underlying modal element that is part of the Aux. The Imperative is thus 'built in'. But it did not escape Stockwell *et al* that a subjunctive on the order of *I insist he be ready on time* is suspiciously like an imperative, and they took the step (687) of assigning it the same modal element: *be ready on time* thus became in effect an embedded imperative. This set the stage for reviving the subordination theme. *Request* might have its disadvantages, but it is one of a class that includes *insist, order, command, demand, require*, etc, all embodying a feature that can be etherealized into an 'abstract governing verb' that embodies whatever it is that sets imperatives apart from other sentences. From this standpoint, instead of a subjunctive being an embedded imperative, an imperative is a liberated subjunctive.

Schreiber 1972 adopts *command* and *suggest* as manifestations of the abstract verb, to take care of a supposed difference between 'command' imperatives and 'hortative' imperatives, for example (*You*) *come down from there this instant* versus *Be glad that we are leaving*. He feels that the latter has to be distinguished from a true command because it does not admit *do*: **Do be glad that we are leaving*. (The problem of this *do* is dealt with in Section 3 below.) The two performative verbs – *command* and *suggest* – are further distinguished by the sentence adverbs – 'style disjuncts' as Greenbaum 1969 calls them – that attach to *suggest* and remain when it is deleted, but not to *command:*

[1] Frankly, (I suggest that you) be glad that we are leaving.
[2] *Frankly, (I command that you) come down from there this instant.

The trouble with this analysis is that it overlooks the function of the style disjuncts as a class, which is transitional. Their origin as modifiers of performative verbs is irrelevant to this except to the extent that the performatives are themselves transitional. A master carpenter arrives to inspect the work of an apprentice. Without preamble, he says, *Hand me that tape*. As an utterance that launches a communication between two speakers, this imperative carries no adverb modifiers. It would be absurd to introduce it with a *frankly* when there was no previous groundwork for a potential *unfrankly*, and so with *honestly, incidentally, personally*, or any of the others listed in Greenbaum (1969, 92). On the other hand, the example with *suggest* – *Be glad that we are leaving* – by its nature comes after a discourse has been initiated, and *frankly* is normal. One could not come on the scene and say out of the blue, *Be glad that we are leaving*. This calls for previous discussion, assessment, or whatever. By contrast, the irate mother who orders her child out of the tree with *Come down from there this instant* is unlikely to have debated the matter either with the child or in her own mind (and if she has, *frankly* would put the debate on the wrong footing – some other illocutionary modifier such as *now you listen to me* would be more to the point).

What the distinction boils down to then is not suggestions versus commands, but initiation (and a concomitant abruptness, where commands are concerned) versus continuation. It is not difficult to rig imperatives that are pretty clearly commands even though they carry a style disjunct, if a proper basis is laid. In the following, the discourse has already been initiated before the command is uttered:

[3] How can I keep the peace with you? – Frankly, stay out of my way.
[4] OK, you've had your fun. Seriously, now, get back on the job; I need those estimates this afternoon.
[5] What are your orders, sir? – Bluntly, bring those bastards in so I can book them.

What needs to be kept in mind is the relationship between two speakers when one presumes to issue an order to the other. Abrupt orders are the exception. Yet an order that initiates a discourse is almost by definition abrupt, because the amenities generally call for a question in that position: *May I pass, please? Would you give me your autograph? Do you mind leaning aside a moment so I can see?* As a discourse builds up, orders seem less peremptory, and by the same token an interior location makes a transitional element more likely. It is in the nature of communication that the longer a given conversational contact is maintained the less abrasive the language seems – and the more like a 'suggestion' rather than a 'command' an order will sound (in any case just a change in intonation will make the difference) – but this is a pragmatic fact, not a grammatical one.

If the *do* test and the *suggest-command* test with style disjuncts really jibed to give us a dependable clue to more than one class of imperative, we would have to wonder why in two such sentences as

[6] Do leave tobacco alone, old pal.
[7] Frankly, leave tobacco alone, old pal.

the supposed contrast is actually reversed – the second sounds more peremptory, more command-like, than the first.

Besides the general transitional nature of the style disjuncts, there are the individual meanings of the words themselves. *Not frankly, be glad that we are leaving* is cited as proof that style disjuncts cannot be phrasally negated in hortative imperatives (Schreiber 1972, 343), and this is seen as further corroboration that they are a distinct class. But the situation in which *Be glad that we are leaving* would be uttered is one that requires frankness. The speaker is suggesting that his hearer do something that is socially unacceptable – be openly glad to see his interlocutor gone. Style disjuncts as a class are not excluded. We can use them after *suggest*, or in a corresponding imperative, if we choose the ones that make sense:

[8] How do you think I shóuld feel about your departure? – (I suggest,) not indelicately or presumptuously, (that you) be glád that we're leaving.

And if we can break out of the straightjacket of the *Be glad that we're leaving* example, many possibilities open up:

[9] How am I to convince the public that I am being fair about this? – Not immodestly, give me a share of the credit and, not unflatteringly, take some of it yourself.

(On the argument that only suggestions will take style disjuncts, this would have to be a suggestion. But again I would say that the distinction is pointless.)

The nature of performative modifiers needs to be investigated more thoroughly before any conclusions can be drawn about the moods that their verbs govern. One unsettled question is the extent to which they ARE modifiers of a higher verb. I have pointed out elsewhere (Bolinger 1972*b*, 94–8) the tendency of the truth modifiers to incorporate themselves in the lower sentence as intensifiers. The classic case is *very*, whose chronological steps can be matched by *truly* in its uses today:

[10] Truly (=I say truly) the work is magnificent.
[11] The work (I say) truly is magnificent.
[12] The work is (?I say) truly magnificent.

But it is not necessary for an adverb to penetrate the inner structure in order to change roles. Some erstwhile modifiers of higher verbs have become intensifiers of the lower sentence as a whole. For all communicative purposes, *in God's name* and *for Christ's sake* are virtual equivalents, yet literally the first can modify only the higher verb (*I ask it in God's name*) whereas the second can be understood either way. There are difficulties even when the modifier is not a fossil. Performative verbs would not be lost so regularly if the adverbs they control did not come partially unstuck, to adhere to the lower sentence. Their advantage is that they CAN face both ways – such Janus-like elements we have already seen in Chapter 6. Take a sentence like *As a favor to me, be careful*. With the adverb construed as a modifier of the higher verb, this is a request:

[13] As a favor to me I ask you to be careful.
[14] ?As a favor to me I order you to be careful.

One does not command a favor. But with the adverb modifying the lower verb, the command interpretation gets by: *I order you to be careful as a favor to me.* The problem does not arise if we do not insist on a dichotomy between commands and requests, commands and suggestions, or commands and any other suasive use of the imperative.

Another problem that does not have to be explained away is the conjoining of different suasive main verbs governing a single subjunctive: *Are you demanding that I be fired? – Not necessarily. I demand, entreat, advise, suggest, or only hint that you be fired. Take your pick, and I hope your boss gets the idea.* If the modal force of the subordinate verb only copies that of the performative, how many things does *be fired* have to be at once? There is nothing to prevent a speaker from EXPLICITLY straddling a command and a suggestion: *As gently as I can put it, which I am afraid is still going to seem as much like an order as like a suggestion, be more tactful in dealing with your subordinates; I can't afford this kind of discord in any of my departments.*

For those who cannot live without a performative verb to make imperatives hang together, I suggest one that is virtually coextensive with the meaning of suasion: the verb *to bid*. It is noncommittal as between commands, requests, suggestions, etc, yet not so broad that it covers declaratives (this is the trouble with *say* and *tell*):

[15] He courteously bade me take a seat. (suggestion)
[16] She entreatingly bade them come in. (request)
[17] They rudely bade me be off. (command)

Bid has other advantages. It is like the older use of *pray*, which we know to have produced imperatives after it became fossilized: *I pray thee go* became *Prithee go*. The infinitive is already there, unencumbered even with *to* – a simple deletion of *I bid you* from *I bid you be quiet* yields *Be quiet.* If the verb *bid* itself is a semantic unit, then so may the imperative be. I propose this as an improvement on the proliferation of subclasses, but I do not advocate it, because I prefer the more comprehensive view of the imperative-as-infinitive.

Returning to the modal notion that was popular before performatives caught on, we might extract some marrow from an oddity in the distribution of *shall*, which is, first, the auxiliary that is used in calling for a command, and, second, is the only auxiliary that is not repeatable in the same sense in which it appears in the question:

[18] Shall I let him in? – Yes, do *or* Yes, let him in (not *Yes, you shall).

[19] Shall we go now? – Yes, let's (not *Yes, we shall).

[20] Shall they report at the same time tomorrow? – Yes, have them report then (not *Yes, they shall report etc).

Contrast these with the readiness with which other auxiliaries are repeated in the same sense:

[21] Must I do it? – Yes, you must.

[22] Could it happen here? – Yes, it could.

[23] Mightn't it be better to ask first? – Yes, I guess it might.

(*Might* is irregular in this respect. In diffident requests, it is not repeatable: *Might I have a look? – *Yes, you might.* But this can be taken care of by saying that what is not repeated is the diffident use of the past tense. The interlocutor replies with the 'same' verb, *may.* The same is true, though less strictly so, of *could-can. Need* is marginal as an auxiliary: *Need I say more? Do I need to say more? – Yes, you do, *Yes, you need.*) This at least is true of American English as I know it, and suggests that *shall* rather than *will* is the auxiliary that belongs to the imperative. So perhaps the imperative could take off from *You shall do it → Do it.* But there is a difficulty here in that *shall* sentences in the same dialects that use *shall* in the way I have described limit it to commands exerted on transcendent powers, not on the hearer. If I say *You shall have it* the *shall* is epistemic: It shall be that you have it – no outward circumstance will prevent you from having it. *You shall go there tomorrow* would not be used at all unless the person spoken to had expressed a wish to go.

Nevertheless, for the game of transformational derivations, *shall* looks more promising than *will.* There are dialects in which *You shall confess* is a command, whereas *You will confess* is a prediction.

It is valuable to point out these resemblances among structures, but 'deriving' one from another, generatively, is another matter. A spurious chopping of many essentially unitary phenomena is only one of the undesirable results, and comes about automatically from the paraphrase relationship that has to be assumed: x comes from y, but there are 'apparent' instances of x that do not mean the same as y, so we have to seek a z to derive them from. If we are diligent we are bound to find it, and since y and z are obviously different, and x has been identified with each, there must therefore be an x_1 and an x_2. The machinery is geared to multiply illusions.

2 The imperative differentiated from the infinitive

Where the imperative and the hypothetical bare infinitive diverge somewhat is in the use of *do*.

In the negative this divergence can be seen in the separation between *don't* and *not*, the latter being normal with the hypotheticals: *You are not to see him again. – Not see him again? That would be unbearable.* (The sentence fragment *Not to see him again?* would be equally normal here, which is evidence, of sorts, that *Not see him again?* is not a fragment.) Whereas a *don't* can be parroted (for example, after *Don't ask questions* either *Don't ask questions? – that would be contrary to my nature* or *Not ask questions? – that would be contrary to my nature* is appropriate), *don't* may otherwise be doubtful: *Stay home. – Hmm. Not take my usual walk; I don't like that idea* (?*Hmm. Don't take my usual walk*, etc.) The negative imperative, of course, is with *don't*.

Actually the asymmetry in the negative is no more a disadvantage in coupling the imperative with the bare infinitive than in basing it on a performative, for the same problem is found in the latter as well. The English subjunctive is in such a state of collapse that this does not show up consistently, but it is present to a large degree in some dialects and probably to a slight degree in most. The best performative verb to use as illustration is *insist*, in third person singular (I realize that in some dialects [25], [27], and [29] are ambiguous):

[24] I insist that he take the medicine. ('He must take the medicine.')
[25] I insist that he takes the medicine. ('I know that he does.')
[26] I insist that he do take the medicine. (emphatic order)
[27] I insist that he does take the medicine. (emphatic statement)
[28] I insist that he not take the medicine. ('He must not take it.')
[29] I insist that he doesn't take the medicine. ('I know that he doesn't.')
[30] I insist that he do not take the medicine. (emphatic order)
[31] *I insist that he don't take the medicine. (a victory for the puristic battle against *he don't*, which has engaged this construction even though irrelevant to it)

Example [28] shows the traditional negative with a subjunctive, exactly the same as with the bare infinitive. In order to get a negative imperative out of it transformationally, the same change is required as to get it from the infinitive. Of course, other performative verbs have dropped the bars to some extent, just as we have seen *don't* spread in the bare infinitive form to situations where *not* formerly prevailed. So *I request that you not do it* sounds a bit formal nowadays beside *I request that you don't do it*. Two things facilitate the step here and not with *insist*. First, request is a bit more obviously quotative: *I request, 'Don't do it.'* Second, *request* can use *don't* without ambiguity, but *insist* cannot (*I insist that they don't do it* may report an act rather than call for one). But with third person singular, *request* runs into trouble too: *I request that he not do it*, too formal; *I request that he doesn't do it*, too obviously indicative; *I request that he don't do it*, in difficulties with *he don't* taboo. *I request that he do not do it* (*read it*, etc) would probably get by as an extremely standoffish utterance.

That *don't* is confusing the situation by gaining ground at the expense of *not* seems fairly obvious. If there is the slightest possibility of viewing a negative hypothetical in a way that would justify *don't*, we tend to use it. I find *What should they do? – Not write that letter* uncomfortably formal; I prefer *Don't write that letter*. There is enough suggestion of a command for it to get by. Similarly in *Please tell him what to do to avoid those emotional upsets. – Just don't (just not) work himself into a lather every time someone criticizes him a bit* – here there is a hint of indirect discourse (*Tell him 'Just don't work yourself . . .'*). The extension of *don't* at the expense of *not* is clearest in the substitution, in some dialects, of *don't let's* for *let's not*.

Don't has another point of infiltration via 'imperative' conditions. We saw some evidence of the possible aphetic origin of these in the last chapter. *Don't* corroborates it. In all conditions where negative *don't* would accord with the number and person of the deleted subject, I find it more or less acceptable:

[32] ([If] I) don't work, (and) I don't get paid.
[33] ([If] they) don't fire him, (and) they won't have to pay him.
[34] ([If] we) don't hang onto our jobs, (and) how do we eat?[2]
[35] ([If] you) don't keep up appearances, (and) it's hard to get ahead.

But not in third singular: *([If] she) doesn't work, (and) she doesn't get paid*. Even with *don't* it is no good: *Don't work, and she doesn't get paid*, and removing the apparent conflict between *don't* and *doesn't* does not help: *Don't work and she won't get paid*. It seems clear that the *don't* in these sentences is from a finite, not from a hypothetical. The latter normally calls for *not*, and is ungrammatical in conditions: *Not work and you don't get paid*. Nevertheless, the more the condition resembles a command, the more acceptable *don't* is in third singular. Thus in *Don't take more than her share, and she'll be OK* the condition is not a gnomic generalization but refers, at least potentially, to a single act of refraining from taking more than her share, and as such is something that can be commanded. Similarly

Don't let herself be fooled, and she won't have to suffer the consequences.[3] The verb *let* has such strong ties with commands that an otherwise unacceptable third singular seems to be able to ride in on it: *Don't ever let anyone help her, and how can she get along?*[4]

So *don't* is spreading to conditions on the strength of imperatives. What is the situation with *do*? In various ways it still seems to be specific to imperatives, and deserves a section to itself.

3 *Do* imperatives

Do with imperatives is characterized by what we think of as most typical of the imperative mood: (1) a *you* subject that is (2) unexpressed. The first condition I think is almost absolute. Whereas *Don't say a word, anybody* or *Don't anybody say a word* is normal, *?Do speak up somebody* would hardly be heard except as a plea of desperation, and **Do somebody speak up* is impossible. Only second person reflexives can appear: *Do help yourself (*himself) somebody, and let's get started.* A third person may appear, of course, if construed with a second person, as in *Do come over, any of you, next time you're here.* The second condition may be violated, as the last example shows, when the subject is postposed. The cases of *do you* cited by Jespersen (3.11.8.43) are no longer current. The difficulty with an explicit *you* is that *do*, as we have seen, has tended to become a courtesy device – it is used to cajole – whereas the explicit *you* has the opposite effect. To combine them we require a contrastively affirmative *do*, and probably also an epithet in apposition to *you*: *All right, then, dó say it, you idiot.* Altogether, *do* thus turns out to be more explicitly imperative in the conventional sense than is *don't*, and this shows up in one other way. *Do* cannot even be parroted: *Do bring your sister, I so want to see her. – Bring my sister?* If possible at all, **Do bring my sister?* would be understood to repeat words more than it repeats meaning: 'Is that the way you put your remark?'

As for hypotheticals and conditions, the first are avoided with *do* and the second are unusual with it – in *Do come tomorrow, and you'll see our new house* the union of the two clauses is forced; the second is an afterthought, and much less like the result clause of a conditional sentence than the one in *Come tomorrow and you'll see our new house*, whose first clause may be a command as well as a condition.

The fact that *do* apparently occurs only with true imperatives led Schreiber 1972 (339–40) to assume that it occurs only with command imperatives (not with anything weaker, such as suggestions), and to propose his *do* test – referred to above, *p* 184 – for true commands:

[36] Be careful.
[37] *Be glad.
[38] Be glad that we are leaving.
[39] Do be careful.
[40] *Do be glad.
[41] *Do be glad that we are leaving.

The reasoning is that since being careful is equivalent to taking precautions, *ie*, is something that can be carried out, it can be commanded, whereas being glad is not subject to control, therefore cannot be commanded. *Do* somehow attaches itself to the former. (We recall that [38] was acceptable because it was supposedly a suggestion rather than a command.)

If *do* is unable to attach at will to imperatives, the limitation must be motivated. I suggest that the motivation is semantic, and that the best way to understand it is to examine the circumstances in which *do* imperatives occur, in the light of what we know about the meaning of *do*. Specifically, *do* is a carrier of emphatic affirmation, and will not be used in contexts which are incompatible with that meaning.

This can be seen most strikingly in situations where *do* imperatives would not be used, even though otherwise they might be normal with the same verbs. If someone knocks on your door and you answer, you may greet him with *Come in* but not with *Do come in;* the latter is normal only after a period – brief or long – of not coming in. If someone enters the room you do not say to him immediately, *Do sit down;* that would come after a moment, or moments, of standing around; *Sit down* is not so restricted. This is predictable from the meaning of affirmation: there is a prior negative on which to base a contrastive affirmative. In Curme's example (1931, 432) the negative is explicit:

[42] Give me a penny, Papa! – I have nothing for you. – Do give me just one penny!

If this analysis is correct, then it should be possible, by building a negative into the situation, to use *do* even with verbs that supposedly forbid it. It is not difficult to find such contexts:

[43] I don't care whether you are successful or not, but do be happy; that is the most important thing in life.

[44] It's all right if you hate each other fundamentally, but do reach an agreement.

[45] I know it's hard for you to be grateful, but do at least be glad that she didn't ask for alimony.

[46] All right, *do* be glad about it! It suits your character.

Do may be used similarly for apostrophizing:

[47] Be indifferent, be stupid, be arrogant. None of these things matter. But do be the man for the job!

The corresponding ordinary commands are unusual:

[48] ?Reach an agreement.
[49] ?Be the man for the job.

The presupposed negative is evident elsewhere in more subtle ways.

1 *Do* is not used with successive actions unless they can be viewed as a unit:

[50] Do bring your friends over here and sit down.
[51] *Do show him the way and come back.
[52] Do go downstairs and fetch them up.
[53] *Do read awhile and then go to bed.

2 *Do* is not used with certain quantitative expressions unless they are made definite:

[54] Eat six cream pies.
[55] *Do eat six cream pies.
[56] Do eat those six cream pies.
[57] Stay two hours.
[58] *Do stay two hours.
[59] Do stay the two hours you promised.
[60] Buy one house.
[61] *Do buy one house.

There is no problem if the quantities are explicitly indefinite:

[62] Do eat a few cream pies.
[63] Do stay a couple of hours.
[64] Do buy a house.

3 Other similar precise expressions are likewise excluded:

[65] Do leave for Chicago on time.
[66] *Do leave for Chicago at 6.15.

but not if some prior basis is established:

[67] Do leave for Chicago at 6.15 in the future.

4 A comparative may make an otherwise doubtful expression acceptable:

[68] ?Do be happy that she is here.
[69] Do be happier that she is here than you were last time.
[70] *Do eat three bagels.
[71] Do eat more than three bagels.
[72] ?Do be confident of success.
[73] Do be a little less confident of success.

Similarly with *at least*:

[74] Remember that I'm here to help you.
[75] ?Do remember that I'm here to help you.
[76] Do at least remember that I'm here to help you.
[77] Own some property. (That's the way to be respected.)
[78] *Do own some property.
[79] Do at least own some property. (That's the only way to be re-
      spected.)

5 *Do* is not used if the time is unlimited. This is most obvious in the
contrast between two such synonyms as *happy* and *cheerful*, which are
lexically unlimited and limited respectively.[5] But the same effect may
be observed when an adverbial modifier renders the time limited or
unlimited:

[80] Be happy.
[81] ?Do be happy.
[82] Be cheerful.
[83] Do be cheerful.
[84] Do be happy just this once!
[85] Be careful.
[86] Do be careful.
[87] Be careful all the time.
[88] *Do be careful all the time.[6]

All these have one thing in common: *do* is acceptable when the circumstances allow for a prior stage of non-doing.[7] In *Do bring your friends over
here and sit down* the person spoken to has been neglecting to perform a
normal social office; in *Do show him the way and come back* the command
would have to refer to something not yet on the boards. The same is true

of specific quantities, except that when an anaphoric element such as *that* is added, the possibility of not having previously performed the action is realized; similarly with indefinite quantities – *Do eat a few cream pies* is based on there not having been any eaten. Leaving for Chicago at a precise time is all right if *in the future* is added because the reference then is to what has not been done in the past. Comparatives are by definition based on prior states that were more or less. *At least* refers to a previous failure to carry out something. An 'all the time' does not allow for a previous opposite state.

If there are actions that cannot be commanded but which can use *do* under the right conditions, there are also actions that can be commanded but can't use *do* if conditions are wrong:

[89] Say that you did it.
[90] *Do say that you did it.
[91] Say that you will.
[92] Do say that you will!
[93] Accuse Mary.
[94] *Do accuse Mary.
[95] Don't accuse John, but do accuse Mary.

These again illustrate the prior basis. *Do say that you will!* presupposes a previous coaxing that has brought negative results. If *Do say that you did it* is said with a coaxing (terminal rise) rather than a demanding (terminal fall) intonation, thus implying a previous state of affairs, then it becomes acceptable. Other examples that I have starred or queried, even those with specific quantities, likewise become acceptable if one can manage to conceive of a prior negation; for example, *Do stay two hours* is acceptable if there has been a previous discussion of staying two hours.

The affirmative use of *do* is clearer in constructions with *let's*. They resemble ordinary commands in *Do let's go over to Jane's*, where the previous non-doing is rather vague; but in *Shall we go over to Jane's? – Let's do!* the *do* is an explicit affirmative in contrast with *Let's not*, adding emphasis to the already weakly affirmative *Let's*. On *do let's* it is also worth citing *Do let's be happy*, *Do let's be glad of it*, etc.

Finally, the affirmative use reveals itself in what would be a paradox if we adopted the *do* test for commands. It ought to be easier to embed *do* after *command* than after *suggest*, but the reverse is true:

[96] I suggest that you do try to be more helpful.
[97] *I command that you do try to be more helpful.

If, as I have argued, suggestions tend to be midway in discourse, then the groundwork for an affirmative can easily be laid: *I suggest that you do try* comes after previous mention of trying and not trying.

Actually the second of the last two examples is not ungrammatical. It only hits us wrong because we tend to think first of *do* with a cajoling intonation – it has become a formula of courtesy. By making *do* contrastively affirmative we can use it after *command* and in peremptory imperatives. In the first example below, the other person has been disputatious, and his negative is being vigorously dealt with. The second example is what Millward calls the imperative of exasperated resignation.

[98] I command that you do try to be more helpful.

[99] All right then. Do tell them. See if I care.

Trying to distinguish command imperatives from other imperatives is a vain attempt to catch metaphors in the bag of grammar. It is true that one cannot command a person to be happy if he has no control over whether he is happy or not; but there is no harm in pretending. *Be happy* is not a literal command; but then neither is *If I lose, I'll eat my hat* a literal promise. The important thing is that *do* has a meaning, from which certain aspects of syntax can be predicted, and not the reverse.

Accepting this frees us to regard *do* in the same light as *please*. Both had their origins as independent verbs (see Jespersen 5.24.2.2-3), but nowadays are verbal fossils. *Do, please, just, now* (*Eat it, now!*, with a fall-rise on *now*) and other such appendages to the infinitive tell us how to view it but are not necessarily any proof of the grammatical independence of the imperative.

4 Conclusion

If attempts to split imperatives in two or more classes consistently fail, then it is reasonable to suppose that they are headed in the wrong direction. Instead of looking for smaller classes we ought to look for a larger one, of which imperatives are a part. I have maintained that the bare infinitive constitutes that inclusive class, with only a shade of a tendency (illustrated by *don't* versus *not*) for imperatives to specialize themselves out of it. When we have something that is identical to the bare infinitive in form (even in the verb *to be*), and shares its meaning of hypothetical action, it makes sense to believe that it is the bare infinitive – and that what differences there are should be put down to variables within discourse. The imperativeness of *Give me your wallet*, spoken as a request in

[100] Give $_{\text{me}}$ $_{\text{your}}$ $\quad$ let.
$\qquad\qquad\quad$ $_{\text{wal}}$

and as a command in

[101] Give $_{\text{me}}$ $_{\text{your}}$ $_{\text{wal}}$
$\qquad\qquad\qquad\qquad\quad$ $_{\text{let.}}$

depends on the intent of the speaker. That the infinitive should take over for the imperative is nothing unusual – it happens in other languages too (for French, see Luker 1916).

I offer one last example of the overlap between infinitives and imperatives, and between *you* imperatives and third-person imperatives:

[102] I can't make my rototiller work any more. – Get a new one, why don't you?

[103] They can't make their rototiller work any more. – Get a new one, why don't they?

The most usual intonations are the ones that imperatives share with questions, which are imperative in their own special way:

$\qquad\qquad$ new

[104] Get ^{a}
$\qquad\qquad$ one, why don't you?

[105] Get $_{\text{a}}$ $_{\text{n}}$
$\qquad\qquad$ $_{\text{e}}$ $_{\text{w}}$
$\qquad\qquad\quad$ one, why don't you?

We sense *Get a new one* as an imperative, yet *why don't you?* is no ordinary tag. This is an inversion of *Why don't you get a new one?*, in which *get* has to be analysed as an infinitive.

Why can't you? and *why shouldn't you?* yield the same results. Even more than *why don't you?*, *why shouldn't you?* reveals how imperativeness is added by exposing the infinitive:

[106] Get a new one, why shouldn't you?

implies 'Get a new one, and nobody has a right to object' – it would be appropriate to add *Go on! Don't let somebody else boss you around!* The uninverted *Why shouldn't you get a new one?* has very little of the imperative about it.

As for the difference between *you* and *they*, it would be odd to insist that *Get a new one, why don't you?* and *Get a new one, why don't they?* are two different constructions.

The infinitive is not the whole answer, because there are still conditions which have to be based on finites. But the influence of the similarity of form is evident even there, in the shared restrictions and the difficulty of telling many imperatives and conditions apart. As Anttila has repeatedly emphasized, one of the overriding tendencies in language is that of 'one meaning, one form'. It makes a good principle to carry as far as one can. With the imperative there is ample reason for doing so.

Notes

1 By 1969 a more sophisticated generative treatment of the imperative had appeared in Stockwell *et al* 1968, 659–97 (the anachronism is due to some peculiarity in the publication schedule of the Stockwell volumes), which asserted that whatever the similarities among commands, requests, hortatives, and the like might be, it was necessary to 'recognize the syntactically distinct class of imperatives' (661), and which drew imperatives and command subjunctives into the same net (*I order that you do it*), thus paving the way for the performative analyses that came along shortly after. For the latter I have taken Schreiber 1972, especially for his discussion of *do* and performative adverbs. An earlier version appeared in *Journal of English Linguistics* 8 (1974) 1–5.
2 This does not have to be inclusive *we*.
3 Compare

Never take more than her share, and she'll be OK.
?Never take more than her share, and she can't make ends meet.

The first is potentially a command. The acceptability of the first and the doubtfulness of the second shows up even more clearly if *never* is replaced by *don't ever*.
4 Similarly with *one*, which we saw earlier was passable where *he* and *she* were not. In the negative, *one* has more trouble getting by except with *let*. I find affirmative

Deny oneself the help of others, and how can one get along? better than negative *?Don't allow oneself the help of others, and how can one get along?* or *?Don't permit oneself to be helped*, etc, but not better than a negative with *let*: *Don't let oneself be helped by others, and how can one get along?*

5 Compare Spanish *Está alegre* 'He is cheerful' and *Es feliz* 'He is happy', with change of verb.

6 As for the examples *Be glad* and *Do be glad*, they are really not relevant because *glad* is semantically incomplete. We no more say *Be glad* than we say *John doesn't look very glad today*. People are only glad about something.

7 The sentence *Do be happy unless you have a real reason for feeling sad* has been proposed as a counter-example. This assumes that *unless* is negative, but as Geis 1973 demonstrates, *unless* is positive, as can be seen using *some* and *any*:

If you don't have any objection, I'll wait.
*Unless you have any objection, I'll wait.
Unless you have some objection, I'll wait.

When *if not* replaces *unless*, *do be happy* becomes acceptable: *If you don't have a real reason for feeling sad, then do be happy.*

Geis deals effectively with another case of false identity. *Unless* and *if not* are not the same in meaning.

References

ANTHONY, MICHAEL. 'Some remarks on *any*'. *Forum Linguisticum* (forthcoming)

ATKINSON, JAMES C. 1973. *The two forms of subject inversion in Modern French*. The Hague: Mouton

BAILEY, C.-J. N. 1969. 'A further example of the manner in which a negative enhances acceptability'. Working Papers in Linguistics (University of Hawaii) 11. 177–8

BARTLETT, J. R. 1848, *Dictionary of Americanisms*. New York: Bartlett and Welford

BOLINGER, DWIGHT. 1961. 'Syntactic blends and other matters'. *Language* 37. 366–81

1967. 'Adjectives in English: attribution and predication'. *Lingua* 18. 1–34

1968a. 'Entailment and the meaning of structures'. *Glossa* 2.119–27

1968b. 'Postposed main phrases: an English rule for the Romance subjunctive'. *Canadian Journal of Linguistics* 14.3–30

1971a. 'Semantic overloading: a restudy of the verb *remind*'. *Language* 47.522–47

1971b. *The phrasal verb in English*. Cambridge, Mass: Harvard

1972a. *That's that*. The Hague: Mouton

1972b. *Degree words*. The Hague: Mouton

1973. 'Objective and subjective: sentences without performatives'. *Linguistic Inquiry* 4.414–17

1974. 'Concept and percept: two infinitive constructions and their vicissitudes'. *World papers in phonetics: Festschrift for Dr Onishi's Kiju*, 65–91. Tokyo: Phonetic Society of Japan

1975. 'On the passive in English'. A. and V. Makkai (eds), *The first Lacus forum, 1974*, 57–80. Columbia, SC: Hornbeam

1976. 'The in-group: *one* and its compounds'. Peter A. Reich (ed), *The second Lacus forum, 1975*, 229–37. Columbia, SC: Hornbeam

1977? 'A semantic view of syntax: some verbs that govern infinitives'. Edgar C. Polomé *et al* (eds), *Festschrift for Archibald A. Hill*. The Hague: Mouton

BREIVIK, LEIV EGIL. 1975. 'The use and non-use of existential *there* in present-day English'. *Forum Linguisticum* 7.57–103

1976. 'A note on the genesis of existential *there*'. Unpublished paper

BRESNAN, JOAN. 1970. 'An argument against pronominalization'. *Linguistic Inquiry* 1.122–3

BROWN, GOOLD. 1884. *A grammar of English grammars*. New York: William Wood

BULL, WILLIAM. 1943. 'Related functions of *haber* and *estar*'. *Modern Language Journal* 27.119–23

CHAFE, WALLACE L. 1970. *Meaning and the structure of language*. Chicago: University of Chicago Press

CHARNLEY, M. BERTENS. 1973 'Formative *there*'. Unpublished paper

CURME, GEORGE O. 1931. *A grammar of the English language*. Vol III, *Syntax*. Boston: Heath

DINGWALL, WILLIAM O. 1971. 'On so-called anaphoric *to* and the theory of anaphora in general'. *Journal of English Linguistics* 5.49–77

EPSTEIN, SAMUEL. 1975. 'A pragmatic account of the "Negative Transportation" phenomenon'. Paper at Linguistic Society of America, Dec

FIRTH, J. R. 1964. *The tongues of men* and *Speech*. (2 vols in one). London: Oxford University Press

FRIES, CHARLES C. 1952. *The structure of English*. New York: Harcourt Brace Jovanovich; London: Longman

GEIS, MICHAEL. 1973. '*If* and *unless*'. Braj B. Kachru *et al* (eds), *Issues in Linguistics: papers in honor of Henry and Renée Kahane*, 231–53. Urbana, Ill: University of Illinois Press

GIVÓN, TALMY. 1976. 'On the VS word-order in Israeli: pragmatics and typological change'. P. Cole (ed), *Studies in Modern Hebrew syntax and semantics*, 153–82. New York: North Holland

GLEITMAN, LILA R. 1965. 'Coordinating conjunctions in English'. *Language* 41.260–93

GREENBAUM, SIDNEY. 1969. *Studies in English adverbial usage*. London: Longman

HAAS, WILLIAM. 1975. 'Syntax and semantics of ordinary language'. Aristotelian Society Supplementary Volume 49, 147–69

HETZRON, ROBERT. 1971. 'Presentative function and presentative movement'. *Studies in African Linguistics*, Supplement 2, Oct, 79–105

1975. 'The presentative movement, or why the ideal word order is VSOP'. Charles N. Li (ed), *Word order and word order change*. Austin: University of Texas Press

HORN, LAWRENCE R. 1974. 'N[egative] R[aising]'. Unpublished paper, Stanford University Project in Language Universals

JESPERSEN, OTTO. 1909–49. *A modern English grammar on historical principles*. London: Allen and Unwin

1933. *Essentials of English grammar*. London: Allen and Unwin

KATZ, JERROLD J. AND PAUL POSTAL. 1964. *Integrated theory of linguistic descriptions*. (Research monograph 26). Cambridge, Mass: MIT Press

KEMPSON, RUTH AND RANDOLPH QUIRK. 1971. 'Controlled activation of latent contrast'. *Language* 47.548–72

KRUISINGA, E. 1931. *A handbook of present-day English*. 5th edn. Part 2, Vol 1. Groningen: Noordhoff

AND P. ERADES. 1953. *An English grammar*. 8th edn. Vol 1, *Accidence and Syntax*, first part. Groningen: Noordhoff

KUNO, SUSUMU. 1971. 'The position of locatives in existential sentences'. *Linguistic Inquiry* 11.334–78

LABOV, WILLIAM. 1972. 'Negative attraction and negative concord in English grammar'. *Language* 48.773–818

LAKOFF, ROBIN. 1969. 'Some reasons why there can't be any *some-any* rule'. *Language* 45.608–15

LANGACKER, RONALD AND PAMELA MUNRO. 1975. 'Passives and their meaning'. *Language* 51.789–830

LEES, ROBERT B. 1960*a*. 'Review of Bolinger, *Interrogative structures of American English*'. *Word* 16.119–25

    1960*b*. 'A multiply ambiguous adjectival construction in English'. *Language* 36.207–21

LONG, RALPH B. 1968. Expletive *there* and the *there* transformation. *Journal of English Linguistics* 2.12–22

    AND DOROTHY LONG. 1971. *The system of English grammar*. Glenview, Ill: Scott, Foresman

LUKER, BENJAMIN F. 1916. *The use of the infinitive instead of a finite verb in French*. New York: Columbia University Press

MCCAWLEY, JAMES D. 1969. 'Tense and time reference in English'. Unpublished paper

MIHAILOVIĆ, LJILJANA. 1967. 'Passive and pseudo-passive verbal groups in English'. *English Studies* 48.316–26

PALMER, F. R. 1965. *A linguistic study of the English verb*. London: Longman

POLDAUF, IVAN. 1964. 'Some points on negation in colloquial English'. J. Vachek (ed), *A Prague School reader in linguistics*. Bloomington, Ind: Indiana University Press

POSTAL, PAUL. 1964. 'Underlying and superficial linguistic structures'. *Harvard Educational Review* 34.246–66

    1970. 'On the surface verb *remind*'. *Linguistic Inquiry* 1.37–120

POUTSMA, H. 1916. *A grammar of late Modern English*. Part 2, The parts of speech, sec. 1B. Groningen: Noordhoff

    1926. *Ibid*, sec. 2. Groningen: Noordhoff

QUINE, WILLARD V. 1941. *Elementary logic*. Boston: Ginn

QUIRK, RANDOLPH, SIDNEY GREENBAUM, GEOFFREY LEECH, JAN SVARTVIK. 1972. *A grammar of contemporary English*. London: Longman; New York: Seminar Press

QUIRK, RANDOLPH AND SIDNEY GREENBAUM. 1973. *A university grammar of English*. London: Longman; (as *A concise grammar of contemporary English*) New York: Harcourt Brace Jovanovich

SCHREIBER, PETER A. 1972. 'Style disjuncts and the performative analysis'. *Linguistic Inquiry* 3.321–47

SCHWARTZ, ARTHUR. 1972. 'Constraints on movement transformations'. *Journal of Linguistics* 8.35–85

SHOPEN, TIMOTHY. 1971. 'Caught in the act'. Papers from the 7th regional meeting, Chicago Linguistic Society 254–63

STANLEY, JULIA. 1972. 'Syntactic exploitation'. Paper at Southeastern Conference on Linguistics VII, April

STOCKWELL, ROBERT, PAUL SCHACTER, AND BARBARA HALL PARTEE. 1968. 'Integration of transformational theories on English syntax'. Los Angeles: University of California under AF Contract 19 [628]–6007

THORNE, J. P. 1973. 'On the grammar of existential sentences'. Patrick Suppes *et al* (eds), *Studies in logic and the foundations of mathematics, Vol 74: logic, methodology and philosophy of science IV*. Proceedings of the 4th International Congress for Logic, Methodology and Philosophy of Science, Bucharest 1971. 863–81. Amsterdam: North Holland

VACHEK, JOSEF. 1947. 'Obecný zápor v angličtině a v češtině'. *Prague Studies in English* 6, 5–64

1976. *Selected writings in English and general linguistics*. Prague: Academia

WASOW, THOMAS. 1975. 'Anaphoric pronouns and bound variables'. *Language* 51.368–83

ZIV, YAEL. 1976. *On the communicative effect of relative clause extraposition in English.* Unpublished dissertation, University of Illinois

Index

abstract: see noun; verb
accent 25, 26, 46, 47, 64, 73, 91, 170, 178;
    see emphasis; prosody
acceptability 125–7, 140; see grammaticality
accomplishment 176–7
accusative 131–2
action vs person, modification of: Ch 7
activity 106–7
adjective 17, 18, 104, 109–10, 122, Ch 7
    adverb, like 103–4
    temporary 149, 151
    see clause, adjective
adjunct 29, 36
admire 68
adverb 80, 88, 98, 110, 120–1, 140, 184, 186,
    194
    directional 75
    sentence see style disjunct
    see clause, adverb; locative
advice 153, 165–7
affirmation 192, 195–6; see negation
afterthought 85, 103, 191
agent 103, 138, 141–3
alegre (Spanish) 199
already 35
ambient *it* 77–87
ambiguity 2, 125, 146–7
anaphora 66, 67, 72, 80, 86, 87, 92, 111, 114,
    118–19, 146
and 29, 159, 164
angry 146
announce 69
annoying, annoyed 147, 150
answer 52, 176
Anthony, Michael 24, 65
Anttila, Raimo 19, 198
any 56, 57, 62–5, 91, 159, 161–4, 180–1, 199,
    Ch 2
anybody, anyone, anything, anywhere 28
aphesis 159–61, 190
apostrophizing 193
apposition 77, 86, 87

approval and disapproval 147–9
article, definite 74, 102, 111, 119; see definite
article, indefinite 25, 29
as 63
asleep 18
assume 178
at all 29, 36, 48
Atkinson, James C. 94
attention, pay no 59
attitude 57, 59, 64, 65, 69, 122, 147–9
Austin, J. L. 183
Aux 156, 176, 183
auxiliary verb 62, 66, 107, 110, 146, 152,
    154–6, 160, 174, 187–8; see modal
averse 33
aware 18
awareness 93–5, 115, 120, 123
awfully 27

Bach, Emmon 123
Baily, C.-J. N. 66
bare infinitive: see verb stem, plain
barely 32
Barmecide feast 58
Bartlett, J. R. 71
be 61, 92, 96, 104–5, 107, 117, 121, 145,
    160–1, 166–7, 173, 175–6, 182
beans, spill the 75
Beatty, John 17
begone 168
behoove 88
believe 110, 125–9
bid, v 187
bifurcation 2
bit 29
blend 77, 81, 86, 133, 154, 172, 175, 181;
    see hybrid
body, -body 14, 15, 23
Bolinger, Dwight 9, 11, 13, 16–18, 121–3,
    135, 143, 151, 180, 186
both 28, 29, 34
Bradley, F. W. 35

Breivik, Leiv Egil 92, 96
Bresnan, Joan 116
brief for, hold no 59
bring 75, 76
Brown, Goold 91, 92, 100
budge 27, 28
Bull, William 116

can, could 37, 154–6, 188
care 27
case 150; see dative; accusative
case, in 30
cataphora 118–19
causative 122
cause and effect 150
certain 110
Chafe, Wallace L. 77–9, 81, 82, 88
Charnley, M. Bertens 96
cheerful 194
Chomsky, Noam 2
Christ's sake, for 186
claim v 181
clause: adjective 121, 158
    adverb 83–5, 87, 158
    main 61
    subordinate 30, 36, 39, 45, 49, 130
    that 71, 73, 74, 77, 84, 124, 149–50, Ch 6
clean v 122
cleft sentence 58, 71–4
clever 148
collocation 43, 54, 55, 59, 60, 146; see idiom
command 184–6, 190–3, 195–8; Chs 8–9
command 184–5, 195–6
comment 73
comparative 194–5
comparison: see degree word; intensifier
compatibility 126–7, 133–4, 139–40, 161, 192
competence and performance 18, 19
complement 88
completely 27
concord 56, 65
condition 28, 30, 84, 90, 118, 153, 158–65,
    173, 177, 180, 190–1, 198; see *if*
conduciveness 24, 25, 31, 59
confess 27
conjecture 70
conjunction 34; see coordination; copula
consider 119, 128–9
constituent 155; Ch 6
context 110–12, 114, 175, 179, 181–2; see
    prior basis
contingency 144, 146–51; see hypothetical
contraction 61, 64

contrastivity 26, 140, 191
convince 151
coordination 158–9, 164–5; see conjunction
copula 176, 181–2; see conjunction
crazy 146–7
Curme, George O. 154, 171, 192

damned 54
dare 173; see threat
dare 170
dative 131–2
deal, great 27
deceived 142–3
declarative 152, 179, 183, 187
deem 151
deep structure 1–4, 16, 66, 125, 140
definite 82, 84, 91, 113–20, 181, 193
definition 42
degree word 123, 148–9
deixis 80, 94, 114, 117, 123
deletion 5, 8, 9, 93, 103; see aphesis
demonstrative 85, 86, 92, 113–14, 119–20,
    154; see *that*
derivation, generative 188
dialect 188–9
difference, to make a 59, 88
Dingwall, William O. 13
disgusted 150
disjuncture 61, 145, 155
distractor 181
distributive 29, 34, 36, 56, 64
Diver, William 20
do 155, 170, 184, 188, 191–6, 198–9; Ch 9
don't 181, 188–91, 197
doubt 68

eager 145, 151
Eisenhower, Dwight 8
either 3, 28, 29, 34, 35
ellipsis 152, 165, 172, 174; see aphesis;
    fragment
else 72
embedding 33, 48, 60, 125, 181; see clause
emergence, verb of 96
emotion, verb of 68, 69, 150
emphasis, emphatic 62, 67, 181, 192; see
    accent
enjoy 2
epistemic 23, 188
epithet 191
Epstein, Samuel 38
Erades, Peter: see Kruisinga
ergative 141–2; Ch 7

euphemism 137
event noun, verb 43, 80, 88, 181
ever 28, 29, 34, 36, 198
existential *there* Ch 5
expect 133
expletive 53, 54, 67
extraposition 71–4, 80, 81, 83, 86, 89, 110;
  see fronting; order; postposition

fact 75, 76
factive 21, 22, 31, 45, 68, 69, 73, 94
fail 122
far 27
feliz (Spanish) 199
fellow 76
few 36
fiddlesticks 46, 64
figure of speech 158, 165, 167, 177; see
  metaphor
find out 69
finite 171, 176–7, 190, 198
Firchow, Evelyn 87
Firth, J. R. 8
fool, nobody's 59
foolish 135–6, 143–4, 148
for 150
forbid 151
foreclosure 56, 63, 64
forget 14
fragment 180–2, 189
frankly 184–5
free variation 24, 72
fresh 149, 151
Fries, Charles C. 116
from 141–2, 151
fronting 109, 112, 136; see extraposition;
  order; postposition
fun, like 55
functional sentence perspective 73
furious 146–7
future 153, 156–7, 165, 167–9, 171, 176, 180

gabby 148–9
galore 18
García, Erica 20
Garvin, Paul 65
gather 88
Geis, Michael 199
generative grammar 183–8
  semantics 15, 16
generic 102
generous 138
genitive, objective 141

gerund 1, 2, 13, 14, 30, 48, 83, 84, 87, 96,
  142
get 166
Givón, Talmy 20, 65, 114
glad 145–6, 149, 199
Gleitman, Lila R. 181
go 160
go and 167
goal 144–6, 148–51
God's name, in 186
gradient 76, 85, 107, 144, 146, 172–3, 177
grammaticality 133, 153; see acceptability
grateful 147
gratuitous 138–9
Greenbaum, Sidney 140, 184
guess 70, 134

Haas, William 4
haber (Spanish) 92, 116
handsome 137–8, 140
handy 18
happen 101
happening 101
happy 146, 148, 194
hardly 23, 32, 62, 63
Harris, Zellig 133
Hatcher, Anna 20
hate 68
Haugen, Einar 87
have: vt 61, 62, 168–70, 175
  auxiliary 105, 169–70
  existential 120
  have done 168, 170
  have it on good authority 75
he 2, 121, 180, 198
  he who 76
  see pronoun
headstrong 149
hear 31
Hetzron, Robert 93, 96, 121, 123
higher sentence 21, 46, 183, 186; see
  performative
homonym 2, 9, 157, 173
Hooper, Joan 20
hope 181
Horn, Lawrence R. 38
hortative 184–5, 198
Householder, Fred W., Jr 180
how come 71
hybrid 135, 137; see blend
hypothesize 70
hypothetical 173, 177–8, 180, 189–91, 197; see
  contingency

I do 8
idea, get the 75
identity 19; see sameness
idiom 42, 43, 55, 60, 75, 76, 88; see collocation
if 9, 30, 158–9, 161–2
   if not 36, 199
   see condition
il (French) 94
illocution 148, 151, 184; see performative
imagine 70, 178
impact 98, 99, 102, 108–9, 111
imperative 8, 50, Chs 8–9
imperative 136
impersonal 137, 158, 162, 180
impertinent 149
impossible 110
inceptive 146
incidentally 12
inclined 145
indefinite 89, 91, 115, 118–19, 154, 173, 180–1, 195
indicate 27
indirect discourse 172, 175
inference 16, 52, 76, 88, 136, 143
infinitive 1, 2, 7, 9, 13, 14, 20, 39, 48, 60, 72, 73, 83, 84, 86, 87, 88, 171, 187, 189–91, 196–8; see verb stem, plain
information: see new information; old information
information, verbs of 74, 110, 122
   nouns of 127
-ing 1; see gerund
initiatory utterance 184–5
insist 189–90
intensifier 151, 186
intonation 6, 7, 12, 35, 44–6, 56, 59, 65, 72, 73, 88, 111–12, 130, 134, 155, 173, 175–8, 182, 196–7; see prosody
intrinsic consequence 162, 173
intuition 153
it 2, 120, 131, 135, Ch 4;
   it says that 81, 82

Jakobson, Roman vii, 20
Jespersen, Otto 14, 21, 34, 37, 92, 123, 135, 167, 171–2, 179–80, 191, 196
joyous 145
juncture 145; see disjuncture
just 63, 174

Katz, Jerrold J. 152–3, 156–7, 165, 179–81, 183

Kempson, Ruth 13
kernel sentence 16
Kirsner, Robert 20
know 12, 21, 31, 68, 69, 110, 125–6, 129
knowledge of the world 53
knownness 88, 117; see old information
Kruisinga, E. 106, 120, 171–3
Kuno, Susumu 91, 121

Labov, William 22–4, 38, 39, 49, 65
Lakoff, George 133–4, 180
Lakoff, Robin 21, 65
Langacker, Ronald 9, 104
least, at 194–5
Lees, Robert B. 21, 24, 25, 30, 33, 34, 135
leftshifting 37, 38, 41
let 191, 198–9
   let on 27
   let's 195
lexicon 24, 35, 85, 91, 120
like 2, 9, 27
likely 110
little 29, 36
locative 81, 82, 84, Ch 5
logic ix, 4, 33, 34, 57, 58
long, long time, long way 27
Long, Ralph B. 115, 121
Long, Dorothy 115
longest element last 117
loose 18
looseness and tightness 140–1, 144, 146, 151
lot, a 27
loth 33
love v 68
Luker, Benjamin F. 197

mad 146
man 23
mandatory 136, 140
many 27, 28
may 171–2, 188; see *might*
McCawley, James D. 19
meaning ix, x, 2, 9, 145; see compatibility; semantic
meaninglessness 121
means 119
Merriam-Webster Third New International Dictionary 71
metaphor 120, 196; see figure of speech
might 188; see *may*
Mihailović, Ljiljana 16
Millward, Celia 180–1, 196
mind v 27, 28

misguided 142–3
misled 142–3
mistaken 139
modal 147–8, 181, 183, 187; see auxiliary
more than, not 32
move 27
much 27, 28
Munro, Pamela 9, 104
Murray, Alexander 91
myself 154

name, personal 119
need 188
negation 66, 67, 90, 122, 130–31, 155–6,
  166–7, 170, 176–7, 189–90, 192, 195,
  198–9, Chs 2–3
  canceled 41, 42
  external 44–55, 60, 64
  formulaic 46–9, 60, 64
  multiple 49, 64, 65
  see polarity item
negative rightshifting Ch 3
neither 29
nervous 147
neuter pronoun 74, 76, 84, 85
never 29, 31, 198
new information 49–51, 57; see old
  information
news stories 111–12
nice 145, 150
Nixon, Richard 8
no 23, 29, 31, 33, 36, 156, Ch 3
  no go 43
  no matter 55
  no such thing 46, 48, 64
  no time, at 54
  no time, in 43
nobody 23, 31, 46, 64
nominalization 181
none 23, 29, 33, 46, 48
nonsense 46
no one 46
no place 47
nor 29, 36
not 31, 61, 62, 64, 177, 189–90, 197
  not any Ch 3
  not at all 46
nothing 46, 59, 64
  nothing but 59
  nothing flat, in 42
  nothing of the sort 46, 64
noun: abstract 54, 55, 64, 75, 76, 96
  concrete 54

  mass 25, 26, 54, 64
  see predicative degree noun; event noun
now 80
nowhere 46, 47, 58, 64
nowise 29

object v 27
obligation expressions 119–20
obviousness 79, 80
occur 101
occurrence 101
of Ch 7
old information 71, 72, 74; see knownness;
  new information
once 158
one, -one 14, 15, 25, 180, 198
oneself 180
only 63
openness 56, 57, 62–4
or 29, 36, 164–5
order 112–13, 120–2, 124, 131–2, 140–1,
  145, 154, 191; see extraposition; fronting;
  functional sentence perspective;
  leftshifting; longest element last;
  postposition; rightshifting
out 79, 80
outrageous 140
overlook 14

Palmer, F. R. 121
paraphrase 16, 38, 78, 86, 125, 140–1; see
  sameness and difference
parenthesis 84
participle: see gerund; past participle
particle 74, 75, 82, 98; see phrasal verb
passive 4, 9, 10, 16, 17, 45, 74, 102–10, 122,
  129, 141–3, 151, 161, 166–7
past 168–9, 177
past participle 104, 107, 142
patient 78, 79, 88
pause 144–5
perception, verb of 131–2
perfect tense 19, 20, 98, 99, 105, 149; see
  have
perfective 88, 168–9, 175
performative 21, 76, 147–8, 183–4, 186–7,
  189, 198; see higher sentence
person 134, 154, 157, 160, 173, 190–1, 197
phrasal verb 17, 95, 98, 99, 108–9
place 92
  take place 92
plan v 132–4
please 168

plural 7, 54, 64, 82, 118
polarity item 26–9, 35, 36
Poldauf, Ivan 65
poppycock 46
possessive 141
possible 110
Postal, Paul 16, 152–3, 180; see Katz
postposition 110, 191; see order
Poutsma, H. 21, 119, 167, 175, 177
pragmatic 137, 144, 185
pray 187
predicative degree noun 123
preposition 180
prepositional phrase 48, 140
presentative construction 93, Ch 5
presume 70
presupposition 21, 24, 50–3, 56, 57, 64
pretend 70
preterite 160
pretty 27
Priestley, Joseph 91
prior basis 194–5; see context; old
    information
prithee 187
privative 43
process 78
pronominalization 5, 7, 66
pronoun 15, 66, 90, 116–17, 119, 121, 130–2,
    153, Ch 4; see neuter
prosody 76, 109, 117, 144; see accent;
    disjuncture; emphasis; intonation;
    looseness and tightness; pause
pun 173–4
purpose 77, 86
puzzled 146

quantitative, quantity 182, 193, 195
question 8, 25–9, 31, 34, 36, 51, 52, 65, 71,
    72, 83, 90, 106–7, 116, 130–1, 133, 153–6,
    175–6, 179, 182, 185, 187–8, 197
    echo 153
    reclamatory 71, 72
    Wh 106–7, 122, 181
Quine, Willard V. 33, 34
Quirk, Randolph 13, 91, 92, 116, 119–20,
    180
quite 27
quotative 190

raising 23, 37–9, 41
rather 27
recall 14
reflexive 152–3, 191

refuse 13, 14
register: see speech level
regret 69
rejoice 150
remind 15, 16
remember 14
repetition 6–8, 191
reporting verb 69
request 178, 183, 187, 198
request 183–4, 189–90
resent 69
result 77
resultant condition 106–8, 111, 122, 142
reveal 27
right 147–8
rightshifting Ch 3
Ross, John R. 133–4

sameness and difference 2–5, 9, 92, 188;
    see identity; paraphrase
Sanders, Lawrence 123
say 110, 178
    it says that 81, 82
scarcely 32
Schreiber, Peter A. 183–5, 191, 198
Schwartz, Arthur 78
Scots 23
see 57, 94
Sellers, Peter 38
semantic: interpretation 125
    weight 74
sentential complement 43
separation 7
shall 37, 178, 187–8
Shopen, Timothy 180
Silverman, Joseph 92
so that 77
some 56, 159, 162, 199, Ch 2
somebody, someone 14, 15, 28
something 28
sometimes 28
somewhat 29
somewhere 28
sorry, be 69, 87
spatial 103, 105
speech level 127–9, 180, 190
spurn 13, 14
staged activity 94, 96, 97, 113
Stanley, Julia 129
state 181; see resultant condition
statement: see declarative
stative 163–6, 175–6; see process
Stockwell, Robert 183, 198

stone unturned, leave no 59
stop at nothing 59
stress: see accent
strike like 16
stupid 54
style 24, 33, 120, 125
style disjunct 184–6
suasion 70, 187
subject 152, 154, 176
subjunctive 180, 183–4, 187, 189, 198
suggest, suggestion 184–7, 195–6
superlative 119
suppletive 22, 56 .
suppose 37, 70, 129, 177–8
supposing 9, 30, 177
supposition 31, 69, 70
sure 110
surface structure Ch 6
surprising 139
suspect 125, 128–9
synonym ix, 3, 9, 40, 135
syntax 124

tag 23, 24, 58, 59, 65, 90, 152, 154–5, 171,
    176, 178, 197
take it that 76, 88
tell 12, 39, 94
temporal 101
tense 70, 73, 74, 88, 98, 99, 129, 138–9,
    156, 167–70, 175, 181; see future; past;
    perfect; preterite
tentative assertion 76
that 10–13, 15, 63, 66, 68, 72, 76, 77, 91,
    113, 120
    that there 84
    that which 119
    see clause
theorize 70
there 84, 89, Ch 5
they 116, 198
things 80, 84, 85
think 125, 129
this here 84
Thompson, Sandra 20
Thorne, J. P. 99, 121–3
those who 119
threat 163–4; see dare
time 79, 80, 85, 158, 194
time: every, any 28
tinpanny 53
to 1, 7, 9, 144, 146, 151, 181; see
    infinitive
today 80

tomorrow 80, 88
too 28, 29, 34, 35
topic 67, 68, 73, 100–2, 110, 112, 114, 133
tough 82, 83, 85, 86
transformation ix, 5, 17, 35, 91, 124–5, 132,
    134–5, 188–9
transition 184–5
transitive 102–3, 121, 150, 168
trifle 29
truly 186
Truman, Harry 35
truth value 4, 33, 41, 57
truth modifier 186

uncertain 110, 122
understand 68, 128–9
unexpected 139
universal 9, 65, 123
unless 36, 199
unlikely 122
unnecessary 138–40
use for, have no 59

Vachek, Josef 64, 65
vagueness 146
valid 104
value judgment 53, 54, 149
verb 78, 96–9, 122, 142–3, 145, 157
    abstract governing verb 184
    stem, plain 160–1, 164, 171–9, 189–91,
        196–7
    see auxiliary; emotion; event; finite;
        gerund; imperative; infinitive;
        information, verbs of; modal;
        perception; phrasal verb; reporting
        verb; suasion; transitive
verb phrase 61, 62
verba dicendi 181
very 27, 186
vocal 148
vocative 8, 155, 179

want 9, 38, 122
wash 122
Wasow, Thomas 116, 121
Waugh, Linda 20
way 181
we 161
weather expressions 66, 79, 80, 83, 85, 86;
    see ambient *it*
Webster, Noah 91
welcome v 68

what 87
  what if 177
when 84, 87
whenever 28
which 10–13, 91, 120
who, whose 12
why 71
will, would 8, 9, 152–7, 171–2, 179–80, 188
wise 144, 148, 150
wish 9
wishes and hopes 153, 165–9
with 43
wont 145
wooden nickels 43
word 16, 56; see lexicon

worried 147, 150
wrong 139

yes 8, 156
yesterday 121
yet 35
you 8, 84, 152, 154–5, 158–61, 165, 171–2, 175, 179–80, 191, 197–8
your grandmother 60
  your old man 49, 64
yourself 152–3

zeugma 82, 83, 87
Ziv, Yael 121